# FRONTIERS IN ANGLO-WELSH POETRY

# FRONTIERS
# IN
# ANGLO-WELSH
# POETRY

~

*Tony Conran*

CARDIFF
UNIVERSITY OF WALES PRESS
1997

© Tony Conran, 1997

British Library Cataloguing-in-Publication Data.
A catalogue record for this book is available
from the British Library.

ISBN 0-7083-1395-7

**Published with the financial support
of the Arts Council of Wales**

Typeset at Dinefwr Press, Llandybïe
Printed in Great Britain by Dinefwr Press, Llandybïe

# Contents

~

Preface     vii

Acknowledgements     ix

## Part I

1. The 'Welsh way of life' and its poetry     1
2. Displaced poets of the way of life:
   W. H. Davies, Huw Menai and A. G. Prys-Jones     12
3. The Anglo-Welsh vanishing point:
   the Eastaway of Edward Thomas     27
4. Pilgrims from a desert land: a study of Idris Davies's
   two sequences and Gwenallt's 'Y meirwon'
   as responses to the Great Depression     42

## Part II

5. Buried treasure     65
6. Gerard Hopkins as an Anglo-Welsh poet     74
7. David Jones and the ironic epic     92

## Part III

8. The advent of modernism     109
9. 'I saw time murder me':
   Dylan Thomas and the tragic soliloquy     121
10. A lonely path: the early poetry of Glyn Jones     142
11. Lynette Roberts     163

# Contents

## PART IV

12. The end of an era     177
13. The new frontier: R. S. Thomas     188
14. Roland Mathias: headmaster, critic and poet     200

## PART V

15. Exile and elegy in the poetry of T. Harri Jones     217
16. Telling the dead go home: the poetry of Leslie Norris     226
17. Funland and the work of Dannie Abse     234
18. An abdication from time:
      the *Collected Poems* of Raymond Garlick     249
19. The Referendum and the poetry of Jon Dressel     259
20. Tony Curtis and the ways of death     265

List of authors and their major works     275

Bibliography     283

Index     285

# *Preface*

~

This book's title includes the word 'frontiers' because Anglo-Welsh poetry is the product of three kinds of frontier between the Welsh and their dominant partners in Great Britain. First, a frontier between two peoples, two ways of life. The Welsh way of life is or was a close-knit structure essentially emanating from the Methodist Awakening of Wales in the eighteenth century. Second, a frontier between two civilizations. Welsh civilization built upon the ruins of Celtic Christianity to achieve classical status in the fourteenth and fifteenth centuries. It was more or less moribund by the seventeenth, but has since been the subject of several renaissances. Third, a frontier between two languages. Welsh is a modern tongue derived from the Celtic that the Britons spoke in Roman times. It is very different from the Low German speech, 'creolized' by Norman French, of their English neighbours.

These three frontiers are related but in themselves very different, and Anglo-Welsh poetry responds to the stresses they occasion in different ways. None of them, however, is to be identified with the historical frontier, the Marches or geographical borderland between Wales and England. Nowadays anywhere in Wales is frontier country.

For the sake of readers who may be unfamiliar with the Welsh and Anglo-Welsh writers mentioned in the book, a list of them, with their dates and their principal works available in English, is appended at the end. An 'Anglo-Welsh' writer means a person from or belonging to Wales (however we interpret that) who yet writes in English. It is fair to say, however, that many authors resent the term, preferring to call themselves 'Welsh writers in English' or even simply 'Welsh writers' (as opposed to 'writers in Welsh').

Tony Conran
1997

# Acknowledgements

~

The author and publisher wish to thank the copyright holders who have kindly permitted the reproduction of the following:

*Articles*

Chapters 1 and 4, based on articles by Tony Conran in *Fires Green as Grass: Studies in the Creative Impulse in Anglo-Welsh Poetry* (1995), edited by Belinda Humfrey; and Chapter 6, which he published in *The Welsh Connection: Essays by Past and Present Members of the Department of English Language and Literature, University of North Wales, Bangor* (1986), edited by William Tydeman, by permission of J. D. Lewis and Sons, Gwasg Gomer.

*Poems and poetry extracts*

Poems and extracts from the work of Dannie Abse, by permission of Dannie Abse.

Extracts from the work of Euros Bowen, by permission of J. D. Lewis and Sons, Gwasg Gomer.

Extracts from the work of Tony Curtis, by permission of Tony Curtis.

Extracts from the work of Idris Davies, by permission of Gwyn and Ceinfryn Morris.

Extracts from the work of David Jones, by permission of Faber and Faber.

Poems and extracts from the work of Glyn Jones, by permission of Doreen Jones.

'Y Meirwon', from Gwenallt, *Eples* (1951), by permission of J. D. Lewis and Sons, Gwasg Gomer.

Extracts from the work of T. Harri Jones, by permission of J. D. Lewis and Sons, Gwasg Gomer.

Poems and extracts from the work of Roland Mathias, by permission of Roland Mathias.

Poems and extracts from the work of Leslie Norris, by permission of Leslie Norris.

Extract from the work of Saunders Lewis, by permission of R. Geraint Gruffydd.

Poems and extracts from the work of John Ormond, by permission of Glenys Ormond.

'Y Llwynog', from R. Williams Parry, *Yr Haf a Cherddi Eraill* (1924), by permission of Gwasg Gee.

Translation of *Y Llwynog* from Joseph Clancy, *Twentieth Century Welsh Poems* (1982), by permission of J. D. Lewis and Sons, Gwasg Gomer.

Poems and extracts from the work of Lynette Roberts, by permission of Angharad Rhys.

Poems and extracts from the work of Dylan Thomas, by permission of David Higham Associates.

Poems and extracts from the work of R. S. Thomas, by permission of R. S. Thomas.

Poems and extracts from the work of Waldo Williams, by permission of J. D. Lewis and Sons, Gwasg Gomer.

# PART I

## 1

## *The 'Welsh way of life' and its poetry*

~

Anglo-Welsh poetry differs from other poetry in the English language in three main respects. First, it has, in its background, a different civilization – it is like English poetry written by Irishmen or Indians. Second, it shares its territory with another linguistic community which regards its tongue as the right and natural language of the country – a claim which Anglo-Welsh writers often accept, and which even if they dispute, they cannot ignore. In this respect, Anglo-Welsh poetry is like English poetry written by Nigerians or Maoris. Third, it derives from a special sort of society, which I shall call the *buchedd* from a Welsh word meaning a 'way of life' or 'ethos'.[1] In this third aspect, it is more like poetry in English written by Americans. American society, like Welsh, was consciously without an upper-class, deliberately egalitarian, puritanical in morals, a product of cultural revolution following the breakup of established social patterns.

The first difference, that of antecedent civilization, is not very marked in most of its practitioners. For the *buchedd*, the Welsh people as a whole, the high civilization of Wales was no more than a vague memory, becoming more than that only in certain metrical habits unique to the country, and possibly in a respect for poets and poetry not otherwise accounted for. Within the *buchedd*, however, the exploration of the lost civilization by scholars and writers was one way in which the aspiration of a new middle class expressed and defined itself in both Welsh and English. Some of this interest rubbed off on to ordinary Welsh people.

---

[1] I borrow the term from a famous study of a Welsh village by David Jenkins in Elwyn Davies and Alwyn D. Rees (eds.), *Welsh Rural Communities* (Cardiff: University of Wales Press, 1962), but my use of it is not the same as his.

1

The second difference, that of sharing its territory with another linguistic community, was again not very important to Anglo-Welsh poetry, except in a negative way, until Welsh-speakers became aggressively defensive of their rights, a development that took place mostly after 1955 or so. Up to that time, Welsh people spoke what language suited them as luck, geography or (what amounts to much the same thing) social pressures dictated; but English- and Welsh-speakers belonged to the same community and very largely shared the same range of outlooks. There is a strong case for regarding William Williams of Pantycelyn (1717–91) and Idris Davies of Rhymney (1905–53) as the two great *buchedd*-poets: Pantycelyn the hymn-writer in Welsh, and Idris Davies the English-language poet of the 1926 miners' strike. One marks the *buchedd*'s rise in the eighteenth century, the other its defeat in the twentieth. Both writers were bilingual and wrote in both languages. It suited Pantycelyn to write much more in Welsh as it suited Idris Davies to write his important sequences in English; but neither felt cut in two by what language he used or necessarily divided from other Welshmen who did not share it.

Of the three differences, the third, its derivation from a unique society, was undoubtedly the overriding one. Anglo-Welsh poetry, quite as much as Anglo-Welsh fiction, was a product of the *buchedd* society, its defeat and breakup. Even a modernist like the young Dylan Thomas (1914–53) wrote his poetry against that background, consciously in rebellion against *buchedd* values. An Anglo-Welsh poet is largely defined by the attitudes he or she adopts to the *buchedd* inheritance. The first chapter in Anglo-Welsh poetry is the stage of *buchedd* sensibility itself, as it glows into new life in the pre-1914 world, and then disintegrates after the defeat of 1926 and the Depression.

The Methodist Awakening in the eighteenth century changed Wales radically. The old culture – Celtic, tribal, hierarchical – was swept away. The unified class-structure of *uchelwyr* (landowners) and peasantry had been undermined by the freedom given the *uchelwyr* by the Act of Union to become an Anglicized and often absentee squirearchy. Methodism over the years re-created what was left into a modern people. Not a populace, not a class structure, not a mass: a people, a *buchedd*, a Children of Israel. In class terms the *buchedd* represented the sub-dominance, beyond the bounds of an upper class that had gone English, of an alliance between the peasantry, the respectable working class and the petty bourgeoisie, together with such capitalists as were not too Anglicized to care.

The *buchedd* was of course not as homogeneous as sometimes it tried to make out. There were class divisions, particularly in the industrial areas: a genuine proletarian consciousness emerged in the south Wales mining valleys, for instance. The breakthrough into proletarian politics is precisely registered in the failure of the Lib-Labbery of Mabon (William Abraham, MP for the Rhondda and first president of the South Wales Miners' Federation) to contain the new socialism of the South within the Liberal Party: the election of Keir Hardie of the Independent Labour Party as MP for Aberdare in 1900 marked the beginning of the end. Mabon's inclusive radicalism was very typical of *buchedd* politics, but it could not survive in the bitterness of the struggle between the coal-owners and the miners. Lloyd George, who did survive, did so partly because his *buchedd*ism was not so threatened in the north; partly because, after the failure of Cymru Fydd and the Welsh Home Rule Movement, he became largely a British Liberal politician, no longer so preoccupied by Welsh issues, even though he kept the aura of a Welsh Moses leading his people to the Promised Land,

> Who strode into London with a dazzling sword,
> A bright St David from the stormy mountain,

as Idris Davies put it.

The *buchedd* was not only ruptured by geography and class: it had its own shadow world as well. The division of the Welsh people into *plant y capel* and *plant y tafarn* – respectable and bibulous – was deep-seated in both ideology and practice. The strictness and the divisiveness tended to vary, of course. In poor areas it might lead to more bitterness (as in the stories of Caradoc Evans, 1878–1945) than in relatively prosperous districts. Moreover the terms of the divide were confused and compounded by Anglicization. Most of the Anglo-Welsh writers of the 1930s and 1940s tended to belong to the lost tribes of Israel, that is, respectable folk who had forfeited their birthright as *plant y capel* by adopting English values as a weapon along with English as their language.

Nevertheless, it is simply not true that only Welsh-speakers belonged to the *buchedd* or shared its values. To some extent it depended where you were: it was probably harder to be a monoglot English-speaking member of the *buchedd* in (say) Bala than it was in Pontypool. Even now the mining valleys are probably the only places in Wales outside the *Bro*

*Gymraeg* (Welsh-speaking areas) where the vestiges of *buchedd* consciousness are still a force to be reckoned with.

The *buchedd*'s archetypal cultural manifestation was the religious revival. Periodically these would sweep the country restoring the ethos of a Chosen People, boosting morale and re-establishing the dominance of *plant y capel* over Welsh life. The poetic counterpart of the revival is of course the congregational hymn, as it is found particularly in the work of William Williams of Pantycelyn. Paradoxically, Pantycelyn's hymns are intensely personal – indeed romantic – expressions of religious longing. Here, for example, he sings of his desire to forsake the values of this world in his eagerness for God:

> 'Rwy'n edrych dros y bryniau pell
>   Amdanat bob yr awr;
> Tyrd, fy Anwylyd, mae'n hwyrhau
>   A'm haul bron mynd i lawr.
>
> Trôdd fy nghariadau oll i gyd
>   'Nawr yn anffyddlon im;
> Ond yr wyf finnau'n hyfryd glaf
>   O gariad mwy ei rym.
>
> Cariad na 'nabu plant y llawr
>   Mo'i rinwedd nac mo'i ras,
> Ac sydd yn sugno'm serch a'm bryd
>   O'r creadur oll i maes . . .
>
> 'Does gyflwr tan yr awyr las
>   'Rwy' ynddo'n chwennych byw;
> Ond fy hyfrydwch fyth gaiff fod
>   O fewn cynteddau'm Duw.
>
> Fe ddarfu blas, fe ddarfu chwant
>   At holl bwysïau byd;
> Nid oes ond gwagedd heb ddim trai
>   Yn rhedeg trwyddò i gyd.
>
> (Always across the distant hills
>   I'm looking for you yet;
> Come, my beloved, it grows late
>   And my sun has almost set.

Each and every love I had
  Turned unfaithful to me at length;
But a sweet sickness has taken me
  Of a love of mightier strength.

A love the worldly don't recognise
  For its virtue or its grace,
But it sucks my liking and desire
  From every creature's face . . .

Nothing under the blue air now
  Would make me want to live
But only that I'll know the joys
  That the courts of God can give.

Relish and appetite have died
  For the flowers of the world that fall:
Only a vanity without ebb
  Is running through it all.)

That love-poem to God is the very stuff of cultural revolution: the old order was rejected, all its dances and folk-songs, its hierarchy and backward-looking abandoned to the unregenerate world that still continued in the pubs, though with less and less confidence as the propaganda against it mounted. When fiddlers believe that playing the fiddle is a sign that they will go to hell, it tends to sap their creativity. Many a violin was abandoned, many a song not sung.

The relation between the individual and the new holy people of God is given by another famous hymn:

Pererin wyf mewn anial dir
  Yn crwydro yma a thraw,
Ac yn rhyw ddisgwyl bob yr awr
  Fod tŷ fy Nhad gerllaw.

Ac mi debygaf clywa' i sŵn
  Nefolaidd raidd o'm blaen
Wedi concwero a mynd trwy
  Dymhestloedd dŵr a thân . . .

(Pilgrim I am in a desert land,
  Wandering here and there,
In expectation, every hour
  That my Father's house is near.

> And I imagine I hear the sounds
> Of a numberless multitude –
> Those that have conquered and gone through
> Fire and tempestuous flood . . .)

It is worth quoting Derec Llwyd Morgan's classic account of the effect of this hymnody on the sensibility of the *buchedd*:

> By means of this sensitive discipline [of theology and Scripture] the Methodist poets got to the point of identifying the archetypes, the stories and the portraits of both Testaments with their own experiences, thus ensuring that they would influence the imagination of their readers in a way that would make their extensive inner experiences resemble the historical and revelatory experiences recorded in the Bible itself . . . What is notably special about the poetry of the Methodists is that there is so much of it, that its influence has been so far-reaching, so that its language has become a tribal idiom, and that this body of poetry has in turn given to its readers a commonly shared imagination . . . The place-names, *Egypt, Canaan, Sinai, Zion*, with their contrasting shades of significance, are repeated over and over, just as the metaphors *balm of Gilead, rose of Sharon*, and others, occur time after time . . . So often are they used that these individual names, the word clusters, and the various references, develop into living symbols of the mind of the converted. (*The Great Awakening in Wales*, trans. Dyfnallt Morgan, pp. 280-2)

When Idris Davies talks about 'deacons dreaming of Gilead' in the first section of *Gwalia Deserta*, for instance, with a single name he can evoke a whole idiom of feeling, the root ideology of the *buchedd*. He does this naturally and many times in his poetry, often (as here) with ironic intention.

*Buchedd*ism, although it starts by dramatically separating the sheep from the goats, the saved from the unregenerate, nevertheless was essentially an inclusive movement, a bit like the Church of England. It tried to contain extremes, rather than separating itself from them. Eventually even cultural manifestations of the old Celtic consciousness – the eisteddfod, the strict metres, the Welsh Folksong Society – which on the face of it were likely to be opposed by Methodists, were in fact enthusiastically supported and 'chapelized'.

The peculiar compromises that *buchedd*ism entailed, however, hardly supported any great art or literature apart from the hymns of Pantycelyn and Ann Griffiths. (I suppose the nearest would be the novels of Daniel Owen from Mold.) In the nineteenth century, *buchedd* poetry was marked by various degrees of compromise. The lyrics of Ceiriog built on folk-song to suggest a stability and human warmth of family life in the countryside – a stability that was in fact being constantly undermined by huge economic and ethnographical change:

> Aros mae'r mynyddau mawr,
>     Rhuo trostynt mae y gwynt;
> Clywir eto gyda'r wawr
>     Gân bugeiliaid megis cynt.
> Eto tyf y llygad dydd
>     O gylch traed y graig a'r bryn,
> Ond bugeiliaid newydd sydd
>     Ar yr hen fynyddoedd hyn.


> Ar arferion Cymru gynt
>     Newid ddaeth o rod i rod;
> Mae cenhedlaeth wedi mynd
>     A chenhedlaeth wedi dod.
> Wedi oes dymhestlog hir
>     Alun Mabon mwy nid yw,
> Ond mae'r heniaith yn y tir
>     A'r alawon hen yn fyw.


> (Still do the great mountains stay,
>     And the winds above them roar;
> There are heard at break of day
>     Songs of shepherds as before.
> Daisies as before yet grow
>     Round the foot of hill and rock;
> Over these old mountains, though,
>     A new shepherd drives his flock.


> To the customs of old Wales
>     Changes come from year to year;
> Every generation fails,
>     One is gone, the next is here.
> After a lifetime tempest-tossed
>     Alun Mabon is no more,
> But the language is not lost
>     And the old songs yet endure.)

Eisteddfod poetry, on the other hand, when it was not versifying theology, tended to stick to safe subjects like Queen Victoria or the Old Testament. A quasi-Wordsworthian idealism – a bit like Idris Davies's 'dreams' – informed the blank verse of his fellow Gwentian poet Islwyn (1832–78), as it did later that of Huw Menai (1888–1961) in English:

> Beth yw heddiw? Mae yr enaid
> Yn hawlu tragwyddoldeb fel ei heddiw,
> Ei briod ddydd, ei ddwyfol ddydd dioriau.
> Y ddoe? Yfory? Darfu am y cwbl.
> Mae'r enaid wedi codi ynddo'i hun
> I'r uchder lle mae'r bythol haul i'r lan,
> Lle mae yn annherfynol ddydd, o'r hwn
> Nid yw pob carreg filter ar hyd ffordd
> Diderfyn fywyd dyn, mesurau bod,
> Ond rhannau o wrthuni amser, rhith
> Ddaduniad o'r anysgaradwy, cysgod
> Colfennau eiddil ar a bythol lif.

(*Y Storm*)

> (What is today? The soul claims
> Eternity as really its today,
> Day proper to it, divinely without hours.
> Tomorrow? Yesterday? All that has ended.
> In itself the soul has risen to the height
> Where the everlasting sun is on the shore
> And it is infinite day; whence every milestone
> Along the road of man's unbounded life,
> All measurements of being, is but part
> Of the defilements of Time, a mere phantom
> Divorced from the inseparable, a shadow
> Of frail branches on the eternal flood.)

Islwyn enabled you to enjoy the emotional gratifications of being Welsh without the responsibility of doing anything about it.

Politics also suffered: a good deal of Welsh nineteenth-century political life seems curiously like very vigorous shadow-boxing. Though great issues – Chartism, the struggle against the Tory squires, the rise of trade unions, the nationalism of Cymru Fydd – were certainly present, for much of the time these were dealt with in terms more appropriate to rural than to industrial consciousness. The only platforms that were able to unite the whole people were those of the national religion, and two in particular: the struggle of the Nonconformist majority against the established Church of the squirearchy, and the pressure that had to be maintained on *plant y tafarn* (the 'drinking classes' of Oscar Wilde's quip) to maintain the dominance of Respectability in Welsh life.

Intellectually the *buchedd* was under threat from the new University Colleges at Aberystwyth, Bangor and Cardiff. The Chosen People were vulnerable at the top to the efforts of the ambitious to improve themselves, which produced an independent Welsh bourgeoisie and intelligentsia, both in Welsh and English. For a time (and indeed even now) the new intellectuals tried to lead a *buchedd*-based movement, much as the old preacher-poets had done. Sir John Morris-Jones, the man who above all put Welsh literary scholarship on a secure intellectual basis for the new age, was assiduous in judging eisteddfod competitions and putting forward his views in the popular press. But the strain was beginning to tell, even in Welsh-language circles. In English, after a Dark Age of ingrowing provincialism and anti-Welsh bitterness represented by (for example) Dylan Thomas's father, the new intellectuals became thoroughly anti-*buchedd*: 'Land of my fathers – my fathers can keep it!' Dylan exclaimed.

But there was a greater and more terrible threat to *buchedd*-values than a dissident intelligentsia. The coal industry, as we say, had been responsible for creating one of the most aware and powerful proletariats in Europe; now the slump in coal meant depression and poverty in the coalfields. Idris Davies's poetry is poised, it seems to me, on the breakdown of the *buchedd*-culture of the South. His greatest work incarnates and mourns *buchedd* values, far more than it does socialism or simply working-class bitterness or hope. As the hymns of Pantycelyn were the poetry of its inception, so the elegies of *Gwalia Deserta* and the quasi-drama of *The Angry Summer* are the real expression of the *buchedd*'s collapse.

These two sequences constitute his chief claim to fame; but it is important to see them in the context of his life as a whole. He was not simply a collier-poet, or even simply a poet of the *buchedd*. He was also an aesthete, who was in love with poetry itself. Beauty is a key word in his work. A lot of his reactions to the strike were aesthetic – he admired the vision and determination of the miners, the pageantry and conflict of the struggle. *The Angry Summer* ends:

> But the battle's end is not defeat
> To that dream that guided the broken feet
> And roused to beauty and to pride
> Toiler and toiler, side by side,
> Whose faith and courage shall be told
> In blaze of scarlet and of gold.

He had a passion for Yeats as well as Shelley; he was not above imitating James Joyce with a Welsh accent:

> Land of my mothers, how shall my brothers praise you? . . . How shall I praise you on the banks of the rhymneying waters, on the abering shores of Gwent? Descend, O tender feet, to the bank of the coal-canal at twilight, at twilight, when vermin fight and toads do bite under the shadows of pit-head light. Descend, O daughters of the land . . . (*Wales*, 4 (March 1938), 143)

His modernism never quite got into top gear, but in the early issues of *Wales* his prose and verse sit quite happily with the craggier work of Dylan Thomas or Glyn Jones (1905–95). To the end he and Dylan Thomas respected and admired each other, even if he found the younger poet sometimes too obscure for his taste.

Idris Davies is, I believe, the poet whose work marks the end of *buchedd* culture, as Pantycelyn's marked its beginning. Like so many *buchedd* poets, however, in Welsh as English – think of Ceiriog or Hedd Wyn – his sensibility was to some extent displaced by his circumstances. He lived in England during his most creative years, studying and teaching English; coming back to work in Wales proved profoundly disillusioning for him. It seems as though this displacement was necessary for his work. It gave him purchase on his subject matter, a quasi-modernist, aesthetic detachment, a sense of belonging to two different worlds at once.

By the time he came back to Wales, he had himself become more middle class, of course; but *buchedd* culture had disintegrated to the point of no return. What Glyn Jones calls the 'beer and skittles culture' of the mid-twentieth-century British working class had taken over, and Idris Davies found he had little in common with it.

As a displaced *buchedd* poet, charting the failure of a culture to survive, his career and his work make sense; whereas if we try and see him in purely class terms, as a writer of the working class, we can only register dissatisfaction. In what sense was Idris Davies a proletarian writer at all? He was never very firmly at the centre of proletarian consciousness, even as a miner. As a teacher he became thoroughly petty bourgeois, more and more alienated from his background. The relations of production behind his art were entirely bourgeois – he took experience as raw material and turned it into commodity for sale in highbrow bookshops. What his two sequences seem to me to lament is the collapse of the *buchedd*, as it held sway in the minds and hearts of the south Welsh working class in the mining valleys. It is very significant that so many of the characters we remember from the *Angry Summer* are petty bourgeois – Dan the grocer, Siencyn Rees the tailor ('I'm only a working man myself'), the vicar of Rhymney, even Maria in the little Italian shop. The feel of his work is quite different from the informed proletarian consciousness in the novels of Lewis Jones, for example, even if Lewis Jones was similarly using bourgeois forms and relations of production.

Idris Davies's presuppositions about poetry, in an English context, could be mistaken for a kind of left-wing Georgianism; but that would be to ignore his power. From a Welsh point of view they seem to me very *buchedd* ideas of what poetry ought to do. They are, of course, full of echoes of English poetry – but what *buchedd* poetry is not, from Pantycelyn down? Idris Davies's peculiar mixture of folk and romantic elements, his stress on the union of all the lower classes against the largely alien squires and mercantile big bourgeoisie, even, ultimately, the way he compromised his art: in all this he seems to me more like Ceiriog – another poet who wrote *buchedd* poetry in exile in England – than any more simply working-class poet. It is fair to say, also, that the two cultural positives in *The Angry Summer* are the great socially uplifting ones, 'Handel mighty and glorious', on the one hand, and the solitary reader in a library or on the hillside, on the other. Surely they are secular displacements (and not all that displaced either) of the two great initiation rites of the *buchedd* – the revival meeting, with its hymns and sermons on the one hand, and on the other the solitary soul wrestling with the Scriptures. The relation between the two is the polarization that produced the *buchedd* in the first place. A Pantycelyn hymn is in its nature an embodiment of that polarization – an expression of individual longing for fulfilment and meaning that is yet sung as an expression of social solidarity and uplift. By the 1920s, of course, the power of the hymn, as of chapel culture generally, was becoming sentimental and nostalgic; but even in 'Let's go to Barry Island, Maggie fach', its emotional potential is still recognizable as a normative experience, part of a rehearsal of the miners' Kingdom of Heaven:

> We'll have tea on the sands, and rides on the donkeys,
> And sit in the evening with the folk of Cwm Rhondda,
> Singing the sweet old hymns of Pantycelyn
> When the sun goes down beyond the rocky islands.
>
> (*The Angry Summer*, 31)

## 2

## *Displaced poets of the way of life:*
## *W. H. Davies, Huw Menai and A. G. Prys-Jones*

~

### W. H. Davies

Anglo-Welsh is a description of a frontier as much as a culture. Anglo-Welsh poets can move across this shadowy no man's land in both directions. They can start as pure Welshmen, sometimes even Welsh-speakers; and then gradually move into the world of English letters, until only a regional accent remains of their birthright. Or, sometimes, they start as Englishmen, and only when they move into Wales do they find themselves as poets. W. H. Davies (1871–1940) is an example of one type, Hopkins (1844–89) and Raymond Garlick (1926– ) illustrate the other. Both types have credentials to be regarded as Anglo-Welsh, in at least some aspects of their work. Of course, other poets do not cross or recross this frontier: Idris Davies, Glyn Jones or R. S. Thomas (1913– ) are never anything else but Anglo-Welsh writers.

W. H. Davies started life as a troublesome schoolboy in Gwent who ran away to seek his fortune in North America. He lost a leg trying to hitch a lift on a train. He became a tramp; but a tramp with literary ambitions. In a London doss-house he managed to publish a book of poems at his own expense, and against the odds it attracted the attention of such literati as Bernard Shaw and Edward Thomas (1878–1917). He became a popular poet, widely read as a 'primitive' and praised for the freshness and charm of his nature lyrics, love-poems and affectionate portraits of beggars. His *Autobiography of a Super-Tramp* was a best seller.

If we look at his career from a Welsh viewpoint, what we see is a poet working at first within *buchedd* expectations of what poetry ought to be about, coupled of course with admiration for the English Romantics.

The longest poems in his earliest books, for instance, are devoted to the evils of drink – 'The soul's destroyer' of his first volume's title. The title-poem is a story, couched in epic style, in a blank verse derived from Wordsworth and Tennyson, about his journey back to Newport to see a childhood sweetheart who had married a friend of his. Davies arrives back just in time to take his erstwhile rival home after a drinking bout and to watch him die raving.

The poem does not deserve its neglect. Davies took fragments from it and worked them into lyrics later:

> We went together side by side to school,
> Together had our holidays in fields
> Made golden by June's buttercups; in woods,
> Where under ferns fresh pulled I buried her
> And called her forth like Lazarus from the grave.
> She'd laughing come, to shake her curls until
> Methought to hear full half a hundred bells.

This very innocent 'Cider with Rosie' scenario becomes curiously blasphemous in its later reshaping:

> Today I acted Christ
>     While Joy played Lazarus;
> I buried her in ferns
>     And heaps of gathered grass.
> And when I cried 'Come forth!'
>     Up from the grave she rose
> And, with a peal of bells,
>     Threw off her burial clothes.
>
> When Sleep this night has come
>     With feathers for our grass
> Shall we reverse our parts
>     Of Christ and Lazarus?
> When I – a buried man –
>     Hear 'Lazarus, come forth!'
> I'll rise and, with both hands,
>     Ring every bell on earth.

(Poem 583)

He's been reading D. H. Lawrence, surely! The image out of a Welsh Sunday school has become a full-scale dirty joke, in an environment governed by half-grasped punning: peal of bells – peel of belles, and so on. The sophistication is only skin-deep, of course. The phrasing in the first couplet of the second stanza is sufficiently clumsy to protect him as a 'primitive' from accusations of blasphemy and bad taste.

'The soul's destroyer' is a sort of matrix for his subsequent development as a writer. The contrast between London (with its stupor and slums) and wandering in the countryside, which is one of its main themes, will be echoed many times, as will the idea of returning to Wales – at least in memory:

> Six days had gone, and I at length near home,
> Where toil the Cymry deep in sunless pits,
> And emptying all their hills to warm the world.

That's in the middle distance, but what really he remembers is the half-country, half-town around Newport:

> Soon saw familiar scenes and saw no change:
> The rookery, where never silence seemed . . .
> And near that rookery a river ran,
> And over it a bridge too small for piers;
> Another crossing, of irregular stones,
> Was seen, which in the springtime flooded o'er;
> And I had heard the river tell their number
> And spell – like letters of an alphabet
> That it would never tire repeating day
> And night. When young I oft had bared my feet
> To go from bank to bank, leapt stone to stone,
> My ankles wetted on a sunken one.

Here again the association is with primary education: the river is like a class repeating its alphabet, so that the boy's crossing the stepping stones is subconsciously compared with the act of reading – leaping from word to word, as it were, and then every so often a word he doesn't know, a 'sunken one' to wet his ankles. (The half-dialectal 'wetted' surely suggests 'whetted' as the problem 'whets' his interest.)

Two things stand out: the fantasy of returning to a childhood sweetheart and the moralizing on the evils of drink. No doubt both are founded on realistic knowledge, but surely they are present in the poem for other than purely personal reasons. The two things are related – two sides of the same coin, we're tempted to say, both being products of a sub-Dickensian Victorian sentimentality. Davies obviously feels that this plot and this kind of moralizing in some way *justify* the sort of poetry he wants to write – full of ambition to get himself out of the human dustbin he was in, as well as nostalgia for his childhood and delight in the countryside. And not only do they justify it, they give it a structure that it would not otherwise possess. The whole poem gravitates towards the final peroration against drink. The theme of the childhood sweetheart revisited seems at last no more than a device to arrive at it:

> Such is this drink that fathers half our sins;
> It makes a simple one responsible
> For deeds which memory makes no count to save,
> And proves man guilty in his innocence.
> When he shall stand before his judging God
> He needs must answer charges strange to him
> And his own mind – to One who sees all things;
> And what He sees, He never can forget.
> May God have mercy on our frailties!
> Sure we, though set a thousand years of pain,
> Nor once should murmur at vicissitude,
> Yet ill deserve those promises fulfilled
> Of an eternity of bliss with Him;
> And who can know the thoughts of him in hell,
> Who sacrificed eternity of joy
> To gratify this little life on earth!
> Were't not for God Almighty's mercy, trees
> Would 'scape the thunderbolt, th' unfeeling rocks
> The lightning's blast; all ills would fall on man,
> Who hides his conscience in a covered cage,
> As dumb and silent as a moulting bird.

Surely Davies's verse here is acting the popular preacher. All the tricks of the trade are imitated – the changes of tone, the rhetorical questions, even the final superb poetic image, off-centre as far as the rhetoric is concerned, yet reaching home as a picture derived from childhood memories of a tame canary. What is more, the preaching tone is completely unironic, as it so frequently was in the Welsh nineteenth-century *pryddestau*, long poems in free metre (now dead as ditchwater) written for eisteddfod competition and as often as not by actual preachers. 'The soul's destroyer' would probably not look out of place in such a rogues' gallery, except that its sensuous freshness might have counted as 'lascivious' and put it out of court!

The sermon is clearly a dominant form at this stage in Davies's development. *The Soul's Destroyer* gravitates towards it. Even so, his preaching might be considered merely opportunist, until one notices that his second book, *New Poems*, is also dominated by a long *pryddest*-type poem against drink called 'Hope abandoned'. True, it is a dialogue in rhyme rather than a blank-verse sermon. The poet argues with a drunkard who mourns his failure to win fame and tells how despair led him to seek intoxication to kill his pain:

> But all Life's play and game is left behind,
> I out of this sad pool no way can find;
> Though hunger doth not make a man his prey,
> Foul air will never leave him night or day.

It is a considerably clumsier piece of work than 'The soul's destroyer' and might be considered a simple expression of his predicament in London, trying to win fame as a poet while living in a doss-house. But the opening stanzas are clearly derived from temperance sermonizing: the insistent morality of that tradition is apparently what the poet feels a long poem ought to be about:

> Enchanter Drink! the world's half, small and great,
> Mock death by lying fearless in Death's state;
> They pawn their finest tools: they know not what
> In life there is to make, why should they not?
>
> Thou leering Imp, create of flame and fume,
> Who quenched such hopes as did yon mind illume,
> Now, like a babe, he is near blind again,
> And sees but from one corner of his brain.

One should not underestimate the extent to which even English-speaking Monmouthshire was still culturally part of Welsh Wales – *buchedd* Wales – in the nineteenth century of Davies's boyhood. One of his headmasters had been Richard Lewis, a translator and anthologist of Welsh lyrics, and it was doubtless at Lewis's school that W. H. Davies first conceived what it meant to be a poet. There was a considerable impulse to put across Welsh values. The language and the textbooks were in English, but the outlook of the teachers was often very Welsh, and many of the important positions were held by Welsh-speakers. (That kind of situation was very familiar to me as a schoolboy in Colwyn Bay nearly a hundred years later.) What is more, Monmouthshire was the familiar stomping ground of one of the most formidable eisteddfod poets, the Revd William Thomas, universally known by his bardic name Islwyn.

You would need a far greater understanding of nineteeth-century

Welsh poetry (not to speak of Welsh elementary education) than I have to evaluate Davies's Welshness: how much, when he came to write poetry, did he instinctively embody a Welsh aesthetic in what he wrote – at any rate in his first two books, before he learned from experience what his English readers required of him? One of the troubles is that he covered his traces. He never reprinted most of the poems in his first book, *The Soul's Destroyer*, which he had privately printed and tried to distribute by hawking it round on his travels. I have never seen a copy even of a reprint. There was a second edition, brought out by a regular London publisher, but it only contained sixteen pieces. The second book, *New Poems*, was similarly degutted in his own collected editions. The posthumous *Complete Poems*, edited by Daniel George, does reprint its missing poems in what amounts to an appendix at the end, though they are numbered consecutively with his later poems and muddled up with rejected poems from later books as well. By the third book, *Nature Poems*, the later middlebrow poet is firmly in the saddle, apart from the trickle of tramp ballads which die out finally about 1922.

I have a copy of *New Poems* (1907) dedicated to Helen and Edward Thomas. To read it gives you a very different picture of W. H. Davies – there's a lot more sense that a poet can speak with authority about traditional moral issues of importance to ordinary people. In my essay on the poet in *The Cost of Strangeness*,[1] I point out how easily the poems fall into the categories of poetry written by the *beirdd gwlad*, the Welsh folk poets: *cerddi natur* (nature poems), *cerddi caru* (love poems), *cerddi cwrw* (literally 'beer poems' – poems against drink), *cerddi i bersonau* (poems to persons – in this case, fellow tramps), *cerddi coffa* (memorials of the dead) and *cerddi moesol* (moral poems). They are probably more sentimental than most folk poets would write, but there do seem to be quite large similarities of approach.

At the centre of the book are various meditations on the cruelty of cities, drink, the fear of death, old age. They deal with moralized nature, sentimental love, *hiraeth* or nostalgia for his old home and his childhood, and moral topics like 'The ways of time', 'The homeless man', 'Dying', and 'A blind child'. These had little appeal to middle-class readers, suspicious of any poetry that has a design upon you and unimpressed with the sentiments of 'banal' morality. *New Poems* was by far the least popular of his books with polite readers. This was partly a matter of

---

[1] See 'The tramp ballads of W. H. Davies' in my book, *The Cost of Strangeness*, (Llandysul: Gomer Press, 1982), pp. 21-51.

timing. Davies made his reputation with his *Autobiography of a Super-Tramp*, published in 1908, the year after *New Poems*. However, it was also a matter of what readers wanted: the exotic flavour and adventure of the super-tramp or the freshness of the lyrical moment, not the commonplaces of an articulate but ill-educated member of the lower orders.

Davies in *New Poems* takes himself seriously as a responsible person, not just one who has lyrical moments of truth. There is a lot that derives from his schooling and ultimately from the *bardd gwlad* (folk poet) tradition, however mediated through English. It is not so much the style as the assumptions about what poetry does, that seem inherited from Welsh nineteenth-century *buchedd* culture.

There were four terms involved in W. H. Davies's attempt to write poetry. First, a derivative layer, from Wordsworth and Tennyson and other English poets. Second, a genuine 'folk-poet' element of the poet as a spokesman for traditional moral values, deriving at least partly from Victorian Wales. Perhaps this element in him did not often produce very good poems but equally it was not humanly despicable. Third, the unique poetry of a beggarman's sensibility, which lies behind what I have called the tramp ballads. And fourthly, the mass of his poetry, written after he had discovered what his English middle-class audience required of him.

His early poems are obviously the products of a man trying to be a responsible citizen. A beggar did not have to forfeit respectability. Though it was stretching the *buchedd*'s ideology of classlessness rather far, there was no reason in theory why a tramp should not be accepted as one worthy of respect. He was not necessarily expected to be a noble savage or a naïve primitive. But W. H. Davies's later verses depend very largely on charm: he seems to be acceding to a view of himself as a 'character'. There is something of the privileged pet of the middle class about his quirky inconsequence:

> Though bees have stings, I doubt if any bee
>> Has ever stung a flower in all his life:
> Neither, my love, can I think ill of you,
>> Though half the world and I may be at strife.

Literally hundreds of short poems isolate a lyric moment, sometimes with genuine power, but quite often not bothering to face the implications of what he is saying. After a while, the lack of real grip wears one down.

The relative integrity and even the dullness of his early *buchedd* work contrasts with the charm and slightly meretricious naïvety that he learnt to exploit for an English middlebrow market; but between the two groups lie what I take to be Davies's most valuable contribution to poetry, what I have described as the 'tramp ballads'. These are poems which relate to his life as a beggar, but they are not always about tramps. They are stylistically bare narratives, unpretentious and direct. In *The Cost of Strangeness* I show that they originated in a sort of praise-poem listing the tramps in the doss-house. It may even be that they derive ultimately from the Welsh praise-poetry tradition, the 'poems to persons' of the folk poets. Some are too clumsy to succeed, but even so they are genuine expressions of beggar sensibilty (where English poetry has not often been before) showing sometimes a fine moral indignation. 'Facts' is one of the more successful of the early ones:

> One night poor Jim had not a sou,
>     Mike had enough for his own bed;
> 'Take it: I'll walk the streets tonight',
>     Said Mike, 'and you lie down instead'.
>
> So Mike walked out, but ne'er came back;
>     We know not whether he is drowned,
> Or used his hands unlawfully;
>     Is sick, or in some prison bound.
>
> Now Jim was dying fast, and he
>     Took to the workhouse his old bones;
> To earn some water, bread and sleep,
>     They made that dying man break stones,
>
> He swooned upon his heavy task:
>     They carried him to a black coach,
> And tearless strangers took him out –
>     A corpse! at the infirmary porch.
>
> Since Jesus came with mercy and love,
>     'Tis nineteen hundred years and five:
> They made that dying man break stones,
>     In faith that Christ is still alive.

The beggar is a familiar image in literature: as the disguised Odysseus he comes to wreak vengeance on those who plunder from him; as Lazarus he is the *agent provocateur* for God's judgement on Dives, the rich man. He is Francis of Assisi, he is Mad Tom in the storm. In the ballads he is often a nobleman in disguise. He can even be Christ. He is able to judge us, not by what he says or does, but by what we say or do to him: that is his power over us, as it is also his livelihood. He is dependent on our kindliness – literally, our sense of kind, our humanity; but it is our humanity, not his, that is in peril. So, 'Facts' contrasts the inhumanity of the workhouse (and the whole civilization it represents and ministers to) with a fellow pauper's spontaneous, heroic kindness. W. H. Davies's slight stylistic clumsiness – which never in this poem gets in the way of what he wants to do – acts as a kind of authenticity which inhibits a merely sentimental response. Mike, for instance, might be a criminal – even a murderer. His act of kindliness still stands as a judgement on us.

The tramp ballads stand out among the general knick-knackery of his poems like good deeds in a naughty world. Here is a later and rather more sophisticated example:

### A child's pet

When I sailed out of Baltimore
   With twice a thousand head of sheep,
They would not eat, they would not drink,
   But bleated o'er the deep.

Inside the pens we crawled each day,
   To sort the living from the dead;
And when we reached the Mersey's mouth,
   Had lost five hundred head.

Yet every night and day one sheep
   That had no fear of man or sea,
Stuck through the bars its pleading face,
   And it was stroked by me.

And to the sheep-men standing near,
   'You see', I said, 'this one tame sheep?
It seems a child has lost her pet,
   And cried herself to sleep'.

So every time we passed it by,
   Sailing to England's slaughter-house.
Eight ragged sheep-men – tramps and thieves –
   Would stroke that sheep's black nose.

In the nightmare of that voyage, the pet sheep has become an image of the men's own affective life, connected as it is with childhood and tenderness and grief. There is a large hinterland of felt connotation behind the narrative – Blake's *Songs of Innocence*, the biblical 'lamb led to the slaughter', even the 'rotting sea' of 'The ancient mariner' – but it is never allowed to interfere with the brutal reality of what happened. And the last phrase 'that sheep's black nose' (though all sheep noses are black) relies partly for its effect on the common idiom, 'the black sheep', the outcast of the family, like the sheep-men themselves. The atmosphere on board this death ship is reminiscent of the slave trade; yet the feeling in the poem is one of refreshment at deep springs.

### Huw Menai

The tramp ballads are in their fashion a product of *buchedd* sensibility, but one displaced in ways alien to most people of the *buchedd* itself. Displaced, literally, in that they have no reference to Welsh life; but also displaced in the kind of society – beggars, prostitutes, paupers – that forms their subject matter. For an undisplaced example of *buchedd* poetry at its finest, we must turn to Huw Menai.

It is an odd place to look: for Huw Menai was himself clearly a displaced person and a displaced poet. He was brought up in Caernarfon thoroughly Welsh-speaking – at a time, however, when English was the language of opportunity and widening horizons. He had educated himself widely in literature and philosophy. In search of work he migrated to the coalfields of south Wales where the shock of human exploitation turned him into an agitator. This meant he lost his job in the mines, and was only given a new one on condition he abstained from politics – in fact, he worked for the bosses against the men, so in effect he had to change sides. He started to write English poetry and published four volumes, from 1920 to 1945, which reputedly contain only a fraction of what he composed.

Most of his poetry[2] seems to me broken-backed, whether it is about conditions in the mining communities – again, one notices the stress on the evils of drink – or, more typically, pseudo-Wordsworthian reflections on nature and the grandeur of life *à la* Islwyn. They give the impression of a grandiloquence hiding inadequacy, reflecting a displacement on

---

[2] See the chapter in Glyn Jones's *The Dragon has Two Tongues* (London: Dent, 1968) and the essay on the poet in my *Cost of Strangeness*.

many levels: language, society, district and class loyalty. The poetry is vague and confused, the metaphors often mixed, unlocalized and leaving the reader without clear feeling. When it is better than usual, it engages you, but only for the sake of a good phrase or two, rarely of anything more.

But there is one poem which almost miraculously escapes these strictures. It was chosen by Gwyn Jones as the opening poem of one of the early (1939) issues of the *Welsh Review* and it fully deserves its eminence. 'When Time the sculptor ...' is certainly the finest single lyric in English produced by the *buchedd*. It is intensely Welsh – Welsh in every nerve. Indeed it is the nearest possible thing to a Welsh poem in English. This very fact may have militated against it: it has been largely ignored by critics and anthologists, who presumably don't have the sensibility to see how fine it is. Instead, Huw Menai is given token representation in our anthologies, usually with the same one or two indifferent sonnets.

When Time the sculptor ...

As Time, the sculptor, deepens
   The lines upon my face
I find my thoughts returning
   To far-off childhood days
When clad in ragged garments
   And hunger was at hand
I combed the tidal leavings
   Of shellfish on the strand –

The strand by wild Coed Alun
   Where oft the poor would spread
The poacher's net for salmon
   And prison risk for bread ...
And big Wil Foundry Morfa
   And Wmffre *bach* the sweep
Now safe from water bailiffs
   In old Llanbeblig sleep!

How Need the latent quickens!
   But what unhappy thrall
To be a man in thinking
   While yet a schoolboy small!

22

And Lord it is no wonder
    They voice an after rage
Who carried on young shoulders
    The burdens of Old Age.

Yet though so full of sadness
    Those days of Long Ago
When carefree joys of childhood
    I was not born to know,
A strange and mighty *Hiraeth*
    Has hallowed since for me
Old haunts by Rhosbodrual
    Llyn Garnedd and Llyn Lli!

Now looms the grave before us
    As we grow old and grey
Hoping that each tomorrow
    Proves happier than today,
Children of fond illusions
    Seeking a magic key
Our hearts for ever yearning
    For things that shall not be!

O! mankind's mighty passion!
    O! pulse that knows the pain
Of going headlong forward
    But to fall back again!
Attila following Jesus,
    Darkness following day,
Yet sunward climbs the primrose
    Out of an old decay.

But all is not yet heartache
    When in the starlight gleams
The sea by Dinas Dinlle
    Whereon I sailed my dreams
A battered bark returning
    Through many a stormy night
To shores of Abermenai
    And Llanddwyn's lonely light.

The first thing to note is the music of the poem: Huw Menai takes a
very simple metre, the 7.6.7.6 of the hymn-writers, and gives it a cadence

and a melody that controls the frequent changes of tone and direction, and articulates what seem on the surface simple statements into a complex expression, wry with lived experience. The music of Welsh place-names has rarely been used to better effect – though it is worth noticing that these are of two kinds: first local Caernarfon names – Llanbeblig, one of the parishes of the borough, Coed Alun (now mistakenly called Coed Elen after Macsen's dream-lady) or Rhosbodrual; and second, names redolent of the high civilization of Wales, like Dinas Dinlle or Dinlleu (the fortress of Lleu Llaw Gyffes from the Fourth Branch of the Mabinogion), or Llanddwyn, the church of St Dwynwen, the patron saint of medieval lovers, on an island off the west coast of Anglesey – its lonely light is a lighthouse to guide shipping into the Menai Straits.

The formality reminds one of Gray; but it has, I think, gone through the hands of Welsh masters like Ieuan Glyn Geirionydd and come out with a Caernarfon accent, so that 'face' and 'days' rhyme, and 'and hunger was at hand' can come after 'when clad in ragged garments'. It is not the formality of an aristocratic culture, but the conscious dignity of a people equal before God with the greatest in the land.

Secondly, this is very much a poem of his relationship to a remembered community – people like big Wil Foundry Morfa (Will of the seashore foundry) and Wmffre bach (little Humphrey) the sweep. It was a world where children had to grow up astonishingly quickly – a world whose consequences he still suffers; and yet for all its misery his *hiraeth* (or longing – Pantycelyn has *hiraeth* for the courts of God) still hallows those places he once knew. We are children now we're old – more than we were then – deluding ourselves with illusory meanings. Attila follows Jesus (he was writing this in 1939 when Hitler's barbarism was being unleashed across Europe). We rush forward only to fall back. Darkness follows day. And yet, he says,

> Yet sunward climbs the primrose
> Out of an old decay.

The ship of his boyhood dreams, he is saying, is now returning to the land of ancient suffering and purpose, to Dinas Dinlle and Llanddwyn, as the primrose climbs out of an old decay. Implicitly, he is linking his own life-story to the oldest strata of his race.

## A. G. Prys-Jones

We have noted that at the end of the nineteenth century the *buchedd* was under threat intellectually from the new University Colleges at Aberystwyth, Bangor and Cardiff. These had been founded largely through the efforts of the *buchedd* itself: in Bangor, for instance, the pennies collected from the quarrymen have become a legend. But higher education meant that the *buchedd* consensus was vulnerable at the top to the efforts of the ambitious to improve themselves, which produced an independent middle class and intelligentsia, both in Welsh and English. For a time (and indeed even now) the new intellectuals tried to lead a *buchedd*-based movement, much as the old preacher-poets had done. But the strain was beginning to tell, even in Welsh-language circles. In English, it led to a Dark Age of ingrowing provincialism and anti-Welsh bitterness. Though few were as flagrant as Caradoc Evans in the short stories published in *My People* (1915), many intellectuals were to become thoroughly anti-*buchedd*. Dylan's distaste for it was flaunted: 'Land of my fathers – my fathers can keep it!' he exclaimed.

For a time, though, before the Depression bled it white, the *buchedd* benefited from the intellectual riches laid before it. A tiny movement of Anglo-Welsh literati was born, which produced the first book-length anthology of Anglo-Welsh poems in 1917, *Welsh Poets*, edited by A. G. Prys-Jones (1888–1937). It begins with translations by Idris Bell from the three leading Welsh poets of the time, R. Williams Parry (1884–1956), T. Gwynn Jones and W. J. Gruffydd, all of them in their different ways Romantic rebels against chapel and respectability. The original poems in English have lines like:

> I come from the realms of Annwn
> On the wings of the drear storm-wind.
>
> (Wilma Buckley, 'Song of Pwyll')

as well as more normal examples of sub-Georgian lyric. (Annwn is the old Celtic Underworld, which Pwyll visits in the First Branch of the Mabinogion.) There is a sense that Wales was at last catching up with the Celtic twilight. T. Gwynn Jones, the arch-poet of the Welsh literary revival, is actually represented by three lyrics in his own right as an English-language poet – not very distinguished, it must be said, though something of his elaborate music comes through:

> Once, she told me, undismaying,
> In our roaming
> Days of old,
> How the Fairy Folk were playing
> In the gloaming,
> By the wold . . .

Among other poets represented are W. H. Davies and Ernest Rhys (1859–1946); but perhaps the best service the editor did for Wales was to introduce his own vigorously patriotic ballads. These gave Welsh children something stirring to read in English about the history of their own country. A good example is 'A ballad of Glyndwr's rising, 1400':

> My son, the moon is crimson, and a mist is in the sky;
> Oh can't you hear the thudding feet, the horsemen speeding by?
> Oh can't you hear the muttering that swells upon the breeze,
> And the whispers that are stealing through the chancel of the trees?
> To-night we two go riding, for the threads of fate are spun,
> And we muster far at Corwen at the rising of the sun.
>
> My son, the winds are calling, and the mountains and the flood,
> With a wail of deep oppression that wakes havoc in my blood.
> And I have waited – waited long throughout the bitter years
> For this hour of freedom's challenge, and the flashing of the spears.
> So we two go riding, riding, through the meshes of the night
> That we hail Glyndwr at Corwen at the breaking of the light.
>
> My son, go kiss your mother, kiss her gently, she'll not wake,
> For a greater mother calls you, though you perish for her sake:
> Lo! the Dragon flag is floating out across the silver Dee,
> And the soul of Wales is crying at the very heart o' me –
> Crying justice, crying vengeance: pray, my son, for strength anew,
> For there's many will be sleeping at the falling of the dew.

It sounds fairly innocent stuff, but the gap is already yawning. A poetry like this is provided by a Romantically inclined middle class for other people. It has a clear educational function. It attempts to teach Welsh people their own history and give it a nationalist direction. Unlike genuine *buchedd* poetry, it is culture handed down from on high.

# 3

## *The Anglo-Welsh vanishing point: the Eastaway of Edward Thomas*

~

Ever since Wordsworth, the philosophy of empiricism (the doctrine that all knowledge comes to us through our senses) with its total emphasis on the individual's experience of the world in a social vacuum, has dominated the English tradition – and still does – so drastically that English poetry has become insular and self-contained, difficult for other traditions to approach or use, except when some accident, like the personality and fate of Byron, renders it accessible to foreigners for what English readers generally see as the wrong reasons.

One of the problems of responding to modern Welsh poetry, for an English reader, is its non-empiricist, 'rationalist' base. The idea is embodied or incarnate in physical existence rather than being discovered there through the senses. Welsh poetry, irrespective of the belief or otherwise of individual poets, is grounded in Christian humanism, of the Word becoming flesh.

This is true also of first-generation Anglo-Welsh poets: what Dylan Thomas, Idris Davies and Alun Lewis (1915–44) have in common – what makes them difficult to fit to English tradition – is precisely their lack of empiricism. Alun Lewis, influenced by Edward Thomas, marks the point where the two philosophies collide, in the overwhelming experience of India and modern war.

There is, of course, an empiricist wing to twentieth-century Welsh poetry. R. Williams Parry is notable. Especially in his first book, *Yr Haf a Cherddi Eraill* ('The Summer and Other Poems'), published in 1924, he found freedom from the stuffiness of nineteenth-century Nonconformity by learning the delightful strangeness of sensory experience, particularly the experience of nature. Take his famous sonnet, 'Y llwynog' ('The fox'):

Ganllath o gopa'r mynydd, pan oedd clych
Eglwysi'r llethrau'n gwahodd tua'r llan,
Ac anhreuliedig haul Gorffenaf gwych
Yn gwahodd tua'r mynydd, – yn y fan,
Ar ddiarwybod droed a distaw duth,
Llwybreiddiodd ei ryfeddod prin o'n blaen;
Ninnau heb ysgog ac heb ynom chwyth
Barlyswyd ennyd; megis trindod faen
Y safem, pan ar ganol diofal gam
Syfrdan y safodd yntau, ac uwchlaw
Ei untroed oediog dwy sefydlog fflam
Ei lygaid arnom. Yna heb frys na braw
Llithrodd ei flewyn cringoch dros y grib;
Digwyddodd, darfu, megis seren wib.

(A hundred yards from the top, as the church bells
Of the slopes called us villageward
And the bright July sun, not a bit worn out,
Invited to the mountain – suddenly
On unsuspecting foot and silent trot
The rare wonder of him came on before us;
And we, stilled, holding our breath,
For a second were paralysed; like a stone trinity
We stood. Then, at a careless mid step,
He too stood stunned, and above
The one poised foot the two fixed flames
Of his eyes upon us. Then, without flurry or fear,
His russet pelt slipped over the ridge;
He was, and was not – like a shooting star.)

But even though 'Y llwynog' is devoted to the value of the unpredictable moment of experience, Williams Parry starts his poem by saying he left the village with its ringing church bells in order to follow the late-setting July sun's invitation to the hilltops. He does not tell us this to share the experience of leaving the bells to ring, as Housman does in 'Bredon Hill',

And I would turn and answer
Among the springing thyme,
'Oh, peal upon our wedding,
And we will hear the chime,
And come to church in time',

but as a symbolic decision in which his 'sincerity' is involved. He deliberately embodies an idea. He becomes agnosticism incarnate, and the poem is his 'I will not serve'. Even in the act of writing an empiricist poem, therefore, Williams Parry assumed some sort of word becoming flesh before he could start. In his later poems, this non-empiricist element grew more, not less, it seems to me, particularly after the burning of Pen-y-berth, the bombing school in Llŷn, and the trial of his friend Saunders Lewis for the first Welsh Nationalist act of violent resistance to thoughtless Anglicization and government disregard for Wales.

It was very hard work for a Welshman, even a monoglot English-speaking Welshman, to write like an English poet. There was, as we say, no traditional bias towards empiricism in the culture he came from. Poems in Welsh were made for a rational purpose, to praise a lord, or God, or to amuse, or edify, or to compete for a prize. They are rarely just records of experience, data presented and knowledge gained. Neither does a Welsh poet usually use his poem to express or practise empiricist attitudes to knowledge. Wandering lonely as a cloud is a fundamentally un-Welsh activity. Again, Williams Parry is the exception or partial exception; but we've seen the difficulty even a poet of his stature had in breaking the mould in which he was reared.

That's in Welsh, of course; but the same difficulty afflicted English-language Welsh poets almost as much. There is a continuous spectrum nowadays, between Anglo-Welsh poets like Idris Davies and Dylan Thomas who write almost totally non-empiricist verse (Dylan's prose is a slightly different matter) and those like Jean Earle or John Davies (1944– ) who mostly seem indistinguishable from English writers in the way they compose.

It is a problem that haunts this whole study, of where to draw the line between Anglo-Welsh and not. I tend to use the term to refer to work, rather than writers. Even so, the criteria of whom to include are not easy. For instance, if one only studied the poetry of Edward Thomas without reference to his influence, it would not make much sense to me to talk of him as Anglo-Welsh, despite his Welsh father and his frequent visits to the country to see Welsh friends like Gwili. Very little of his poetry refers in any way to Wales, Welsh people or Welsh traditions, compared with the mass of it that describes and embodies a vision of England. If Edward Thomas is to count as Anglo-Welsh, the grounds have to be more than genealogical. Otherwise every writer with Welsh blood – the metaphysicals Donne and Herbert, for example, or possibly even

Shakespeare – becomes eligible and the term grows so unwieldy as to be useless as a critical tool. There are Anglo-Welsh aspects to Edward Thomas, certainly, as there are to Shakespeare. But he became important to Anglo-Welsh poets like Alun Lewis and Leslie Norris (1921– ) in the middle decades of the twentieth century; and it is probably there, rather than as a writer in his own right, that he concerns this history.

Nevertheless, and with misgivings, I decided to include a brief notice of his work, for three reasons. The most important is that he represents a vanishing point: if Anglo-Welsh writing represents a pilgrim's progress towards the New Jerusalem of blue-blooded English, then Edward Thomas is the success story. The second reason is that he was tempted to become Anglo-Welsh, and the temptation remained open. In a letter to his future wife Helen Noble in 1898 he speculated on what would have happened to him had he been born in Wales instead of London:

> Certainly, I think a poet, especially a lyric poet, has an infinitely greater chance here than in England, a greater chance of perfection in his art and in his fame; I myself, if only I were greater, might lament that I came to London to be born. Certainly my present writings would have given me a sort of name if written in Welsh; even in English I might do something by writing of Wales. At present, however, I have no impulse at all. (quoted in R. George Thomas, *Edward Thomas,* 70-1)

'I might lament that I came to London to be born . . .' This half-joking sentiment seems to me very Anglo-Welsh. The temptation to be Welsh is not usually open to real English poets in quite this casual fashion. It is also true that two or three of Edward Thomas's poems, 'The child on the cliffs', 'The ash grove', possibly 'The coombe', do use Anglo-Welsh material, even if they do not constitute an Anglo-Welsh œuvre in any considerable sense.

The third reason is that Welsh poets like Gwili (John Jenkins, 1872–1936) the future Archdruid, recognized him as in some sense a fellow Welshman, and that this recognition has persisted among Welsh people to this day. Gwili wrote an English elegy for 'Edward Eastaway', the pseudonym under which Edward Thomas published his poems: the name itself looks as though it was invented in a Welsh context, for where else would 'Eastaway' refer to someone away in England? Gwili's poem shows real Anglo-Welsh feeling, that is, it approaches the frontier between the two cultures in a living, 'insider' way:

But most of all I miss thee on the road
To Carreg Cennen, and the castled steep
Thou lovedst in all weathers, and the cave
Of Llygad Llwchwr and Cwrt Bryn y Beirdd.
Thither we wandered in thine Oxford days,
When there were hours of gladness in thy heart
That seemed a hoard thy childhood had conserved
When song burst out of silence, and the depths
Of thy mysterious spirit were unsealed.
Thither we sauntered in the after-years,
When London cares had made thy Celtic blood
Run slow, and thou hadst sought thy mother Wales
Full suddenly – for all too brief a stay.
Lore of the ages, music of old bards
That would have soothed the ear of Golden Grove
And its great exile priest, and brought delight
To Nature's nursling bard of Grongar Hill,
Beguiled the footsore pilgrims many an eve
Past Llandyfân and Derwydd, past Glyn Hir.
It is October, but thou comest not
Again, nor hast returned since that wild night
When we were on this road, late lovers twain,
And thou saidst, in thy firm and silent way,
That all roads led to France, and called thee hence
To seek the chivalry of arms.

Tonight,
The road is lonelier – too lonely far
For one. I turn toward set of sun, since thou
Hast journeyed west, dear Edward Eastaway.

(Gwili, *Poems,* 92-4)

Gwili's poem is old-fashioned *buchedd* poetry, of course; but it deals very movingly with Edward Thomas as a Welshman – a side of him we do not usually find expressed. Wales and England are confronting each other in the elegy, the strength of the feeling for the *bro* or native district that the Welshman uses place-names to invoke, 'the cave / Of Llygad Llwchwr, and Cwrt Bryn y Beirdd', contrasted with the life Edward Thomas lived at Oxford and London. But the *bro*'s strong links with English tradition are also remembered: the 'great exile priest' is Jeremy Taylor who once lived in Gelli Aur, Golden Grove, a celebrated house in the area; and 'Nature's nursling bard of Grongar Hill' is of course the eighteenth-century poet John Dyer. This is what it felt like to be on the

Anglo-Welsh frontier in the year Edward Thomas died, before it lost its innocence in the abrasive mockery of Caradoc Evans.

Edward Thomas was born at Lambeth in 1878. His father came from Tredegar, his mother from Newport (though she was half-English). He went to Lincoln College, Oxford, where he studied under O. M. Edwards, historian and popular writer in Welsh. He became an author and journalist, mostly about the countryside. He married Helen Noble in 1899, and supported her and their three children by literary hackwork until the Great War broke out in 1914. They were often very poor, though by the end he was an established writer and earned enough to live on, in the process frequently working himself into nervous exhaustion. He and his family lived in the country, particularly in the Steep district of Hampshire which will always be associated with his poetry. Throughout his life he made frequent visits to south Wales, where he had many relatives and friends – Gwili, as we've seen, was one. He was, as well, a familiar figure in the London literary scene. He was a highly influential poetry reviewer, being one of the first to notice such widely different poets as W. H. Davies, Ezra Pound and Robert Frost. He forced the reading public to recognize Frost as the important poet he was, and later became his greatest friend. More than anyone else Frost seems to have had a formative influence on Edward Thomas, giving him encouragement and the vital sense of direction he needed to find himself as a poet.

The war broke out in August 1914, and for some time Thomas was undecided what to do. He had plans to join Frost in New England, but in July 1915 he surprised everyone by enlisting. He spent some months as a map-reading instructor, but was commissioned as a second lieutenant and volunteered for overseas service in December 1916. He was killed by a shell-blast at the Battle of Arras early on Easter Monday, 9 April 1917.

Edward Thomas wrote his first serious poetry in December 1914, when he was already thirty-six and a prose-writer of long standing. His last complete poem was written on Christmas Eve 1916, just before he left for France. In the intervening two years he produced 144 poems, some of them fairly elaborate pieces that entailed much revision. It seems like a great release of pent-up energy: during the first four months of 1915 Thomas was writing, on average, a poem every two days. He also completed, during the same two years, a 75,000-word life of Marlborough, which took him twenty-six days; and he was, of course, being trained and working as a soldier for three-quarters of the period. Even if we allow that Thomas had long been a hack-writer and could contemplate an amount of work that would leave most people gasping, it is still extraordinary how many poems – how many good poems – he managed to produce in such a short time. His collection is equal in volume to many another's that took a lifetime to produce.

By nature, Edward Thomas was an introverted, meditative man, full of complex sadness and despair. He was passionately observant and committed to the truth, and yet unsure of himself and reticent of expressing emotions that might break through the web of responsible friendship which – on one level at least – was vital to him. He would not have found possible D. H. Lawrence's kind of outgoing expressionism. He is a poet of detachment as much as commitment, whose best poetry tends to define by negatives, insistent on the awkwardness of feeling:

> What does it mean? Tired, angry, and ill at ease,
> No man, woman, or child alive could please
> Me now. And yet I almost dare to laugh
> Because I sit and frame an epitaph –
> 'Here lies all that no one loved of him
> And that loved no one.' Then in a trice that whim
> Has wearied . . .
>
> ('Beauty')

It was primarily the Great War that turned this worried, overworked writer of purple prose into a poet. His poems in a real sense are all war poems, though none of them were written in the trenches and few are ostensibly about warfare at all. The presence of war is everywhere implied, however, and in many poems actually explicit:

> And salted was my food, and my repose,
> Salted and sobered too, by the bird's voice
> Speaking for all who lay under the stars,
> Soldiers and poor, unable to rejoice.
>
> ('The owl')

Like the owl's cry, the war 'salted and sobered' him. It imposed a polarity – 'Now all roads lead to France', he says, the living soldiers going out, the dead ghosts returning:

> Now all roads lead to France,
> And heavy is the tread

> Of the living; but the dead
> Returning lightly dance:
> Whatever the road bring
> To me or take from me,
> They keep me company
> With their pattering,
>
> Crowding the solitude
> Of the loops over the downs,
> Hushing the roar of towns
> And their brief multitude.
>
> ('Roads')

The world was filled with ghosts, both of the past and of the future – 'old griefs, and griefs not yet begun'. These ghosts, these griefs, altered the texture of experience. Edward Thomas had been writing prose about the English countryside for years. It was only with the coming of the ghosts along the roads from France that that same English countryside became for him the new subject matter that original poetry like his demanded before it could exist. The accounts of him as a soldier show that he had rid himself of much of his melancholy and indecision. It was the war that sharpened his apprehension of the moment and made him even more intensely aware of what recurred with the seasons:

> And now again
> In the harvest rain,
> The Blenheim oranges[1]
> Fall grubby from the trees
>
> As when I was young –
> And when the lost one was here –
> And when the war began
> To turn young men to dung.
>
> ('Gone, gone again')

The typical Edward Thomas experience begins as a rapt meditation on some aspect of rural life. The country had become for him a kind of guarantee of integrity, a sign to himself that he was being sincere. But though it all starts happily in the countryside, the final discovery is likely to be of melancholy, or void, or the threat or release of death.

---

[1] A variety of apple.

Discontinuity, not the unfolding of generations, is the keynote. When human beings appear in his work, they often come from nowhere and just as suddenly disappear. In Edward Thomas the English countryside and its inhabitants seem somehow in hiding and therefore mysterious – almost a fairy country, a timeless Otherworld, where you can understand the language of birds – the 'pure thrush word' that he talks about.

And yet, that's not it either. Edward Thomas is not Thomas the Rhymer, stolen away to fairyland, but a very human person, whatever his psychological problems, a lover, a father and a soldier. At the end of his life he wrote a poem, 'As the team's head-brass', in which he sits on a fallen elm in his soldier's uniform and watches a ploughman plough a field. The two men shout to each other as the plough-team turns at the end of its furrow. They are on terms of complete equality. It is no longer anything like fairyland, but a countryside undergoing serious disruption. I think of that strange, spasmodic conversation as very close to the centre of Thomas's work. He moves *into* normality, in these last poems; he comes from the Otherworld into our own, without denying either. In a sense, though he clearly derives from Romanticism, he is the opposite of a Romantic. He misquotes Keats's 'half in love with easeful death' and deliberately turns its meaning inside out:

> And yet I still am half in love with pain,
> With what is imperfect, with both tears and mirth,
> With things that have an end, with life and earth,
> And this moon that leaves me dark within the door.
>
> ('Liberty')

Raymond Williams is impatient with poems like 'Lob' for spreading a myth about country people:

> All countryman, of all conditions and periods, are merged into a singular legendary figure. The varied idioms of specific country communities – the flowers, for example, have many local names – are reduced not only to one 'country' idiom but to a legendary, timeless inventor, who is more readily seen than any actual people. And this is the point at which the Georgian imagination broke down: the respect of authentic observation overcome by a sub-intellectual fantasy: a working man becoming 'my ancient' and then the casual figure of a dream of England, in which rural labour and rural revolt, foreign wars and internal dynastic wars, history, legend and literature, are indiscriminately enfolded into a single emotional gesture. Lob or Lud, immemorial peasant or yeoman or labourer: the figure was now fixed and its name

was Old England. The self-regarding patriotism of the high English imperialist period found this sweetest and most insidious of its forms in a version of the rural past. (*The Country and the City,* 308–9)

He sees Thomas as implicated in a conspiracy, along with writers like Kenneth Grahame and J. M. Barrie and the folk-song collector Cecil Sharp, to propagate the myth of the 'remnants' of the 'peasantry':

> It is then not only that the real land and its people were falsified; a traditional and surviving rural England was scribbled over and almost hidden from sight by what is really a suburban and half-educated scrawl.
>
> This is the damage which can never be forgotten. But it is ironic that some of it was done by men who did look and learn in rural England, and who, like Edward Thomas, had so much genuine feeling in them. (ibid., 309–10)

Williams does mention 'As the team's head-brass' as an example of this genuine feeling and picks out the finely observed land and the scraps of convincing talk; but I am not sure he does justice to what is going on in the poem. In fact, he does to Edward Thomas what he accuses Thomas of doing to rural England – treating his work as if it was all of a piece, as if there was no change or progression in it, 'a version of history which succeeds in cancelling history'. But in fact Thomas was changing rapidly during the two years in which he wrote poetry. The change was masked for readers of the old *Collected Poems* by its lack of chronological order; but now R. George Thomas has put them in the order of their composition we can see the extent and the rapidity of his development. The prose Thomas, to which poems like 'Lob' were still umbilically joined, fell away and a much more objective and tougher poet began to emerge. Compare two poems about old, deserted houses – a favourite symbol of tragic unease from July 1915 and September 1916 respectively. The first ('Two houses') is about a living farmhouse next to a ruin. They grow together in the imagination so that the living and the dead (i.e., the poet and the 'remnants of the peasantry') are in a kind of symbiosis:

> . . . another house stood there long before:
> And as if above graves
> Still the turf heaves
> Above its stones:
> Dark hangs the sycamore
> Shadowing kennel and bones
> And the black dog that shakes his chain and moans.

> And when he barks, over the river
> Flashing fast,
> Dark echoes reply,
> And the hollow past
> Half yields the dead that never
> More than half-hidden lie:
> And out they creep and back again for ever.

This is more real than 'Lob' and certainly than most of the prose, but it still answers to Raymond Williams's description: 'authentic observation overcome by a sub-intellectual fantasy' of a timeless past. But in the later 'Gone, Gone Again' the deserted house, the peasant symbol, stands in open sunlight:

> Look at the old house,
> Outmoded, dignified,
> Dark and untenanted,
> With grass growing instead
>
> Of the footsteps of life,
> The friendliness, the strife;
> In its beds have lain
> Youth, love, age, and pain –

that is, real history, not a timeless past. The poet tentatively identifies *himself* as 'something like that':

> I am something like that;
> Only I am not dead,
> Still breathing and interested
> In the house that is not dark:
>
> I am something like that:
> Not one pane to reflect the sun,
> For the schoolboys to throw at –
> They have broken every one.

The poet has become one with the peasants of his Otherworld – his fairyfolk – not by becoming an elf or changeling as perhaps Walter de la Mare did, but by seeing these seeming fairies as human beings on a par with himself.

What happened to Edward Thomas was that he became a common soldier. At a stroke the objective conditions that separated him from the mass of the people, including country people, were done away with. Thomas was very aware of the economic and cultural consequences of enlisting. In a letter announcing it, he ends: '. . . in a few months I expect to go to France to finish my training. Here then ends reviewing & I suppose verses, for a time' (*Letters from Edward Thomas to Gordon Bottomley*, no. 154). He found a new kind of life in the society it forced upon him: '. . . in camp I found I could get on with people I had nothing in common with & almost get fond of them. As soon as we were in London the bond was dissolved & we had blank looks for one another' (*ibid.*, no. 159). As he says in 'Home',

> we knew we were not friends
> But fellows in a union that ends
> With the necessity for it, as it ought.

The alienation that he suffered as a soldier, though it alleviated his habitual anxiety and depression, was not without cost. Soldiering introduced him to new kinds of relationships; it enforced distances between himself and the relationships he was used to. He was made intensely aware of himself, both as a private and as a social being. He had to clarify his position in relationships that he had formerly been able to take almost for granted, even though some of them, like those with his father and possibly his wife, were very unsatisfactory. He wrote a series of personal poems – they amount to a poetic Last Will and Testament – which are almost without parallel in the language. Along with these he produced six or seven love-lyrics, and a number of poems of self-analysis, concerning his own melancholy and foreboding of death. They are among the most searching and introspective poems of our literature; but he is just as objective analysing himself as confronting others.

He starts with two poems to his father. 'This is no case of petty right or wrong' dissociates himself from his father's jingoism; the other is more crucial, cutting himself away from the guilt of not loving:

> I may come near loving you
> When you are dead . . .

'No one so much as you' – the poem to his mother (or alternatively to his wife, if we follow John Pikoulis's plausible argument[2]) – is a tender

---

[2] See 'Edward Thomas as war poet', in Jonathan Barker (ed.), *The Art of Edward Thomas* (Bridgend: Poetry Wales Press, 1987).

and very loving acknowledgement of, once again, his failure to love. Then follow the bequest poems to his children and his wife; and finally 'The sun used to shine' about his friendship with Frost, and 'The Shieling' about the house of Gordon Bottomley.

The passionate objectivity he was able to achieve in these 'testament' poems enabled him to treat even the most casual relationships with a new realism. 'As the team's head-brass', in its quiet way, has actually caused critics to be confused by its treatment of the ploughman as a thoughtful person on fully equal terms with the poet. The best treatment of the poem is in W. Cooke's *Edward Thomas: A Critical Biography* (pp. 238–41). He points out that the scene described is of a countryside under pressure: cultivation is matched against sterility in words like 'charlock', 'fallow', 'the fallen elm' that will not be moved until the war is over. Thomas creates a sense of a rural community undergoing serious disruption from the effects of war:

> 'Have many gone
> From here?' 'Yes'. 'Many lost?' 'Yes, a good few.
> Only two teams work on the farms this year.
> One of my mates is dead. The second day
> In France they killed him . . .'

To the ploughman, the soldier sitting in the fallen boughs of the dead elm is an equal: they discuss the chances of war very much on equal terms. The soldier must be in uniform for this to have happened. The ploughman starts:

> 'Have you been out?' 'No'. 'And don't want to, perhaps?'
> 'If I could only come back again, I should.
> I could spare an arm. I shouldn't want to lose
> A leg. If I should lose my head, why, so,
> I should want nothing more . . .'

As R. George Thomas shows in his notes, 'This poem reflects the poet's maturing decision to abandon his job as a map-reading instructor and to apply for a commission with the possibility of a posting to France. His chief concern was the financial plight of his family' (*The Collected Poems of Edward Thomas*, 415). That's on a personal level; but 'As the team's head-brass' is more than a personal poem. By its very casualness, it marks a new depth, a new sense of history as it impinges on ordinary people, rural or not. Its lack of class prejudice is strikingly original.

The protest poems of Wilfred Owen and Sassoon are still basically those of a ruling class that has got itself into a mess. Edward Thomas, though, shows us a distinctively middle-class sensibility uncertain of its bearings, whether to go on following the lead of the ruling class (squires and big bourgeoisie) or to fall back on its own resources; or even whether to throw in its lot with a new-found companionship among the 'Tommies'. It is symptomatic that he hesitated for a long time before claiming his class privilege and becoming an officer. His poems made a permanent contribution to middle-class consciousness, showing how sensitivity and individualism could survive the regimentation and horror of world war. But they also seem to me to mark the precise point where middle-class proponents of high culture dissociated themselves, if only in principle, from emotional identification with the 'top people'.

The basic feeling of Thomas's poetry is one of discontinuity and nothingness, hesitant, groping, fearful:

> How weak and little is the light,
> All the universe of sight,
> Love and delight,
> Before the might,
> If you love it not, of night.

('Out in the dark')

Obviously this is the expression of the sort of person, the sort of poet he was; but a poet's personality – as we see and appreciate it in his work – like any artist's is never merely personal or idiosyncratic. Why should this vein of uncertainty or hesitation suddenly become relevant? Why does a Beethoven come when he does? The creation of art is an immensely subtle mesh of the time, the potential of the time, the artistic milieu, the personality of the artist and the society in which he or she lives; and the appreciation of art by those who find it relevant is scarcely less complex.

Whether his Welshness had anything to contribute to Thomas's ability to express dissociation is doubtful; but it certainly made it easier for Welshmen of the professional class in the 1940s and later – Alun Lewis, Leslie Norris – to identify with his work and use it as a 'backdoor' to English poetic tradition. It both gave them a language in which to talk about individual experience – for Edward Thomas is rooted in empiricism – and a sense of alienation without the need to rebel. Simultaneously they could be English and not-English, as well as contributors to high culture without being 'high' themselves.

M. Wynn Thomas (personal communication) remarks that

> Edward Thomas discovered his very Englishness (and with it his creativity as a poet) when he turned away from his romantic obsessions with his imagined Welshness. That is, his otherwise purely residual Welshness paradoxically exists most strongly in him as the very ground of his Englishness as man and poet.

This fits in very well with my feeling that he is an Anglo-Welsh vanishing point. There is no poet more English, and yet Edward Thomas is still perceptively Welsh. Poets who were preparing to enter English culture and to leave behind them the constraints and the claustrophobia (as they increasingly saw it) of the *buchedd*, the Welsh way of life, were emboldened and charmed by his example. Without denying their nationality, they too could succeed as English poets. The brief and tragic Odyssey of Edward Thomas documented a progress away from English upper-class ideology (even if it was tinged with *hiraeth* for Wales) into an honesty of feeling that felt almost beyond class, so that its Englishness no longer seemed alien to Welsh petty-bourgeois aspirations.

# 4

## Pilgrims from a desert land: a study of Idris Davies's two sequences and Gwenallt's 'Y meirwon' as responses to the Great Depression

~

Idris Davies was born in 1905 into a Welsh-speaking family in Rhymney. His father was a pit winderman, with a responsible and secure job. Idris learnt English at elementary school, which he left at fourteen to go down the pit.

The coal industry was enjoying a brief post-war boom and wages were buoyant; but there was a sudden slump in demand for British coal, partly due to a widespread change to oil fuel but partly also to government policy. In trying to curb inflation, they raised the price of sterling so that British goods were priced out of the market. The coal-owners responded by trying to cut wages. In 1921, and most catastrophially in 1926, an attempt at a general strike collapsed, leaving the miners feeling betrayed. They went on strike by themselves, but were finally defeated after eight long months in late autumn 1926.

Idris Davies had lost a finger in a pit accident early in 1926, and was only just back at work when the strike began. He had started to read poetry – Shelley he admired greatly – and now the enforced idleness encouraged him. Afterwards, the pit where he worked closed down and it was virtually impossible to find other work as a collier. He decided to educate himself for a career as a teacher, took a correspondence course, matriculated, and then went on to train at Loughborough College and Nottingham University. In 1932 he found a post in a London primary school. His poems began to be published in magazines, particularly in the new *Wales* edited by Keidrych Rhys (1915–87).

By this time of course Wales was suffering the extreme deprivation and poverty of the Depression. Nearly half a million people left the country in the decade or so before the outbreak of the Second World War. Idris Davies's first book, *Gwalia Deserta*, was a loosely structured sequence, a mosaic of poems about the desert that Wales had become. It was published in 1938. When war broke out, he was evacuated with the schoolchildren to Northamptonshire. It was here that the idea of writing a major work about the 1926 strike occurred to him. It was published as *The Angry Summer* in 1943 by Faber and Faber.

Other transfers in both England and Wales followed. A third book, *Tonypandy and Other Poems*, followed in 1945, and a fourth, *Selected Poems*, in 1952. Shortly afterwards at the age of forty-seven, he died from cancer at Rhymney in January 1953.

If we open *Gwalia Deserta*, Idris Davies's first book, we may be struck by what seems artless simplicity. The first poem is like a list, every line except the last a new sentence or and-clause. It all seems very predictable:

> The Commissioners depart with all their papers
> And the pit-heads grin in the evening rain;
> The white deacons dream of Gilead in the Methodist vestry
> And the unemployed stare at the winter trees.
> The parallel valleys crawl to the Severn shore,
> And adolescents jazz in the mining village,
> And somebody's only daughter is in trouble.
> The Sabbath choristers in Bethel praise the Lord;
> And young men at street-corners are aimless and ragged,
> And the old, old miners sit and dream
> Of the mirth and the pain of the distant years.

Predictable, that is, until one notices what is being connected with what. The first line is straight documentary: the bureaucrats go home; the moral is, having failed to do anything. But then, pit-heads grinning? That's not documentary. Almost surrealist in fact. And is it a description of the pit-heads or a sardonic comment on the Commissioners? The third line changes perspective again: the 'white' deacons in the chapel vestry dream of Gilead. Why *white*, first of all? The obvious answer, that it means 'white-haired' and therefore elderly, has some relevance, but it doesn't seem idiomatic to talk of white deacons in that way; anyhow, deacons don't have to be ancient. The off-centre use of the word throws up other connotations. In Welsh, which Idris Davies spoke as a child and which was the Chapel language *par excellence*, the word for *white* is *gwyn*, which can also mean blessed or holy or sincere. But *white* in the twenties and thirties was often opposed to *red*: White Russia of the counter-revolution against the Red Russia of the Soviets. Lily-white, innocent, but also bloodless, lacking in spunk. And so on. The adjective undermines these deacons as much as it describes them.

And what about *Gilead*? Gilead was a district to the east of Israel, in what is now Jordan. It was a fertile country, famous in antiquity for its medicinal herbs. Balm of Gilead became a metaphor of healing – and particularly spiritual healing – in Old Testament times. The Welsh hymn-writers used it constantly. It is worth quoting again Derec Llwyd Morgan:

> By means of this sensitive discipline [of theology and Scripture] the Methodist poets got to the point of identifying the archetypes, the stories and the portraits of both Testaments with their own experiences, thus ensuring that they would influence the imagination of their readers in a way that would make their extensive inner experiences resemble the historical and revelatory experiences recorded in the Bible itself . . . What is notably special about the poetry of the Methodists is that there is so much of it, that its influence has been so far-reaching, so that its language has become a tribal idiom, and that this body of poetry has in turn given to its readers a commonly shared imagination . . . The place-names, *Egypt, Canaan, Sinai, Zion*, with their contrasting shades of significance, are repeated over and over, just as the metaphors *balm of Gilead, rose of Sharon*, and others, occur time after time . . . So often are they used that these individual names, the word clusters, and the various references, develop into living symbols of the mind of the converted. (*The Great Awakening in Wales*, trans. Dyfnallt Morgan, 280-2)

With a single name, therefore, Idris Davies can evoke a whole idiom of feeling, the root ideology of the *buchedd*, the Welsh way of life. He does this naturally, and many times in his poetry, often (as here) with ironic intention.

The deacons dream about Gilead; the unemployed stare at the winter trees. Each line changes and opposes and contrasts not simply subject matter but manners and registers of discourse. There is something of the actor about this poet, and if he were reciting the poem I am sure every line would have its own different style of delivery. Dreaming about Gilead involves you in intellectual puzzles as well as a knowledge of hymns, a reading of life in terms of biblical allegory; whereas the unemployed staring at the bare winter trees is the sort of symbolism and mood-painting you would be likely to find in a modern film.

A similar dislocation and contrast of registers occurs in the next couplet too. 'Parallel valleys crawl to the Severn shore' is a mixture of a geography lesson and the overtly poetic: at a pinch it might come from a travelogue. But 'adolescents jazz in the mining village'? The words could come from a newspaper article, except that a journalist would be more precise about where they danced – in the working men's club, in the dance-hall, or wherever. By saying they jazz in the mining village, the poet makes it sound more archetypal, more of a contrast to the parallel valleys crawling to the shore. And then the next line is pure gossip – '*Somebody's* only daughter is in trouble'. You can almost see the knowing look! Or that's one way to read it: the kind of put-down use of 'somebody' you get in 'Somebody round here's too big for their boots'. You ought to be able to hear the aunts and uncles blaming all this jazz music for what's been happening to their Blodwen.

Then, just as the white deacons were juxtaposed with the unemployed, so the Sabbath choristers at Bethel are with the aimless and ragged young men. The old order of the chapel (isn't it implied?) is losing its grip. The young drift in an economic and spiritual limbo. Finally, Idris Davies frames his little collage with a whole couplet about the old, old miners dreaming about the past – a commonplace, but it does not pretend to be anything else. Actually, if we read the next poem, we'll find Idris Davies taking a much more critical view of the past. He often uses *dream* – meaning both daydream and aspiration to be striven for – as a framing mood for his sequences. We shall see later something of the dangers as well as the advantages of this 'dream'. We've been taught to be suspicious of that kind of language: *dream* is a word the popular press thrives on, a code-word that signals 'human interest' and the sob-story. But we mustn't be put off by snobbery or nervousness. Let us give the 'old, old miners' (the phrase would be quite normal in Welsh though in standard English it sounds like gush) the response they require, and wait for the next poem.

What we have in this collage is a series of snapshots of *buchedd* culture disintegrating. Bureaucrats and halted pit-heads, deacons and unemployed, 'parallel' valleys – the term is more than geographical – adolescents, jazz, girls in trouble, Sabbath (only) choristers praising the Lord – all is as aimless and ragged as the young men at street corners. Contrast this opening with Idris Davies's picture of the purposive bustle of the Valleys in the opening poem of *The Angry Summer*:

> Now it is May among the mountains,
> Days for speeches in the valley towns,
> Days of dream and days of struggle,
> Days of bitter denunciation.
>
> Now it is May in all the valleys,
> Days of the cuckoo and the hawthorn,
> Days for splashing in the mountain ponds,
> Days for love in crowded parks . . .

I have not analysed the opening of *Gwalia Deserta* because it exemplifies a typical Idris Davies poem, or a typical Idris Davies style. There is no such thing. He has a very wide range of styles available to him: wider, indeed, than any other English-language poet I can think of since the sixteenth century. Such a spread of diverse styles is often a feature of a young poet learning his craft. In the case of Idris Davies, however, the more successful and mature his art, the more it is diversified. In his two long sequences, at any rate, and in *The Angry Summer* even more than in *Gwalia Deserta*, the whole strategy of the work consists in juxtaposition, style against style, viewpoint against viewpoint. He lacks almost entirely the power to build a sustained poetic edifice on the basis of a single, consistent style, such as we find satisfying in such varied works as Edward Thomas's 'Old man' or the Dantesque passage in Eliot's 'Little Gidding' describing the meeting with the 'familiar compound ghost'. When Idris Davies does attempt such a consistency of style, as in 'Tonypandy', the result is depressingly poor: though admittedly that might not only result from the stylistic endeavour, for he was a tired and defeated man by the time he wrote it.

Here are some of the styles he uses in *Gwalia Deserta*: the comedy of manners,

> In Cardiff at dawn the sky is moist and grey
> And the baronets wake from dreams of commerce
> With commercial Spanish grammar on their tongues . . .

(iii)

The high romantic mood, out of Shelley,

> The insistent language of the dream would ring
> Through the dear and secret places of the soul.
> O fresher than the April torrent, the words of indignation
> Would clothe themselves in beauty, and be heard
> Among the far undying echoes of the world.

(xxix)

46

The deflationary, modern, ironic use of anticlimax,

> I seek in the faces of men glimpses of early joy,
> I seek in the sounds of human speech
> The echoes of some far fogotten rapture . . .
> Alas, the wind from the moor squeaks through deserted machinery,
> And pulls at the edges of tawdry advertisements,
> Shakes patched-up shirts and drawers on backyard lines,
> Shakes the last brown leaves on the hawthorn hedge;
> And many eyes are fixed on 'our expert tipster'.[1]

(xiv)

Then, the secular hymn,

> Ten million stars are burning
> Above the plains tonight
> But one man's dream is greater
> To set the world alight.
>
> The gods of great disasters
> May crack the hills tonight,
> But one man's dream is greater
> To set the world aright.

(xxxii)

Nursery rhyme,

> Who made the mineowner?
> Say the black bells of Rhondda.
>
> And who robbed the miner?
> Cry the grim bells of Blaina.[2]

(xv)

---

[1] I took it that the 'many eyes fixed on "our expert tipster"' were reading the racing papers. But my neighbour, Mr Williams from Rhymney, gives a different explanation. Betting off the race-track was illegal in Idris Davies's time. Bets used to be placed with a 'bookie' (a fellow miner) down the pit, out of reach of the police. But when the miners were on strike or unemployed, of course, this system could not operate. Men used to gather in some out-of-the-way spot and wait for the 'bookie' to appear. I am told that the 'bookie' was also called a 'tipster', so the line might refer to him. But my guess that they were reading tips in the paper may still be correct. In any case the phrase carries a greater punch than mere reportage. All human endeavour is being trivialized into the attempt to outwit luck. The poem is one of the first where the poet voices his disillusion with the culture of the Valleys in their decline – a disillusion that greatly increased when he came back to them during the last years of the war.

[2] In this lyric made famous as a 'folk-song' by Pete Seeger, the arbitrary attachment of slogans to place-names is strikingly reminiscent, in a different key, of Old Welsh gnomic poetry. The poem is a sort of historical tour of 'Gwalia' in nursery-rhyme terms.

And the literary lyric from Housman's *Shropshire Lad*,

> He is digging in the dark,
>   Jude who would the poet be,
> And dreaming of the distant isles
>   And the summer on the sea.
>
> Not for always shall he grope
>   In the galleries of grime –
> 'Tis sure he shall be shouldered,
>   And need nor pick nor rhyme.
>                                                    (v)

To quote bits like this is to make him more derivative than he is: all these extracts, even the secular hymn, are in fact justified in their context. The Jude lyric, for example, ironically comments on the poet's own history: he too had been a miner who had dreams of being a poet. Unlike thousands of others, he had escaped, up the ladder of education. The overall shape is Housmanesque, and the use of 'shouldered' is probably borrowed from 'To an athlete dying young', where similarly 'shoulder-high' means both being carried in triumph and being carried in a coffin:

> The time you won your town the race
> We chaired you through the market-place;
> Man and boy stood cheering by,
> And home we brought you shoulder-high.
>
> Today, the road all runners come,
> Shoulder-high we bring you home,
> And set you at your threshold down,
> Townsman of a stiller town.
>                                  *(A Shropshire Lad, xix)*

Though poets, unlike athletes, are not usually carried shoulder-high, they *are* chaired, at least in Wales; and that was probably what connected the Housman lyric to his own. But Housman is by no means the only element. Hardy's *Jude the Obscure* is certainly referred to in the name. Housman's poems are pastoral in the sense that the characters and events only pretend to be low-life, while in fact they connote Housman's own middle-class despair. The collocation of this pastoral 'pretending' with Hardy's novel about a working man's aspiration to higher things thwarted by the class structure is itself a rich metaphorical hinterland to this poem about a collier. But the two lines

> And dreaming of the distant isles
> And the summer on the sea

have little to do with either Housman or Hardy. They are pure modern escapism, and ironic as an image of poetry: it is abundantly clear that Idris Davies did not see poetry as simply a substitute for a Mediterranean cruise. 'Jude who would the poet be', not 'Jude who wanted to be a poet': the definite article means that *be* is used with the meaning *act* – 'Jude, will you be the poet?' as a producer in a play-reading might say. And this would-be role-playing itself shows that the conception of poetry that Jude has is limited and egotistical: 'Look at the so-and-so being "the poet"!' where, as it were, we put 'the poet' in quotes.

The lyric follows a piece about 'timbers from Norway and muscles from Wales' which ends:

> O what is man that coal should be so careless of him,
> And what is coal that so much blood should be upon it?
>
> (iv)

The reference is to the eighth Psalm, verses 4-5:

> When I consider thy heavens, the work of thy fingers, the moon and
> the stars, which thou hast ordained;
> What is man, that thou art mindful of him? and the son of man, that
> thou visitest him?

What to the psalmist (and therefore to the orthodox *buchedd* also) had been a sense of awe and humility before divine providence, becomes, for Idris Davies in the desert of Gwalia, bitterness and a sense of the careless cruelty of things. It is not God's mercy that visits man now, it is affliction and the 'blood' upon the coal. There is no God but Coal. 'Blood' in this context echoes back to the New Testament – to the blood of Christ, through which we are saved, and to the Chief Priests saying of the thirty pieces of silver that Judas threw down before he hanged himself, 'It is not lawful to put them into the treasury, because it is the price of blood'.

So to the first question 'What is man that coal should be so careless of him?' the Jude-lyric answers that man may be a poet, a creative imagination; and that his creativity is itself bled to death, trivialized by the coal. The next poem rejects Jude totally, therefore. It is a harsh bit of sloganizing, stigmatizing the imagination's escapism as a cop-out:

> For the dreamers of dreams are traitors
> When wolves are at the gate.
>
> (vi)

But this is no answer either. In what is one of the most deeply felt and serious poems of the sequence, Idris Davies presents us with a 'straight' vision of life down a coal-mine, what the imagination means in such a place:

> There are countless tons of rock above his head,
> And gases wait in secret corners for a spark;
> And his lamp shows dimly in the dust.
> His leather belt is warm and moist with sweat,
> And he crouches against the hanging coal,
> And the pick swings to and fro,
> And many beads of salty sweat play about his lips
> And trickle down the blacked skin
> To the hairy tangle on the chest.
> The rats squeak and scamper among the unused props,
> And the fungus waxes strong.

A 'correct' writer would have missed out all those 'ands': the description would then have been externalized, a series of events and actions in sequence. What the 'ands' do is to act out the Gestalt of the whole experience, so that you are aware of the leather's sweatiness and the crouching against the 'hanging' coal and the pick swinging back and forth, not as discrete moments but as all the same thing, the hard work of hewing coal.

The miner, Dai, pauses to wipe his sticky brow; and in those few moments thoughts and images streak across his mind. He worries about whether his sons will have to go down the pit, whether he is earning enough to feed his family; and he thinks sardonically about the under-manager going to church with the curate's aunt – he'll have to 'clean his mouth', stop using bad language! These images and worries surface and disappear in a trice. They are indeed the stuff of which dreams are made on. And then?

> Again the pick resumes the swing of toil,
> And Dai forgets the world where merchants walk in morning streets,
> And where the great sun smiles on pithead and pub and church-steeple.
>
> (vii)

It is a remarkable poem, not so much about mining as about the imagination; but this point may well be missed if we do not attend to the form of the unfolding sequence, or have not followed the argument from poem to poem. This is what those blinkered critics always miss who criticize Idris Davies for stylistic faults within sections, as if he didn't know what he was doing. The unit of discourse is not the individual lyric but the whole sequence: it is the logic of the whole that controls the details of expression, not the gearing of a single section to our ideas of what constitutes a good short poem.

So, in turn, this leads to the famous 'Do you remember 1926' (the year of the General Strike) which has been made into a poster. It is often read as simply a collection of bitter reminiscences about the strike and its aftermath. In its context, however, it picks up the last sentence of poem vii, where Dai has to forget the world of the merchants and the great sun. It refers to the last time that the miners – Dai and his mate Shinkin among them – did challenge that merchant's world and did try for a place in the sun:

> 'Ay, ay, we remember 1926', said Dai and Shinkin
> As they stood on the curb in Charing Cross Road,
> 'And we shall remember 1926 until our blood is dry.'
>
> (viii)

Forgetting and remembering, blood and coal, sun and darkness. The themes weave in and out, one poem answering another, one style challenging its fellow.

The mosaic structure of the sequences explains why Idris Davies is so difficult to anthologize. He is the most quotable of Anglo-Welsh poets. Very many of his lyrics are memorable. Yet if we extract them from their context, most of them fade like seaside pebbles left to dry. Time after time, performances of his poetry miss this essential point. The producer thinks he knows better than the poet the right order of the poems; and he never does. The great art of Idris Davies is highly formal: it develops through the angles that lines and poems and *personae* make with one another, and the imaginative space thus produced.

Critics have not fully realized the implications of the fact that in the Anglo-Welsh poetry of the inter-war period we are essentially dealing with a new language. English in the families of Vernon Watkins (1906–67), Glyn Jones, Dylan Thomas and Idris Davies was no more than a generation or two old. Before that, people no doubt spoke it, but it was a foreign speech to them. And this is true in spite of the fact that all four writers used English as their first language, and the two from Swansea spoke no Welsh at all.

I would stress the importance of this newness in two ways. First, in matters of vocabulary the actual words are often without the *patina* that English writers would instinctively give them. The big words – 'father' or 'love' or 'death' – when an English writer uses them are worn like stone steps in a cathedral. They are fitted into the intimacies of the language, they gather nuances. Trace elements of pathos, irony or snob-value control their usefulness. In Dylan Thomas's poetry nothing is half-said, words are sounded at full power. Not since the Elizabethan dramatists has English verse been able to strut like that. The English culture of the Thomas family was 'all in the head', as Lawrence would say. It hadn't had time to be natural. Dylan's Welshness is a lack of Englishness as much as anything homespun from Wales.

And much of this applies to Idris Davies also, though of course his Welshness is obvious and he took no pains to conceal it. He wasn't 'Lord Cut-Glass'. Idris Davies was an ex-miner, not a scion of a ferociously Anglicizing professional class. Nevertheless I think one of our responses to his poetry is a feeling of shameless verbal nakedness. Words like *vision, truth, battle, wonder, passion,* are used without any of the restraint that English writers of comparable skill would employ. Perhaps this is partly a working-class boldness with rhetorical abstractions, a lack of inhibition that has never been taught polite hesitancy. But similar trust in the big words also occurs in middle-class poets from south Wales: Alun Lewis is full of it.

The second effect of the newness of their language on the Anglo-Welsh between the wars was stylistic in a different way. They were very rarely able to build long structures out of a consistent and idiomatic English style. This may not be entirely due to the effects of a new language: social causes may also have operated so that, for example, they had contradictory expectations of what their poetry ought to do; and there are clearly exceptions, or apparent exceptions. Dylan Thomas did indeed produce some quite large, sonorous poems; but his method of producing them was as formal as writing villanelles, not a matter of style but of a kind of dialectic. One image (so he tells us) was allowed to give birth to an opposite image, and the conflict between them resolved by a third into 'the momentary peace that is a poem'. Any attempt to wrest a sustained meaning out of this play of imagery is almost bound to seem arbitrary and only locally effective.

Now Idris Davies quite early in his career as a poet opted for total clarity of expression. In Welsh poetry of the twentieth century the main fault-line has been between those who expected poetry to be quickly understandable – i.e., those who belonged to *buchedd* culture with its distrust of the divisive effects of élitist literature – and the advocates of 'dark' poetry, appealing to the tastes of a new intelligentsia. Ease of understanding was for Idris Davies a moral and political necessity. There is no doubt which side of the fault he was on. He could never have countenanced in himself the deliberately obscure grandiloquence of *18 Poems*:

> These boys of light are curdlers in their folly,
> Sour the boiling honey;
> The jacks of frost they finger in the hives . . .
>
> (Dylan Thomas, 'I see the boys of summer')

Having said that, he too builds his long sequence out of a sort of dialectic – of styles, images and *personae*. It is not often that we can vouch for the author's own indisputable opinion or personal style, as we commonly can, for instance, in the work of Edward Thomas. All we can say is that his position is 'somewhere over there' behind the mosaic of short lyric structures.

Losing one language and acquiring another is a complicated process. Welsh critics have naturally tended to see it as largely one of cultural loss. The result, they say, is neither English nor Welsh, but a kind of limbo creature of the wasteland. There's a lot of truth in what they say. The process is accompanied by a great deal of silly snobbery. There's often a sense of cultural deprivation, a truculence that betrays an inferiority complex; even a wholesale failure to articulate more than bread-and-butter meanings. Patterns of thought which in the parent speech would have been integrated into a whole way of life are left loose and noisy on the surface of the mind. People become linguistic opportunists, at the mercy of short-term emotions. Style becomes either a conformity to standards borrowed from elsewhere and only partially assimilated; or a series of 'existentialist' gestures, what is 'hip' or 'flashy'. I once hitch-hiked a lift from a traveller in paints and wallpaper, and I asked him if there was any difference between suburban tastes in north Wales and in England. I thought in my innocence that visually we all belonged to the same spectrum these days; but no, he said, the north Welsh were renowned in the trade for the garishness of their tastes. Once they had left behind the homeliness and decent poverty of their background, they had no visual culture to modify their desire for flashiness and ostentation.

That's not the whole story, though. If the linguistic change accompanies a mighty convulsion in the fabric of society or a great widening in social opportunity, as it did among immigrants to the United States or in the coal-mining valleys of south Wales, the parent languages – Welsh or Lithuanian or Yiddish – may not be able to confront the situation at all adequately. Some sort of atavistic response, seeing the new world only in terms of what is lost, may be a temptation written into the language you use. Most of the time indeed, the old culture may just forget that the new situation exists at all. There are no rules in the matter. Some Welsh poetry certainly confronts the industrial revolution in the South. One thinks of Gwenallt especially. But there is not the feeling, as there often seems to be in Anglo-Welsh writing, that anything not to do with coal and the Depression is somehow a bit unreal. The obsessions are elsewhere.

And because the obsessions are elsewhere, and because the basic element of the situation *is* an exploding fragmentation of what it has meant to be human, the new language may in fact be stronger, more culturally apposite, than the old. English in the Valleys had certainly a gusto that was partly a product of explosive industrial growth and its aftermath, but partly also derived from the linguistic change itself. Transforming yourself from a community that speaks one language into a community that speaks another – if it takes place in an expanding world where social contacts are ramifying and becoming ever more complex – can be a source of power. You turn a lot of your cultural baggage into a blank credit-note to meet the future. A lot gets wasted in the process, of course; but human learning is never acquired without waste or without an overall increase in energy. In America, as in modern Israel, the power released by whole communities changing their language was surely one factor in the dynamism of the new nation.

True, there was a vast waste of human potential in the melting-pot of America, but the surplus energy did have somewhere to go. Success was as much a fact of life as failure. South Wales was not so lucky. The energy largely leaked away, the power was wasted. Even so, there were poets and writers who could seize on it to respond to the epic history of their time. Dylan Thomas found his subject matter in the imaginative frontier situation of suburban Swansea; Vernon Watkins in the trauma of vision betrayed by time; Alun Lewis in the erosion of traditional priorities by modern war; and Idris Davies in the dereliction of the mining communities and the dramatic struggle in the strike of 1926 to avert disaster. Nor should we forget the novelists and story-writers – Jack Jones, Lewis Jones, Glyn Jones, Gwyn Jones, Dylan Thomas and Alun Lewis (again) and, not least, Gwyn Thomas.

What these writers share is a power that comes from social and linguistic convulsions churning in and around the individual consciousness. They are a remarkable movement. Our virtual neglect of most of them has done us no sort of good. Partly our trouble is that we do not have the critical apparatus to deal with them. Even critics who see literature in a social context have tended to stress the importance of the organic community in shaping a writer's vision and moulding his style. But the south Wales valleys are exciting precisely because they are so new, so inorganic to the history of Wales. As we have seen, style – the fitting of a viewpoint to a subject matter – tends to be fragmentary and opportunist in all these writers. None of them, it seems to me, had the ability to build large-scale structures 'naturally', that is, on the basis of a consistent and authoritative style. The poets tended to evade the problem: Dylan Thomas – at least in *18 Poems* – with his dialectic of imagery; Idris Davies by constructing a mosaic. Vernon Watkins confronted it head-on, however. He had been to a public school, and therefore felt the pressure to be bourgeois English, even to the point of nervous breakdown. He worked obsessively all his life to assemble a consistency of style that should assert eternal order against time's fragmentation.

I want now to illustrate what I've been saying by comparing a representative bit of Idris Davies with a poem written out of a long poetic tradition – a poem built 'naturally' on the basis of a consistent and authoritative style. I have chosen a poem by Gwenallt (D. Gwenallt Jones, 1899–1968) who was from Pontardawe in the western Valleys as Idris Davies was from Rhymney in the east. Both were brought up Welsh-speaking, but whereas Gwenallt became a Welsh-language poet and academic, Idris Davies left Wales to become a teacher in London and already thought of himself as an English poet before he left. One might have expected, prima facie, that Gwenallt would have stressed continuity, while Idris Davies would have mourned the tragic break that the Depression had caused. In fact, the reverse is true. It is Gwenallt's poems of the Depression that really close the account, draw a line under the Valleys' experience and see it in purely historical terms. Gwenallt, it is true, calls his book *Eples*, which means 'yeast' or 'ferment'. The Valleys' experience is still a leaven in his spiritual life; but only as a touchstone, an abiding talisman of human suffering and sacrifice – what made him the sort of person he is – not as the Valleys saw themselves, as struggling to assert the political hope of socialism in the selfish desert of capitalist exploitation. Gwenallt begins his book of leavenings with a poem called 'Y meirwon', 'The dead':

## Y meirwon

Bydd dyn wedi troi'r hanner-cant yn gweld yn lled glir
   Y bobl a'r cynefin a foldiodd ei fywyd e',
A'r rhaffau dur a'm deil dynnaf wrthynt hwy
   Yw'r beddau mewn dwy fynwent yn un o bentrefi'r De.

Wrth yrru ar feisiglau wedi ei lladrata o'r sgrap
   A chwarae Rygbi dros Gymru â phledrenni moch,
Ni freuddwydiais y cawn glywed am ddau o'r cyfoedion hyn
   Yn chwydu eu hysgyfaint i fwced yn fudr goch.

Ein cymdogion, teulu o Ferthyr Tydfil oeddynt hwy,
   'Y Merthyron' oedd yr enw arnynt gennym ni,
Saethai peswch pump ohonynt, yn eu tro, dros berth yr ardd
   I dorri ar ein hysgwrs ac i dywyllu ein sbri.

Sleifiem i'r parlyrau Beiblaidd i sbio yn syn
   Ar olosg o gnawd yn yr arch, ac ar ludw o lais;
Yno y dysgasom uwch cloriau wedi sgriwio cyn eu pryd
   Golectau gwrthryfel a litanïau trais.

Nid yr angau a gerdd yn naturiol fel ceidwad cell
   Â rhybudd yn sŵn cloncian ei allweddi llaith,
Ond y llewpart diwydiannol a naid yn sydyn slei,
   O ganol dŵr a thân, a wŷr wrth eu gwaith.

Yr angau hwteraidd: yr angau llychlyd, myglyd, meddw,
   Yr angau â chanddo arswyd tynghedfen las;
Trôi tanchwa a llif-pwll ni yn anwariad, dro,
   Yn ymladd â pherau catastroffig, cyntefig, cas.

Gwragedd dewrfud â llond dwrn o arian y gwaed,
   A bwcediaid o angau yn atgo tan ddiwedd oes,
Yn cario glo, torri coed-tân a dodi'r ardd
   Ac yn darllen yn amlach hanes dioddefaint Y Groes.

Gosodwn Ddydd Sul y Blodau ar eu beddau bwys
   O rosynnau silicotig a lili mor welw â'r nwy,
A chasglu rhwng y cerrig annhymig a rhwng yr anaeddfed gwrb
   Yr hen regfeydd a'r cableddau yn eu hangleddau hwy.

Diflannodd yr Wtopia oddi ar gopa Gellionnen,
   Y ddynoliaeth haniaethol, y byd diddosbarth a di-ffin;
Ac nid oes a erys heddiw ar waelod y cof
   Ond teulu a chymdogaeth, aberth a dioddefaint dyn.

## The dead

When he's turned fifty, a man sees with fair clarity
   The people and places that made him what he is,
And the steel ropes that tether me strongest to them
   In one village of the South, are the graves in two cemeteries.

I rode a bicycle pilfered from the scrap,
   Played rugby for Wales with the bladder of a sow,
Little dreamt I'd hear how two of those playmates
   Would throw up their lungs in a bucket of red spew.

Our neighbours, they were a family from Merthyr,
   'Y Merthyron' – the martyrs – was our name for them,
Five by turns had a cough that crashed the garden fence
   And broke upon our chatter and darkened our fun.

We slunk into Bibled parlours and looked amazed
   At cinders of flesh in the coffin, at ash of a voice;
That's where, over lids screwed down beforetime, we learnt
   Red revolution's collects, and litanies of rape.

It was not Death on his natural rounds, like a gaol warder
   With a warning in the clink of his damp keys,
It was industry's leopard leaping, sudden and sly,
   From the midst of water and fire, on men at their work.

Hootering death; dusty, smoky, drunken death;
   Death with the terror of grey destiny on it;
Where fireblast and flood turned us into savages
   Fighting catastrophic primordial powers.

Mute and brave women with a fistful of bloodmoney,
   With a bucketful of death, forever the rankling of loss,
Carrying coal, chopping firewood or setting the garden,
   And reading more and more the passion of the Cross.

This Sunday of Flowers we place on their graves a bunch
   Of silicotic roses and lilies pale as gas,
Between premature stones and the curb never ripened
   Gather from their funerals old blasphemy and curse.

Utopia vanished from the peak of Gellionnen,
   Abstract humanity, without frontier or class:
Today nothing's left at the bottom of memory
   Save family and neighbourhood, man's sacrifice and pain.

Gwenallt runs through what we are accustomed to think of as a typical Valleys scenario – the children playing rugby, the colliers dying of 'dust', the 'Bibled parlours'. We hear of the death that afflicted men like his own father at the steelworks at Pontardawe, 'industry's leopard' that leaps sudden and sly. We hear the din of it, we smell the heat. The poet joins the widows 'with a fistful of bloodmoney' who are going to the cemetery on Flowering Sunday (*Sul y blodau*), the Sunday before Easter – Palm Sunday in English – when it is traditional in Wales to deck the graves of your dead with flowers. The flowers become almost surreal at this point, the roses (out of season?) are 'silicotic', red with the blood of the disease's victims, while the lilies are 'pale as gas'; and this alerts us to a kind of exaggeration of poetic speech which has modified the realism throughout and is sometimes reminiscent of Dylan Thomas in English – 'Bibled parlours', 'ash of a voice', and the use of ecclesiastical terms like 'collects' and 'litanies' about red revolution and violence – a strain of imagery that leads through the women reading of Christ's passion to the 'aberth a dioddefaint dyn', 'man's sacrifice and pain' of the last line. The imagery is vigorous and draws attention to itself, which is one reason for a certain chunkiness of the style: you have to know what you're doing with these blocks of simile and metaphor, otherwise they'd take over, as they sometimes do with Dylan. It is the slightly harsh, idiomatic and decisive voice of Gwenallt the *prifardd* that does not allow this to happen.

So the poet mourns his dead, and the culture and the hope that died with them:

> Utopia vanished from the peak of Gellionnen,
> Abstract humanity, without frontier or class . . .

Gwenallt's name is an inversion of that of the village of Alltwen, 'Whitewood' or 'Whitehill', where he lived as a boy, on the eastern slope overlooking Pontardawe, the 'bridge on the Tawe'. Gellionnen, 'Ash Grove', is the still wooded slope opposite. So when he says Utopia vanished from Gellionnen he is actually thinking of himself looking out of his window over the valley, 'dreaming' (as Idris Davies would say) of a socialist world 'without frontier or class'. That's all gone. But it is important to remember that Gwenallt had been to prison for the sake of it: he refused to fight for the capitalist state in the First World War, not as a pacifist but as a Marxist. The image of death as a 'gaol warder going his rounds' earlier in the poem is taken from life.

'Utopia', he calls it now, 'abstract humanity'. The words are satirical, even if only gently so. It was a socialist Utopia which had replaced 'my Father's House' of the Pantycelyn hymns as the sacred object of pilgrimage for the 'gwareiddiad a diwylliant y De' – the civilization and culture of the South – as he calls it[3] – that is, the *buchedd* culture of the mining valleys. Utopia is dead. The humanity it looked towards was 'abstract' because it was 'above' the contradictions of nation or class, as of course a *buchedd* Utopia would have to be. (Marxists would probably agree with Gwenallt here: 'Utopian socialism' is, for them also, a satirical term. But Gwenallt is using their own terminology against them.) What is left 'at the bottom of memory' is family and neighbourhood, the sacrifice and suffering of man.

The terms are carefully chosen. Family and neighbourhood were the elements of the older, tribal Wales that survived most unchanged into the new order of the Methodists. Kinship is still vestigially important among Welsh people, even if shamefacedly so; but neighbourhood, whether in the sense that most English people would mean, the immediate social environment where you live, or extending outward to the *bro* or native district, or even to the whole *gwlad* or country, is a still growing feature of Welsh ideology. If ever there was a growth industry in Welsh poetry, it is the poetry of *bro*. So, as against the 'abstract' humanity of *buchedd* socialism, Gwenallt bases his new nationalism of the Welsh intelligentsia on 'family' and 'neighbourhood'. The missing item, which an intellectual from Gwynedd (say) would have been sure to include, is of course *yr iaith* – the language. Though Pontardawe was (and is) partly a Welsh-speaking area, no one from the Valleys could possibly exclude English-speaking compatriots from 'the bottom of memory'.

Theologically also, 'the sacrifice and suffering of man' replaces Methodist viewpoints with something older. Although certainly Methodists do sacrifice and do suffer in the course of their pilgrimage to the Promised Land, they would find it difficult to put ultimate value on this, without stirring up the hornets' nest of justification by good works. Only the Christian's faith in the crucified Jesus justifies him in the sight of God. No sacrifice or suffering other than that of Christ has anything but incidental value. And the socialists in this respect were heirs to the Protestants, though without the supernatural Saviour. Suffering, sacrifice and martyrdom had no value in themselves, though they might exemplify social conditions or good or bad responses to them. For a Catholic, though, the sacrifice of Jesus takes to itself all suffering and all sacrifice, and by that offering renews and deifies the worth that, poor things as they are, they always had in themselves.

---

[3] 'Y Dirwasgiad' ('The Depression'), *Eples* (Llandysul: Gwasg Gomer, 1951), tud. 12.

Gwenallt, therefore, is blessing what remains 'in the bottom of memory' – surely a phrase redolent of the cup of Communion – in the name of nationalism and Catholicism, two of the escape routes of the Welsh intelligentsia from the catastrophic collapse of the *buchedd* society between the wars.

'Y meirwon' is a magnificent poem. If Gwenallt had written it in a more familiar language than Welsh, it would be counted as one of the great elegies of our time. Partly its triumph is one of style. It belongs to a poetic tradition that is eminently used to the elegiac mode; but it assimilates a wealth of modern experience and vocabulary to this age-old, deeply felt mourning. It has a boldness of imagery and a sense of purpose that can take itself for granted. It builds 'naturally' a towering lyric structure on the basis of a style consistently maintained and developed from the very first phrase. By means of it, the poet takes into himself the experience of the dead, and their defeat is his defeat. And yet, he is still here, in the poem, and they are not. He may be tethered to them, but he has certainly survived. And that, of course, is both his responsibility and his freedom.

It would be impossible to find any single lyric by Idris Davies – and difficult to find any Anglo-Welsh poem, for that matter – with that kind of power. But Idris Davies did write sometimes about graveyards. According to his biographer Islwyn Jenkins, he wrote several poems about a cemetery called Cefn Golau on the moorland road between Rhymney and Tredegar, where Aneurin Bevan's father was buried. Perhaps this is one of those:

> Tonight the moon is bright and round
> Above the little burial ground
> Where father of Dai and father of John
> After the sweat and blood sleep on.
>
> They do not hear your voice tonight,
> O singer on the slaggy height,
> They do not know the song you sing
> Of battle on this night of spring.
>
> But in their blood in Maytimes past
> The armies of the future massed,
> And in their dreams your dreams were born,
> Out of their night shall break your morn.

> Shine softly, moon, upon their sleep,
> And, poet, in your music keep
> Their memory alive and fair,
> Echoing through the electric air.

*(The Angry Summer, 4)*

It is a pleasing poem, attractive for its clarity and music. By the side of the Gwenallt, however, and in isolation from its fellows, it is bound to seem lightweight. Most of the phrases in it are commonplace: the moon is *bright and round*, the burial ground is *little*, the hardships of the miners are *sweat and blood*. At first when I read the third stanza I thought that *blood* equals *semen*, as it does in aristocratic genealogy:

> But in their blood in Maytimes past
> The armies of the future massed.

But this blood–semen equation works only at a third remove. The main meaning is something like, 'Their warm-blooded response to former oppressions made possible future resistance to later ones, including this that you are suffering.' *Maytimes* is a figure of speech for strikes, since the 1926 strike – what *The Angry Summer* is about – started in May. The same thought is more or less repeated three times: *their blood, their dreams*, and *their night* are cognate with each other, in opposition to *armies of the future, your dreams* and *your morn*.

As I say, if we put it against the Gwenallt, the poem will seem too lightweight to count. There is nothing of the felt particularity, the weight of experience, that the Welsh poet so effortlessly deploys. Surely, we say, there are better poems to represent Idris Davies than this! And indeed there probably are; but before we reject this one utterly, it catches at us, refuses to be put out of court, even in Gwenallt's company. 'Father of Dai and father of John', it says obstinately. Not, as we would normally find, 'Dai's father and John's father' – for clearly the emphasis is not on the fathers at all, but on Dai and John themselves, and on the enigmatic figure of the singer. We suddenly realize that in spite of a context that wellnigh forces elegy on us, Idris Davies's poem is not elegiac. It refuses to be about the past. On the contrary, it is almost totally future-directed. The poet is told to keep their memory alive and fair; but that is because they were and are the womb of what is to come. Their struggle made possible this struggle and the struggle after this.

And then, such is the power of the matrix, the mosaic that Idris Davies fashions, we begin to be aware that the poem is not just a thing by itself. It carries within it, like Wagnerian leitmotivs, seeds and hints of growth from many others. If we go back to the first poem of the sequence, it begins:

> Now it is May among the mountains,
> Days for speeches in the valley towns,
> Days of dream and days of struggle,
> Days of bitter denunciation . . .

And so on. Our poem is the night of those insistent days. The first poem announces much more than this, of course – the sheer enjoyment of the strike, in some of its aspects:

> Days for splashing in the mountain ponds,
> Days for love in crowded parks . . .

and the self-help of growing vegetables in square allotments, the roaming through the countryside begging, and the 'beauty born of sacrifice'. It is like a symphonic exposition. We remember that Idris Davies was a great lover of Beethoven. At any rate, in our graveyard poem, many of the themes are already familiar: night and Maytimes, dreams and struggle, the mountain heights. And what of the singer and his song? We've had that too, in section 3:

> Now is the month of marching,
> Valley to valley calling,
> Bugle to bugle replying,
> Tra la la la la la . . .

The singer, the poet, the dead fathers, the archetypal miner Dai – in fact the whole *dramatis personae*[4] – echo across the cycles. Indeed, we meet Dai again in the very next poem (5), and, as his conscience, question him:

---

[4] Except for John. Is John another miner, perhaps an English mate for Dai the Welshman? One might be tempted to think there is an older antithesis implied here, usually pointed in English songs as a contrast between Jack the workman and John the boss, with the poet glancing at a reconciliation between them in death as in Eliot's 'Little Gidding':

> These men, and those who opposed them
> And those whom they opposed
> Accept the constitution of silence
> And are folded in a single party.

But if this was ever in his mind he did not develop it. Of course a great many Welsh miners are christened John. Perhaps we should just accept the name as suggested by the rhyme.

> And how will you stand with your honesty, Dai,
> When the land is full of lies,
> And how will you curb your anger, man,
> When your natural patience dies?

We will come back to the cemetery in section 25, for the funeral of the broken old man who was a sort of 'folk remembrancer' of the Valleys, their hopes and their heroes: 'Now falling like a wrinkled apple into a ditch . . .' So we are given flesh for the abstractions of our poem: 'And in their dreams your dreams were born / Out of their night shall break your morn.' The felt weight of the experience clothes the abstract words, and the abstract words illumine the particulars. They reverberate as we read. I have heard it said that in all the epics of Homer there is only one half-line that does not recur somewhere else. It is a bit like that with this poem from *The Angry Summer*.

And of course it could be a prescription for the merest cliché-mongering. Too many poems that merely used the stock words of his work would have destroyed the vision. But even in this little poem as it stands – to say nothing of its place in the grand symphony of the whole – there is enough to save it from banality. We have already felt the tug of 'Where father of Dai and father of John' resisting any tendency to facile elegizing. Nor is the music of the piece to be despised, the way it shimmers as the iambics break down at the end into flickering short syllables, vowel eliding into vowel:

> keep
> Their memory alive and fair
> Echoing through the electric air.

Many people may have felt this tenderness towards the dead, but it is certainly not a cliché. Above all, there is the sense we have in any poem by Idris Davies (at least before his final phase of disillusionment, and even there in some fashion) that the poetry is open-ended, refuses to draw a line under life and call it finished, even if the good is defeated and the beautiful ravaged by greed.

It is for these sorts of reason that we have to balance Gwenallt's 'Y meirwon', 'The dead', not just with any single lyric of Idris Davies but with one or other of the sequences, with the whole mosaic, *Gwalia Deserta* or *The Angry Summer*, for anything less botches his form. And in that sort of balance, with the teeming sense of life, the good humour, the hope, the very healthy kind of anger, the compassion that does not lose its bearings in the sufferings of others, with all that on one side of the scales, it is not at all obvious that the Gwenallt – for all its power – is the greater poem of the two. On the contrary, it is Idris Davies who emerges as what we always knew he was, the poet of the Valleys, that unique society in its travail and dereliction, its hope and its betrayal.

# PART II

## 5

### *Buried treasure*

~

So far we have been dealing with Anglo-Welsh poetry as the product of a social system and a culture which existed mainly through the medium of the Welsh language, but also in English. This society we have called the *buchedd*, and we have seen how its values in various ways were being displaced by the time they found expression in the work of English-language poets like W. H. Davies, Huw Menai and Idris Davies. In the next chapters we shall consider the full-scale repudiation of *buchedd*-values by the modernists.

But there is another side to Anglo-Welsh poetry. It differs from other poetry in English not merely in originating in a peculiar people, but because there lies behind it a different antecedent civilization. It is difficult to know how far back we should look for the first Anglo-Welsh poets: it is not impossible – to say the least – that they had a hand in the Harley lyrics and the fourteenth-century alliterative revival. Certainly there is a poem to the Virgin written in English according to the rules of the Welsh strict metres by a fifteenth-century Welsh poet; and by the sixteenth and seventeenth centuries Anglo-Welsh poetry was common and included at least one major writer, Henry Vaughan. This early Anglo-Welsh poetry (which is not part of my subject in this book) was written while Welsh civilization was still more or less in place – it was becoming moribund by the late sixteenth century, but there wasn't any mystery about it. The civilization was either still alive or had been within living memory; and its last great achievement – its dowry, as it were, to succceeding generations – the translation of the Bible into Welsh, was not completed until 1588. All the same, its products – poems, stories, translations, some music – were becoming collectors' pieces, carefully copied by the patriotic gentry into the great manuscripts which now adorn our libraries.

It is no part of my purpose here to describe Welsh civilization,[1] save to say that its chief cultural manifestation was the praise-poetry, music and story-telling of the bardic orders. That was, so to speak, its official centre; but round the periphery of that circle, particularly in its earliest period, various other, more mysterious processes radiated outward. The whole body of poetry connected with Myrddin (Merlin) and Taliesin is one such process: prophecy, religious literature, poetry that might or might not reflect ancient Druidic beliefs. From our point of view – but not, as far as we can see, from that of the bardic orders themselves – these processes constitute Welsh 'unofficial' literature, together with a mass of folk-tale and folk poetry, legends such as that of Madog discovering America, and so on.

Welsh scholarship has always found it easier to deal with the 'official' culture, and until recently has tended to treat the other with various degrees of impatience as something to be circumspect about, and if possible explained away. Too many wild theories have ballooned out of it for academic comfort. English readers, on the other hand, in search of ancient esoteric lore, have tended to go to the 'unofficial' literature and to describe the official bards as dull and sycophantic – which they are not – and the miracles of metrical form on which they prided themselves as mere artifice and misplaced ingenuity. There are exceptions to both these generalizations, of course: Barnes and Hopkins were both inspired by the bardic poetry and its metres; while Taliesin is still a name to conjure with, even in Welsh.

By the eighteenth century the bardic orders had collapsed, and even on a folk level (comparable to Irish in Connemara) the civilization was being swept away by the Methodists, as we have described. The institutions of the newly formed *buchedd* were intolerant of old hierarchies and customs; and though some features of the civilization – the eisteddfod, for instance – were later revived, they were often in a form that would have been unrecognizable to their original exponents.

So the civilization became a quarry for antiquarians. It was buried treasure. Who knows what keys to future greatness it might contain? Welsh scholars became witch-doctors against the national malaise, their work a bulwark against the increasingly rapid deracination of the Welsh

---

[1] The introduction to my *Penguin Book of Welsh Verse* (1967), particularly in the later expanded editions published by Seren Books (*Welsh Verse*, Bridgend: Poetry Wales Press, 1986, 1992), probably gives the easiest overview.

people. At the same time, it became the weapon of a new middle class trying to secure its markets against English and imperial penetration. The *buchedd*, like the chapel, relied for its survival on Britishness as the overarching political fact of life. The new middle class needed space of its own: either space to become totally Anglicized and compete with English business and institutions on equal terms, or space to develop its own Welsh market and nationality. The compromises needful to the cohesiveness of the *buchedd* inhibited both these ambitions. A common reaction of middle-class people to *buchedd* culture was increasingly a sense of claustrophobia and betrayal.

The typical cultural manifestation of the *buchedd* phase had been the religious revival, and the typical hero the preacher or his secular equivalent, the charismatic political speaker, Lloyd George or Mabon or A. J. Cook, the miners' leader. But in the second phase, that is, the search for the lost civilization, the characteristic cultural manifestation was the great work of scholarship. The hero was the scholar or poet who made past glory live.

This phase was crucial to twentieth-century culture in the Welsh language, though it had begun as long ago as the eighteenth century with the Morris brothers and Goronwy Owen from Anglesey, Evan Evans from Cardiganshire and Iolo Morganwg from Glamorgan. The establishment of the Welsh University Colleges from 1872 onwards gave a great boost to accurate scholarship. John Morris-Jones, Ifor Williams and Thomas Parry were giants who made possible a real assessment of Wales's literary past, and are still household names. The new life they found flowed into the work of the poets, who were thus enabled to break free of *buchedd* expectations into imaginative freedom. The creative use of myth and legend in the narratives of T. Gwynn Jones and the lyrical genius of R. Williams Parry are among the finest things in the language.

Some of this activity spilled over into English. In the eighteenth century, Thomas Gray's ode, 'The bard', gave new life to the spurious legend that Edward I had ordered a massacre of the bards. (I am told that a Hungarian poet János Arány made the story into a major poem of defiance against cultural oppression in Eastern Europe.) In the nineteenth century, Southey the friend of Coleridge wrote an epic poem about the Madog who was supposed to have discovered America in the twelfth. Lady Charlotte Guest translated the *Mabinogion*. William Barnes, the Dorset poet, learnt Welsh, translated from old Welsh poetry and experimented with *cynghanedd*.

Easily the most remarkable confrontation of an English poet with the buried civilization of Wales was that of Gerard Hopkins in the 1870s, even if it lay off the beaten track and had little effect on Anglo-Welsh sensibility till much later. I will argue that as a poet he was formed by this experience in three ways. First, his identification with Wales released the affective and creative life that his consciousness suppressed when he became a Jesuit. Second, his attempt to write in *cynghanedd*, albeit in an archaic form, provided the technical challenge he needed, revolutionized his style and allowed him to write the great poems of his maturity. And third, the praise-poetry of the princes provided him with a poetic stance that suited his profession as a Jesuit in a way that English poetry of his own time could not.

Finally Matthew Arnold found in Celtic literature a style, a melancholy and a natural magic which he claimed English poetry inherited also. The way was open for the Celtic revival, mainly organized by English-monoglot Irishmen like W. B. Yeats and Scotsmen like William Sharp. It was a movement largely based on a misapprehension of the nature of Celtic art, favouring mystical aloofness and vague outlines, the so-called 'Celtic twilight'. Celtic twilight was not often created by Welsh writers, even in English; though the work of Ernest Rhys, friend of Yeats and co-founder of the Rhymers' Club, made a distinctive contribution to the poetry of the Celtic school before he achieved a very different kind of immortality as editor of the Everyman Library.

W. B. Yeats describes how he and Ernest Rhys founded the Rhymers' Club:

> I had already met most of the poets of my generation. I had said soon after the publication of *The Wanderings of Oisin*, to the editor of a series of shilling reprints, who had set me to compile tales of the Irish faeries, 'I am growing jealous of other poets and we will all grow jealous of each other unless we know each other and so feel a share in each other's triumph'. He was a Welshman, lately a mining engineer, Ernest Rhys, a writer of Welsh translations and original poems, that have often moved me greatly though I can think of no one else who has read them. He was perhaps a dozen years older than myself and through his work as editor knew everyone who would compile a book for seven or eight pounds. Between us we founded The Rhymers' Club, which for some years was to meet in an upper room with a sanded floor in an ancient eating-house in Fleet Street called the Cheshire Cheese. (*Four Years: 1887–1891*)

Half a century later Yeats included two of Rhys's translations from Llywarch Hen in *The Oxford Book of Modern Verse*, that impressive and eccentric Rhymers' Club and Celtic Revival rearguard against prevailing

English literary norms. And with justice, for Ernest Rhys was indeed a modern poet, who used Welsh themes as part of his modernity and played an important part in the Celtic nineties. He is to be sharply distinguished from his Anglo-Welsh literary successor, A. G. Prys-Jones, who was always out of date, even in 1917.

Rhys was born in London in 1859. His father was Welsh, his mother English. The family returned to Carmarthen where Ernest was taught Welsh 'on the sly' by a pretty maid called Hannah. He was apprenticed as a mining engineer in Durham, but abandoned it for a literary career, becoming 'Mr Everyman', one of the most successful publisher's editors of all time. *A London Rose and Other Rhymes* was published in 1894, *Welsh Ballads*, his major collection, in 1898. He continued to write verse, but not in any quantity; his last collection, *Song of the Sun*, appeared in 1937, the same year as *In Parenthesis*, and was reviewed in the second issue of *Wales* next to Dylan Thomas's *25 Poems*.

Ernest Rhys says of himself:

> Yeats' imagination of Ireland set me wondering whether I could not give to Wales, country of the Druids and the Mabinogion, her new deliverance. But I was complicated in ways he was not. A Londoner born, as well as a Welshman in exile, I suffered from the mixed sympathies that are bound to affect a man of mixed race. (*Wales England Wed*, 104)

*Welsh Ballads* contain three classes of poem: first, the ballads themselves, about heroic incidents in Welsh legend or history: the deaths of Hywel ab Owain, and of the last prince, Llywelyn ap Gruffydd, for example. The poem about Hywel incorporates adaptations from the prince's own poetry. They are very picturesque, but over-literary and too conscious of their Welsh sources to stand up in their own right. Rhys's lack of a firm viewpoint means that ultimately they don't seem to be saying very much. At the end of the Hywel poem, for example, the prince's ghost appears (like the Revd Eli Jenkins) to sing his evensong, 'mountain-wild and sweet':

> 'I love at eve the seaward stream,
>   Where the seamews brood;
> And the sighing vale of Cwm Deuthwr
> Where the nightingale sings in the privet wood!'

It is not a message that warrants such an apparition – and in any case Hywel has already sung it in a version of his 'Gorhoffedd' ('Exultation') incorporated into the poem; but the poet concludes:

He was gone;
Poised high, amid the mountain night,
Beneath the stars, we stood alone.

But down the track the shepherds take,
      As we clung
On the torrent's brink, benighted,
And the mountain-fox gave tongue –

Night, nor Time, nor David's dagger,
      Gave a pause
To your deathless rhyme, O Hywel,
And, O Wales, your ancient cause!

But that seems to be the first mention of Wales's 'ancient cause' and what the phrase is meant to imply is not immediately apparent.

The second class of poems in *Welsh Ballads* consists of rather facile lyrical pieces, not much to the point. But the third category, of translations from ancient Welsh poetry, is more important:

The Eagle of Aeli is up and abroad,
At dawn he will feast in the breast of the wood:
And his feast shall be on my new-slain lord.

The Eagle of Aeli is up and abroad,
He lifts his beak from Cynddylan's blood;
Tonight, his eyrie's in Brochwael's wood.

It is here that Ernest Rhys's bookishness comes into its own. The true heroes of *Welsh Ballads* are not the legendary or historical figures themselves, but the original Welsh poems where Rhys encountered them. It is not the ghost of the real-life Hywel that appears to him, so much as the personified memory of Hywel's poetry. If anything is to be identified as Wales's 'ancient cause', it is the hope that her poetry – what she has given to the imagination of mankind – will be handed on from generation to generation. As he says about his poems in 'Envoi i'r Cymry ar wasgar' ('Envoi to the Welsh in exile') if you can find in them 'some lingering cadence' of what Wales means:

then is the lyric dream
Not given to them in vain! Old death-wounds still
Set free the spirit for eternal life;
In every dirge there sleeps a battle-march;
And those slain heroes of the past may tell

How they attained, who only seemed to fail;
And they that fell of old, on those grey fields,
By their red death, enable us to live.

It is surely Rhys's nearest approach to a subject matter. Had he been as dedicated as his friend 'Willie' Yeats, this is where his journey would have started. The vision of Wales and Welsh poetry that this 'Envoi' conveys does not seem very inferior to the vision of Ireland in, say, Yeats's 'Rose of the World'. Yet Yeats went on to become the greatest poet of the English-speaking world, whereas Ernest Rhys edited Everyman's Library.

Perhaps Ernest Rhys came too soon, or was too easily deflected into mere literature. But he is the only Anglo-Welsh poet of his time who was conscious of the greatness of his task, even if he failed to live up to it.

## *David Jones and the* traddodiad

With Ernest Rhys, one has the sense of his turning away from a promised land, and yet of its haunting him always. He knew in his heart that there was great poetry to be found in these Welsh 'deposits'. Indeed, the main work of the Anglo-Welsh writers of the nineteenth century (apart from Hopkins) had been to make old Wales an accessible country: it was waiting its poet. And when he came, in the shape of an infantryman and artist called David Jones (1895–1974), it found a dedication and commitment as great as Willie Yeats ever had, within a hermit-like absorption that remembered going over the top at Mametz Wood in 1916 as though it was coeval with the men who went to Catraeth in the sixth century. David Jones lists three books as decisive in bringing him into a knowledge of Wales, three 'Everymans' as it happens: '. . . *Wild Wales,* along with Lady Charlotte Guest's translations called *The Mabinogion* and Sir Richard Colt-Hoare's translation of Giraldus Cambrensis became, at that time, the main printed sources from which I began to learn something of my father's *patria' (Epoch and Artist,* 70).

As with Hopkins and Ernest Rhys, David Jones's Welshness came from his father, James Jones, who was from Holywell (the town round St Winifred's Well) in Flintshire. His family had discouraged James from learning Welsh though they were all Welsh-speaking themselves. He had married Alice Ann Bradshaw, a boatbuilder's daughter from London. David Jones, as he said himself, was a Londoner, brought up entirely in an English setting, though he always felt one with his father's people. Wales was a memory of holidays, little more; but when war broke out in 1914 he enlisted in the Royal Welch Fusiliers. It was about the war service he saw with that regiment that his great work, *In Parenthesis*, was written.

Welsh civilization – let us adopt another Welsh word as a technical term for it and call it the *traddodiad* ('tradition') – means different things to different people. Whereas Hopkins's interest in it was largely bardic and metrical, and Ernest Rhys's was aesthetic, David Jones was drawn by political and religious affinities. That is to say he felt acutely the tension which from the beginning has pulled it in two directions at once. For embedded in Welsh tradition was the memory both of Rome and of the attempt by the British to take over the mantle of empire, at least in these islands and in Brittany. This lies behind Geoffrey of Monmouth's largely fictional *History of the Kings of Britain* and the growth of Arthurian legend, the Matter of Britain.

The Welsh have often tended to see their culture as a kind of interlude, always about to be superseded. As in the story of the Assembly of the Head, in the Second Branch of the *Mabinogion*, you spend an age in the Otherworld feast of Gwales; but then the door opens, the dolorous stroke is struck, Gwales becomes a waste, a gannet colony, an unrememberable dream. You remember Britain and scurry off to London to bury the Head – the life of the civilization – under the white hill. You protect Britain – never Wales – from harm. Brân's command to feast with the head in the Otherworld and finally to bury it in London is the myth that expresses best the great paradox at the root of Welsh civilization, its inspiration and its bane.

The *traddodiad* was distinctive in taking over from tribal poetry and its own remote past the notion that poetry was praise or boasting about your lord, your God, your lady or yourself. It built round that idea a way of feeling and a way of thinking that was surprisingly sophisticated and varied. It was, moreover, rather like Byzantine culture in that antiquarianism always played a large part in its make-up. It looked back to Roman and Arthurian Britain as the golden age. It was never content to be merely Welsh – it longed to be British; and that longing was of course one of the ways it articulated itself, and the way it was eventually destroyed.

Little in the plastic arts can be labelled as indigenous to Wales; and this absence is certainly disconsolate, compared with the relative wealth of Ireland in this respect. Perhaps the work of David Jones – particularly the late drawings and letterings – marks a tardy entry of Welsh civilization into the visual arts. Both as a poet and as a thinker, he echoes the *traddodiad*'s abiding preoccupations. What other English poet, for instance, would emphasize so much the Rome–Britain–Wales axis of his world; or see in the mixture of Wales and London in himself so much symbolic importance? Yet both emphases are at least as old as the *Mabinogion*. The Emperor Macsen comes from Rome to Caernarfon to find his love Elen who then rules Britain in his name; and Brân the Blessed instructs his Welsh followers to bury his head under the white hill in London, where it will protect Britain from invasion. In some ways, David Jones is far more a Welsh writer than an Anglo-Welsh one, in spite of his 'ignorance' of the Welsh language. He is like one of those one-man renaissances – Iolo Morganwg is the most famous in Wales – who from time to time revive or even reinvent worlds that to all appearances have been moribund for centuries. So I do not think it is entirely stupid to call those late drawings and letterings a tardy product of a civilization that for all the ages of its growth and decay had been visually unfulfilled, waiting for them to happen.

# 6

## Gerard Hopkins as an Anglo-Welsh poet

~

In September 1874 when Gerard Hopkins had been three weeks at St Beuno's College near St Asaph, north Wales, he wrote to his mother, 'I have always looked on myself as half-Welsh.' On the face of it this would seem to argue that he regarded himself as what would now be called Anglo-Welsh – at least in a cultural sense, if not by blood. I shall try to show that his claim to be so regarded is a strong one and casts light on both his personality and his poetry.

It is not, let me admit at the start, an easy claim to uphold. Genetically – if that is important – his father came of Welsh stock; but they had been London Welsh for generations. The letters Gerard wrote and received reveal an almost exclusively English social milieu. Politically, at any rate towards the end of his life, his English nationalism was disquietingly strident. If it were not that four letters from Sir John Rhys, the Welsh scholar, have survived, we would be hard put to it to point to any contact with Welsh intellectual society. In another letter to his mother, when he was on holiday in north Wales eight years after he had left St Beuno's, he noted as if it were a novelty for him: 'By the bye I saw a bard in the flesh. I made also the acquaintance of the genial and learned antiquary Mr Howel Lloyd.'[1] If his life as an English poet is marked by general isolation and lack of any public appreciation of his genius, his life as an Anglo-Welsh one is so personal and unknown to anyone but himself as to be virtually private.

Partly this is because the central episode in that life, the three-year sojourn at St Beuno's, lacks the sort of intellectual documentation that the rest of his life provides. His letters to Bridges were interrupted from

---

[1] C. C. Abbott (ed.), *Further Letters of Gerard Manley Hopkins*, 2nd edn (London: Oxford Univesity Press, 1956), 126–7. Henceforward referred to as *Further Letters*.

early 1875 to 1877 because of the latter's suspicion of censorship; and when they were resumed it was after Hopkins's rebirth as a poet. His letters to Dixon and Patmore had not begun, and there is only one letter to Baillie from this period. His journal ends in mid-sentence, in February 1875. In fact from then until February 1877 virtually our only documents from his pen are the poems, which he started to write in December 1875, and the letters to his parents.

Not that he leaves us in any doubt that Wales and her language and poetry were important to him, or that he felt drawn to commit himself to her by working for the conversion of the Welsh people. He talks of the landscapes of north Wales as if he were in love with them, as Fr A. Thomas remarks.[2] Whether to learn Welsh or not was a problem that engaged him in a spiritual and psychological crisis. As his journal narrates:

> Looking all round but most on looking far up the valley I felt an instress and charm of Wales. Indeed in coming here I began to feel a desire to do something for the conversion of Wales. I began to learn Welsh too but not with very pure intentions perhaps. (Humphry House (ed.), *The Journals and Papers of Gerard Manley Hopkins,* compl. by Graham Storey (London: Oxford University Press, 1959), 258. Henceforward referred to as *Journals and Papers*)

When the Rector discouraged it unless it was purely for the sake of labouring among the Welsh, Hopkins saw that he must give it up. At the same time his music seemed to come to an end.

> Yet, rather strangely, I had no sooner given up these two things (which disappointed me and took an interest away – and at that time I was very bitterly feeling the weariness of life and shed many tears, perhaps not wholly into the breast of God but with some unmanliness in them too, and sighed and panted to Him), I had no sooner given up the Welsh than my desire seemed to be for the conversion of Wales and I had it in mind to give up everything else for that; nevertheless weighing this by St Ignatius' rules of election I decided not to do so. (ibid.)

Coming to Wales presented Hopkins with typically all-or-nothing choices. One notices the dichotomy, Welsh and music on the one hand, his profession as a Jesuit on the other.

Why, then, did he so tremulously desire to learn the Welsh language

---

[2] 'Hopkins, Welsh and Wales' (*Transactions of the Hon. Soc. of Cymmrodorion,* 1965, 272–85).

that it presented itself to him almost as a temptation? He tells us that it was at least partly to help convert the Welsh; but that only throws the question back one step: why the Welsh? We can, I think, discount the allurements of Welsh prosody at this stage. In his lecture-notes of 1873–4, just before going to St Beuno's, he discusses rhyme and alliteration in detail as structural features of poetry. If he had knowledge of *cynghanedd* at that time, he would surely have mentioned it, as he does Chinese, Arabic, Icelandic etc. There is no such mention. He has looked up Gaelic rhyme 'in a grammar' but that is all.[3]

In fact, for all his obvious passion for Wales and Welsh, he only once in all his letters, papers or poems gets round to giving us any information about what he thought of the Welsh people he was so anxious to convert. This is in the letter to his mother I have already quoted at the beginning of this chapter, the one written three weeks after he arrived at St Beuno's in which he says he has always looked on himself as half-Welsh. The whole passage is crucial to our understanding of Hopkins at this time:

> I have got a yearning for the Welsh people and could find it in my heart to work for their conversion. However on consideration it seems best to turn my thoughts elsewhere. I say this because, though I am not my own master, yet if people among us shew a zeal and aptitude for a particular work, say foreign missions, they can commonly get employed on them. The Welsh round are very civil and respectful but do not much come to us and those who are converted are for the most part not very stanch [*sic*]. They are much swayed by ridicule. Wesleyanism is the popular religion. They are said to have a turn for religion, especially what excites outward fervour, and more refinement and pious feeling than the English peasantry but less steadfastness and sincerity. I have always looked on myself as half-Welsh and so I warm to them. The Welsh landscape has a charm and when I see Snowdon and the mountains in its neighbourhood, as I can now, with the clouds lifting, it gives me a rise of the heart. I ought to say that the Welsh have the reputation also of being covetous and immoral: I add this to forestall your saying it, for, as I say, I warm to them – and in different degrees to all the Celts. (*Further Letters*, 126–7)

Hopkins had wounded his parents by his 'sudden' decision to become a Catholic, and in turn had been wounded by them. Although there was no break in their relationship, for about eight years he had been, as he said in a later sonnet, at a remove from home and the sources of affection:

> To seem the stranger lies my lot, my life
> Among strangers. Father and mother dear,

---

[3] *Journals and Papers*, 283-8.

> Brothers and sisters are in Christ not near
> And he my peace my parting, sword and strife.[4]

He had given up poetry, burnt his poems, deprived himself of the intellectual companions he was used to. There is a sense in which he seems an exile, during those years, from his own feelings. But now, in north Wales, the springs of feeling flowed again. He was enchanted with the place, and at home there as he had not been for years. The grumbles and despair about his lot seem lightened for those years at St Beuno's. He actually seems happy for much of the time.

That is the first component of his complex feelings: a sense of being at home, a 'rise of the heart'. And with this flow of renewed feeling, a sense of danger. For he was at home among his father's people, half-Welsh himself. In December 1869 he had ferreted out some details of his father's Carmarthenshire ancestry;[5] it is probable that a certain amount of Welsh versus English teasing went on, as between mother and father. This would explain Gerard's writing that he is forestalling his mother's moral reservations about the Welsh. Certainly the Welshness he describes himself as warming to, and half-identifying with, is opposite in its moral emphases to everything he had stood for since his conversion to Catholicism eight years ago. The Welsh are civil and respectful, but not interested in Jesuits. If they are converted, they are not staunch. They are swayed by ridicule. They have 'a turn for religion', for what excites outward fervour. Their approach seems aesthetic rather than moral: they have refinement and pious feeling rather than sincerity and steadfastness. It is said they are covetous and immoral – that is, sexually loose. They certainly are not good examples of the three monastic virtues, obedience, poverty and chastity. It makes not a ha'porth of difference, of course, that Hopkins's experience of them three weeks after he arrived could not possibly have given him adequate grounds for these generalizations. They are obviously based on hearsay and the opinions of his fellow Jesuits. The point is not their truth or falsity, but the fact that Hopkins says that he is half-Welsh, meaning by that that he is half of him like these generalizations. It is as if all the sides of his personality that for eight years had been ruthlessly suppressed had suddenly reappeared along with the 'rise of the heart' as he looked at the clouds lifting over

---

[4] W. H. Gardner (ed.), *Poems of Gerard Manley Hopkins*, 3rd edn (London: Oxford University Press, 1948), 109. Henceforward referred to as *Poems*.

[5] *Further Letters*, 109.

Snowdon. It is small wonder that he was anxious to convert the Welsh! Small wonder, either, that he felt that his motives were impure and that the work was too dangerous for him to undertake.

The experience of coming to Wales, then, was, in Jungian terms, a confrontation with the Shadow, that part of the personality which the conscious ego banishes to the subconscious. The Jesuit ego of Hopkins, his will and his intellect, was shaken but not uprooted. A compromise was reached. His superiors must have realized that he needed careful handling. He was allowed to learn Welsh with Miss Jones, the sister of a Jesuit and ex-student of St Beuno's, Fr John Hugh Jones, parish priest of Caernarfon and at that time (as Fr Thomas tells us)[6] the only priest in Wales able to preach in the language. That was the first concession in Hopkins's compromise with his Shadow, and it probably defused the situation a great deal. The Welsh language became a reality to him, a task that he was not really very good at, instead of being the secret Shadow language of his buried half.

The second concession was to have more far-reaching effects. In December 1875 the *Deutschland* was wrecked and five Franciscan nuns who were sailing in her to escape persecution were drowned. Hopkins says in a letter to Dixon of 5 October 1878:

> I was affected by the account and happening to say so to my rector he said that he wished someone would write a poem on the subject. On this hint I set to work and, though my hand was out at first, produced one. (C. C. Abbott (ed.), *The Correspondence of Gerard Manley Hopkins and Richard Watson Dixon,* 2nd edn (London: Oxford University Press, 1955), 14)

Hopkins took it as a sign, though with some trepidation, that he could write verse again – he had given it up, he says, as not belonging to his profession unless it were by the wish of his superiors. He started to write the great poems of his maturity. Partially, at any rate, he began to live the life of a poet. These two concessions to his Shadow, learning Welsh and starting to write poetry, were connected by the beneficent presence of Gwenfrewi or Gwenffrewi Santes, St Winifred of Holywell, and her uncle Beuno, the patron saint of the Jesuits' College. He first became interested in her well, as far as I know, as early as 1867 when he mentioned in his journal that Fr Renelm Yaughan had been saved from consumption by drinking water from it. Fr Yaughan was a favourite of Hopkins at

---

[6] Op. cit.

that time, the brother of the future cardinal.[7] On 8 October 1874 he walked over to Holywell with another novice and bathed in the well. They returned 'very joyously':

> The sight of the water in the well as clear as glass, greenish like beryl or aquamarine, trembling at the surface with the force of the springs and shaping out the five foils of the well quite drew and held my eyes to it. Within a month or six months from this (I think Fr di Pietro said) a young man from Liverpool, Arthur Rent, was cured of rupture in the water. The strong unfailing flow of the water and the chain of cures from year to year all these centuries took hold of my mind with wonder at the bounty of God in one of his saints. (*Journals and Papers*, 261)

In 'The wreck of the *Deutschland*' of just over a year later, he uses two images juxtaposed without comment to describe his life as a Jesuit after the initial spiritual experience when his heart fled into the terror of God, 'dove-winged' and 'carrier-witted' to 'flash from the flame to the flame then, tower from the grace to the grace'. The first image is that of sand in an hourglass, mined from within by God's terrible erosion. It is the same quality of image as when he calls himself 'Time's eunuch'. The other is of St Winifred's well:

> I am soft sift
> In an hourglass – at the wall
> Fast, but mined with a motion, a drift,
> And it crowds and it combs to the fall;
> I steady as a water in a well, to a poise, to a pane,
> But roped with, always, all the way down from the tall
> Fells or flanks of the voel, a vein
> Of the gospel proffer, a pressure, a principle, Christ's gift.
>
> (*Poems*, no. 28, st. 4)

The very violence of the juxtaposition – for as images the two are totally opposed to one another – is in itself proof of spiritual advance. Gwenfrewi's well gave him an image of reconciliation with what we have been calling his Shadow. It was both a flowing, a welling-up, and a containment; both an image of stillness – 'steady . . . to a poise' – and of energy – 'a pressure', 'trembling at the surface with the force of the springs', as he put it in his journal. But neither image denies the other. Out of the creative tension between them his best poetry proceeds, both an expression of tragic aridity and a welling-up of hope as a spiritual force.

---

[7] See *Journals and Papers*, 157, and notes on pp. 575–7.

But this is to anticipate. Hopkins walked back with his fellow novice to St Beuno's. Perhaps he had already started to learn Welsh with Miss Jones. At any rate he did so soon after. He settled down into the routine of his theology course.

Among Hopkins's papers was found a cutting from the *Montgomeryshire Mercury*, which Gardner[8] dates 8 July 1875, but Paddy Kitchen, who quotes from it,[9] as 7 October 1874 just before the trip to Holywell we have just described. It contains a *cywydd*, a Welsh poem in couplets in full *cynghanedd* by Tudur Aled, a late fifteenth-century poet, in honour of Gwenfrewi Santes and her well. Apart from one short epigram (it is not an *englyn*, though it looks like one) that he noted in an early diary for 1864 (*Journals and Papers*, 34), this is the only specific Welsh poem that there is even circumstantial evidence that Hopkins read. It could well have been his first acquaintance with classical Welsh poetry. As such, it would have interested him both for its subject matter and for its form. Even if it was his first acquaintance with *cerdd dafod* (strict-metre poetry) he certainly searched out and tried to pick his way through other examples. His analyses of rhyme and alliteration in his lecture-notes of 1873–4[10] show him to have had considerable delight in such things as Norse 'shothending', assonance, and richness of what he calls 'lettering'. He quotes both an Icelandic example – lines like 'remma rimmu gloðir / randa grand ofjarli' – and an English imitation, with his own italics:

> *Sof*tly now are *sif*ting
> *Snows* on landscape *fro*zen.
> Thic*kly fall* the *flake*lets,
> *Feathery*-light tog*ether*.
>
> (ibid, 287)

It is abundantly clear that he was equipped to appreciate and respond to the intricacies of Welsh poetry, and in particular the 'lettering' that is called *cynghanedd*.

Some technical discussion of Welsh metrics is now necessary, though I shall try to keep it down to a minimum.[11] Roughly speaking, the history of bardic verse is divisible into two periods: an archaic period dominated by the *awdl*, and a modern period by the *cywydd*. The transition

---

[8] *Poems*, 270n.

[9] Paddy Kitchen, *Gerard Manley Hopkins* (London: H. Hamilton, 1978), 153–4.

[10] Loc. cit.

[11] I am grateful to Professors Bedwyr Lewis Jones and Gwyn Thomas for curbing some of my wilder ideas on *cerdd dafod*, and for their helpful comments on the essay.

occurred in the lifetime and practice of Dafydd ap Gwilym in the mid-fourteenth century.

The *awdl* was essentially a primitive form, an accumulation of longish lines (usually from eight to nineteen syllables each) in groups of up to fifty (or exceptionally up to a hundred or more), all with one rhyme. In writing, lines of over ten syllables are usually written as two or more separate lines. The *awdl* was strongly stressed, usually having four or six stresses to a line. The habit grew up from very early times of decorating at least some of these stressed words in each line with cross-alliteration or internal rhyme, or a combination of the two. This gave rise to archaic *cynghanedd*. Here is an example from the twelfth-century poet Cynddelw, with the 'lettering' under-lined, and the divisions it makes in the line marked by a stroke:

> Dôr / ysgor, / ysgwyd ganhymdaith.
> Tarian / yn aerwan, / yn eurwaith.
> Twrf grug, / yng ngoddug, / yng ngoddaith.
> Tarf esgar, / ysgwyd yn nylaith.
> Rhwyf myrdd / cyrdd, / cerddorion obaith.
> Rhudd, / ddiludd, / ddileddf gydymdaith.
> (*Oxford Book of Welsh Verse* (Oxford: Oxford University Press, 1962), 39)

The main purpose of this type of *cynghanedd* is to decorate and pick out the stresses in the body of the line, before you get to the main rhyme. Save that it is generally more complex, it is on the whole comparable in function to Anglo-Saxon alliteration. It helps to isolate the stressed words. We may therefore call it isolating stress *cynghanedd* and regard alliteration as a variety within it. Notice that the *cynghanedd* is not full *cynghanedd* in the modern sense, and (as in Anglo-Saxon) need not reach to the last stress of the line, and therefore need not be involved in the main rhyme-word of the passage.

Hopkins, as we shall see, almost certainly knew about archaic *cynghanedd*; but if you don't know the rules of modern *cynghanedd* it is not immediately obvious that the modern variety is different. If you come with an innocent eye to a modern *cywydd*, or poem in couplets, the *cynghanedd* may seem to you actually simpler and less rigorous than that of the archaic *awdl*. Take this section from Tudur Aled's poem to Gwenfrewi Santes (which is where we and Hopkins started this digression): let us imagine Hopkins trying to make sense of its 'lettering':

Tra fu'r mab ar i aberth,
A'i weddi'n Nuw iddi'n nerth,
Arwain afon o'r nefoedd,
A chwys gras, a chysegr oedd;
Teilynged, pan goded Gwen,
Tarddu ennaint Iorddonen . . .

(T. Gwynn Jones (ed.),
*Gwaith Tudur Aled* (Cardiff, 1926), II. 524)

Hopkins would probably have spotted the internal rhyme *mab* – *ab*erth in line 1. In line 2 he would have got the alliteration Nuw – *n*erth, and most probably we*ddi* – i*ddi* also, though he might have regarded this as a rhyme. In the third line, looking at the words, he might have thought there was rather weak alliteration on the vowel *a* in *a*rwain – *a*fon. In the fourth line he would have seen the alliteration *ch*wys – *ch*ysegr. The fifth line, like the first, he would probably have analysed correctly as internal rhyme plus alliteration (*cynghanedd sain*): Teilyng*ed* – god*ed* – *G*wen. Unless he mistook the *i* of *I*orddonen for a vowel, in which case it might be said to alliterate with the *e* of *e*nnaint, he would probably not have seen any lettering in line 6 at all.

It is important to realize that this is the sort of verse on which the rules of modern *cynghanedd* are based; and yet, despite that, if we come to it with an innocent eye (or perhaps more accurately, with the sort of expectations aroused in us by other forms of 'lettering' – including archaic *cynghanedd*), then it is likely that only two or three lines would be analysed correctly. In one line the lettering might be missed altogether, and in at least two others the perceived lettering might well be quite misleading. Here is the correct analysis of the *cynghanedd* in these six lines:

| | |
|---|---|
| Tra fu'r m<u>ab</u> / ar i <u>ab</u>erth, | -ab / ab- |
| A'i we<u>ddi</u>'<u>n</u> <u>N</u>uw / i<u>ddi</u>'<u>n</u> <u>n</u>erth, | dd-n-n- / dd-n-n- |
| A<u>r</u>wai<u>n</u> <u>af</u>on / o'<u>r</u> <u>n</u>e<u>f</u>oedd, | r-n-f- / r-n-f- |
| A <u>ch</u>wy<u>s</u> <u>gr</u>as, / a <u>ch</u>y<u>seg</u>r oedd; | ch-s-g-r- / ch-s-g-r- |
| Teilyng<u>ed</u>, / pan <u>g</u>od<u>ed</u> / <u>G</u>wen, | -ed / g-ed / g- |
| <u>T</u>a<u>r</u><u>dd</u>u e<u>nn</u>ain/<u>t</u> Io<u>r</u><u>dd</u>o<u>n</u>en ... | t-r-dd-n / t-r-dd-n- |

The difficulty Hopkins would have had in construing modern *cynghanedd* in ignorance of the rules has something to do with the way these rules to a great extent ignore the integrity of the word, even if it is stressed. What you have to look for is not simply words that answer each other, sound for sound, but rather you look for sequences of phonemes. It does not matter, within limits, what words these phonemes are in. In line 6, for example, the *t* of tarddu is not answered by the first letter of Iorddonen but by the last letter of ennaint, which properly belongs in the first part of the line and not in the second at all. It is this concentration on phoneme-sequences, rather than on words connected by their sound, that makes *cynghanedd* in its modern form unique to Wales.[12]

Is there any evidence that Hopkins ever knew the rules of *cynghanedd*? Where would he have found them? In English? Well, William Barnes, the Dorset poet, had published a simplified description of one kind of *cynghanedd* in *Macmillan's Magazine*[13] where he calls it 'the matching of clippings'. If Hopkins had seen this or anything similar he would have mentioned it in his 1873–4 lecture-notes. From printed sources in Welsh? It is difficult to be certain but if we look through the list (given by Fr Thomas in his *Cymmrodorion* article[14]) of Welsh material that was probably available to Hopkins, it seems unlikely. From talking to Welsh people? None of the Jesuits was proficient in Welsh. He did not meet Dr (later Sir) John Rhys the Celtic scholar until the summer of 1877. It is probable that Miss Jones, his teacher, would have known in general what *cynghanedd* was (and certainly Hopkins frequently uses the word in correspondence) but she was unlikely to have been familiar

---

[12] I do not in this section mean to imply that Hopkins never at any time knew the rules of modern *cynghanedd*, with its emphasis on sequences of phonemes rather than on words answering each other sound for sound. By the time he returned from his holiday in north Wales in the autumn of 1886, the evidence is that he knew about *cynghanedd groes*, the most typical form of it, and that he rather disliked it, at any rate in English. He wrote about William Barnes's experiments to Coventry Patmore:

> However his employment of the Welsh *Cynghanedd* or chime I do not look on as quite successful. To tell the truth, I think I could do that better, and it is an artificial thing and not much in his line. (I mean like *Paladore* and *Poly dear*, which is in my judgment more of a miss than a hit.) *(Further Letters, 371)*

The contrast between this wry disillusionment and his earlier enthusiasm for *cynghanedd* may not be simply a matter of a craftsman rejecting a technique which excited him before. The two attitudes may be based on different conceptions of *cynghanedd*: first, a delighted appreciation of the way archaic *cynghanedd* decorates and savours the stressed words in a line; and second, a suspicion of the arbitrary order implied by the phoneme sequences of modern *cynghanedd*, which in a typically English way he judged to be 'artificial'.

[13] 'The old bardic poetry' (May–October 1867), 306–17.

[14] Op. cit.

with the whole gamut of rules. The only person likely to have told him about that was a Welsh poet; and as we have seen, he did not meet a bard in the flesh until 1886.

More significantly, in the English poems he started to write in 1875 and 1876 there is considerable evidence of exposure to Welsh strict-metre poetry. We see him responding to the various types of *cynghanedd* he found there, understanding their function even when he probably didn't understand what the Welsh meant, and translating that function (but not the rules as such) into his own poetic grammar. Only one kind of *cynghanedd – sain –* is used strictly in his work with any frequency. What is more, in 1876 he wrote a Welsh *cywydd* to honour the Jubilee of the Bishop of Shrewsbury. Only two lines are correct according to modern rules. The poem shows considerable patterning, however. Every line is 'lettered' in some way, besides the rhyme at the end. It is hard to imagine that a poet who could write a line as ornate as 'Fardd a lif i'r hardd brif dda' could not have managed some easy *cynghanedd draws* or *lusg* at least in one line of each couplet. My guess is that the poet was not so much incompetent as blissfully ignorant. Or, to put it another way, Hopkins is the only Welsh nineteenth-century poet to use *cynghanedd* as though he was learning his craft in the thirteenth. I am sure that Hopkins thought he was writing a *cywydd* with *cynghanedd*. I am also sure that he thought 'The wreck of the *Deutschland*' embodied 'certain chimes suggested by the Welsh poetry I had been reading' not spasmodically but in practically every line of the poem.

Miss Gweneth Lilly[15] has tried to catalogue the different ways that Hopkins embodies or approximates to *cynghanedd* – and indeed other features of Welsh poetry. She found that his usage is reminiscent of early Welsh poets, rather than the fully formed art of modern strict-metre bards. It seems to me odd to describe Cynddelw in the twelfth century as though he was trying to be like Tudur Aled in the fifteenth, failing because the art of *cynghanedd* had not attained its true perfection yet. I prefer to think that Cynddelw knew very well what he was doing, perhaps better than Tudur Aled. But aside from that, Miss Lilly and I agree that Hopkins's *cynghanedd* is in general reminiscent of the archaic period. The question is, why?

There would seem to be two reasons. One is the availability of texts. According to Fr Thomas, St Beuno's possessed copies of *The Myvyrian*

---

[15] 'The Welsh influence in the poetry of Gerard Manley Hopkins', *Modern Language Review*, 38 (1943), 192–205.

*Archaiology of Wales* and *The Four Ancient Books of Wales,* both of which contain ancient and medieval Welsh poetry (mainly before 1350), but nothing much later. Those would seem to be the only printed books containing Welsh verse available to Hopkins, though Dr Geraint Gruffydd[16] has suggested that he might also have had access to a seventeenth-century manuscript of Welsh poetry, which seems to have been at St Beuno's at the time. On the whole I think it more likely that he stuck to the *Myvyrian Archaiology.* He only had limited time, after all, and to decipher a manuscript would probably have been less inviting to him than to read from a book. He wrote to Baillie on 6 January 1877:

> I have learnt Welsh, as you say: I can read easy prose and can speak stumblingly, but at present I find the greatest difficulty, amounting mostly to total failure, in understanding it when spoken and the poetry, which is quite as hard as the choruses in a Greek play . . . I can make little way with. (*Further Letters,* 241)

If he was trying to read the mediaeval poetry from the *Myvyrian Archaiology,* and in particular that of the twelfth and thirteenth centuries where he would have found archaic *cynghanedd* exemplified most, then it is no wonder he could make little way with it! It is indeed fiendishly hard, deliberately so. The poets liked it that way. On the other hand, if he had poetry of the sixteenth century before him, then his remark would be surprising. It would present him with many and severe local difficulties, certainly; but even with a poorish dictionary he should not have found it totally impossible. Such, at least, has been my own experience in circumstances not totally dissimilar to Hopkins's at that time.

The other reason why Hopkins's practice is similar to archaic *cynghanedd* is that both are concerned with making us linger over stressed words. Hopkins's sprung rhythm was based solely on counting stresses: any lettering he used would have to be there to strengthen their impact. The *cynghanedd* he uses is almost always of the isolating stress type.

Let us now imagine Hopkins poring over the *Myvyrian Archaiology,* a huge block of incomprehensible verse. Probably he makes the mistake of thinking that the early poetry will be more difficult than the section called medieval, and he starts turning over the pages, recognizing the odd word here, the odd name there. Let us suppose that he studies the following poem by Gwalchmai. It would be a good place to start, partly because it isn't too long, partly because it is certainly easier than anything

---

[16] *Y Faner* (6 Mawrth 1981), 'Llawysgrif Heythrop a Brân Maenefa'.

else for many pages, and partly because he might have remembered it in Gray's translation. It is on the fifth or sixth page into the medieval section, depending on which edition he was using:

Gwalchmai ai cant i Owain Gwyned

Ardwyreaf hael o hil Rodri
Ardwyad gorwlad gwerlin teithi
　Teithiawg Prydain
　Twyth afyrdwyth Owain
　Teyrnain ni grain
　　Ni grawn rei.

Teir lleng y daethant liant lestri
Teir praf prif lynges wy bres brofi
　Un o Iwerdon
　Arall arfogion
　O'r Llychlynigion
　　Llwrw hirion lli.

A'r dryded dros for o Nordmandi
Ar drapherth anferth anfad idi
A draig Mon mor drud ei eissillud yn aer
　A bu terfysg taer i haer holi.

A ragdaw rewys dwys dyfysgi
A rewin a thrin a thranc cymri
　Ar gad gad greude
　Ar gryd gryd graende
　Ac am dal Moelfre
　　Mil fanieri . . .

He would have noticed that the opening line is characteristic of Gwalchmai. No less than five out of his twelve poems extant start with the words, 'I exalt the generous one of the line of . . .' whoever it is. Something like it was surely in Hopkins's mind when he wrote in 'The wreck of the *Deutschland*': 'I admire thee, master of the tides' (st. 32).

Rhythmically he would have found that the longer lines mostly have four beats and the shorter two or three; but that the pattern is 'sprung', as he called it. He would have noticed that the longer lines have fairly elaborate patterning, sometimes simple alliteration as in 'A'r dryded dros for o Nordmandi' (line 13), sometimes what Wilfred Owen called pararhyme – 'hael o hil' in line 1; and sometimes a combination of alliteration and rhyme, as in 'daethant liant lestri'. In the second line of the second stanza, there is double patterning, for 'praf prif' is followed by 'lynges ... bres brofi'. The shorter lines are sometimes patterned separately, sometimes in groups: for example, 'Teithiog Prydain' alliterates and rhymes with 'Twyth afyrdwyth Owain'. In some cases, as in the third and fourth lines of stanza 3, a word at the end of a line is patterned not with that line but the middle of the next.

Let us now compare this with a couple of stanzas chosen at random from 'The wreck of the *Deutschland*', one from the first part and the other from the second. I mark the Gwalchmai-type patterning with italics:

> Not out of his bliss
> *S*prings the *s*tress *f*elt
> Nor *f*irst from heaven (and *f*ew know this)
> *S*wings the *stroke* dealt –
> *Stroke* and a *st*ress that *st*ars and *st*orms deliver,
> That guilt is *hushed by*, *h*earts are *flushed by* and melt –
> But it *r*ides time like *r*iding a *r*iver
> (And here the *f*aithful waver, the *f*aithless *f*able and miss).
>
> (st. 6)

(I have ignored the assonances – the long a's in 'the faithful waver, the faithless fable', for example, undoubtedly contribute to the effect.)

> With a mercy that outrides
> The *a*ll of water, an *a*rk
> For the *l*istener; for the *l*ingerer with a *l*ove glides
> *L*ower than *d*eath and the *d*ark;
> A *v*ein for the *v*isiting of the *p*ast-*p*rayer, *p*ent in *p*rison,
> The *last-br*eath *p*eni*t*ent *sp*irits – the uttermost mark
> Our *p*assion-*p*lunged giant risen,
> The Christ of the Father *c*ompassionate, *f*etched in the *st*orm of his *st*rides.
>
> (st. 33)

It seems clear that in every line (except optionally the first of each stanza) Hopkins is patterning his verses in a way that is more or less equivalent to Gwalchmai's. There is far more simple alliteration than there is in the Welsh, and the alliteration on vowels in the beginning of stanza 33 would not be in his model; and there is far less rhyme-plus-alliteration (*cynghanedd sain*). But it is not true to say merely that every line contains simple alliteration. Every line contains simple alliteration or some other, complicated patterning, or else continues the patterning at the end of the line before. These two stanzas are by no means the most elaborate in the poem. They contain nothing as ornate as, for example, 'Warm-laid grave of a womb-life grey' of stanza 7. But, allowing for some licence due to enthusiasm and some perhaps to ignorance, such a consistency of patterning must be deliberate. I think myself that Hopkins thought he was writing a poem in *cynghanedd*. The fact that he might afterwards have realized that Welshmen did not agree with him might have prevented him later saying anything about his full intentions.

This is even more true of his *cywydd*, though in this case the *cynghanedd* (even if incorrect) is often more like the sort you would find in a *cywydd*. He might have looked at one – such as that to Gwenfrewi Santes, for example – before he started to write his own:

> Y mae'n llewyn yma'n llon
> A ffrydan llawer ffynon,
> Gweddill gwyn gadwyd i ni
> Gan Feuno a Gwenfrewi.
>
> (*Poems*, no.135, p. 190)

Writing as he was, out of a dictionary in a poetic language half-understood, as one might do an exercise in Greek verse, Hopkins here too, it seems to me, was applying in his own poetic grammar the lessons he had learnt from such poets as Gwalchmai in the pages of the *Myvyrian Archaiology*. That is, he thought he was writing *cynghanedd*.

As far as other features of Welsh poetry affected him it was mainly to confirm and exaggerate tendencies that were in Hopkins already, such as the use of compound words and 'expressionist' breaks in syntax and normal word order. Rhythmically, though, he did note in a letter dated 21 August 1877: 'Such rhythm as French or Welsh poetry has is sprung, counterpointed upon a counted rhythm' (C. C. Abbott (ed.), *The Letters of Gerard Manley Hopkins to Robert Bridges*, 2nd edn. (London, 1955), 46.)

I cannot find much Welsh influence on his own sprung rhythm. The nineteenth century witnessed a gradual breakdown in the usefulness of the iambic, due in part to the changing structures of the English verb. Hopkins's sprung rhythm is only the most extreme attempt to find a viable substitute before the whole question collapsed into the metrical no man's land of free verse. Nor would there seem to be any Welsh element in the large-scale structure of his poetry, its architectonics. I am inclined to agree with Todd K. Bender[17] that he probably designed 'The wreck of

---

[17] Todd K. Bender, *Gerard Manley Hopkins: The Classical Background and Critical Reception of his Work* (Baltimore: John Hopkins Press, 1966).

the *Deutschland*' according to his understanding of Greek choral odes. The poem is complex in a way that no Welsh *awdl* could match.

There is, however, another way in which a poem like Gwalchmai's could well have pointed the way forward for Hopkins in 1875. As a Jesuit, we know, he often doubted whether poetry-writing sorted with his profession. He gave it up entirely during his noviciate until it seemed to be his superior's wish that he should write. That is familiar ground. Less so is the other side of the question, namely, whether having that kind of profession made normal English post-romantic bourgeois poetry impossible for him to write at all. Ever since poets like Chaucer ousted the professional minstrels from the court, English poetry has been more or less an amateur's domain. That is, the poet wrote because he had it in him to write, not because it was his job to do so. The wind bloweth where it listeth. Except poetry come as naturally as leaves to a tree, said Keats, it had better not come at all. The romantic stress on the primacy of the poetic imagination was a climax to four hundred years' development away from professionalism in poetry. To put it another way, the poet set up as his own master, dependent on the market forces he called fame, but having no allegiances other than to his genius. His style as a poet, his point of view, his opinions and moods, were on offer as a personalized commodity, so to speak; but apart from that use of himself as marketable, he was free to go wherever his inspiration led him.

Now Hopkins was not his own master, in poetry or in anything else. His membership of the Society of Jesus took away his amateur status for ever. He might pursue music or Welsh as 'interests' or hobbies; but he had too great a respect for poetry, and ultimately for his own talents as a poet, to lower it to that level. He had to write a kind of poetry, if at all, which his profession as a Jesuit allowed, and which his superiors had the absolute right to demand or forbid. Anything like selling himself or his opinions on the market would be deeply repugnant to him. Those who have read his letters, particularly to Dixon, will remember the mixture of confused hope and resignation whenever one of his poems had a chance of being published; and the obvious relief as well as disappointment when that chance faded. The model behind 'The wreck of the *Deutschland*' is not a personal expression of a point of view but a boast of God's mighty deeds. First Hopkins boasts of God's mastery as he has known it and responded to it:

> Thou hast bound bones and veins in me, fastened me flesh,
>    And after it almost unmade, what with dread,
>       Thy doing: and dost thou touch me afresh?
> Over again I feel thy finger and find thee.
>
>                                                        (st. 1)

It is this experience which qualifies him, as it were, to make the second and greater boast, of God's redeeming power through the persons of the five drowned nuns:

> Surf, snow, river and earth
>    Gnashed: but thou art above, thou Orion of light;
> Thy unchancelling poising palms were weighing the worth,
>    Thou martyr-master: in thy sight
> Storm flakes were scroll-leaved flowers, lily showers – sweet heaven
>                                           was astrew in them.
>
>                                                        (st. 21)

It is the kind of boast that a Catholic priest makes every day at the altar, for the Mass centres upon it:

> Vere dignum et iustum est, aequum et salutare: Te quidem, Domine, omne tempore ... gloriosius praedicare, cum Pascha nostrum immolatus est Christus ...

> It is truly meet and just, right and availing to salvation that at all times ... we should extol thy glory, Lord, when Christ our Pasch was sacrificed. For he is the true Lamb who hath taken away the sins of the world. Who by dying has overcome our death ... (Preface for Easter)

The consecration of the bread and wine and its transubstantiation into the Body and Blood occurs during the relation by the priest of God's great deeds. It is entirely set in the context of the boast, which itself echoes the boast of the Jewish people at the Passover feast. (The point is a little obscured in the Tridentine Mass by the number of supplicatory prayers which are allowed to interrupt the exalting of God's works.)

Now although this kind of boast was as familiar to Hopkins as his own face, it is nevertheless not an easy thing for an English poet to imagine his poetry doing. Gentlemen – and amateurs have to be gentlemen – don't boast. Even Herbert's religious poems do not exactly brag of God's mercies. For that you have to go back, perhaps to Dunbar with his 'Done is a battell on the dragon blak'. When Hopkins first picked out such poems as Gwalchmai's in the *Myvyrian Archaiology* it must have acted like a lightning conductor for him. Even if he could scarcely make out their drift, two things would have been abundantly clear. First, that the poems are boasts, usually about the prince or tribal leader of a people: 'Ardwyreaf hael o hil Rodri', begins Gwalchmai, 'I exalt the generous one of the clan of Rhodri.' And secondly, the poet is boasting because it is his job to boast. He isn't an amateur paying compliments to his leader, flattering him with flannel. It isn't that kind of praise. He boasts of his lord's prowess in battle, and of his generosity, or he laments him when he is dead, because that is what poets do, that is why the tribe maintains them as poets, and that is how they keep their status and self-respect.

Hopkins's position as a Jesuit, pledged to submit in everything to his superiors, made amateur poetry impossible for him. He had to be professional or nothing. Like Gwalchmai, the only poetic function he could justify professionally was to boast of his master's mighty deeds, when the occasion called for it. He was already being pulled into the orbit of this 'world of Wales'. He found in the early Welsh poets a way of celebrating (we use the same word for praising heroic deeds as for saying Mass) that was deeply familiar to him and which consorted with his profession as a Jesuit priest. He found a rhetoric and a mode of versification that answered his needs. Both in English and (as far as he was able) in Welsh he created praise-poetry that related more to Taliesin, Gwalchmai, Cynddelw and Tudur Aled than to anything English poetry had seen for centuries. It is very largely the Welsh element in him that makes his work so eccentric and so challenging from the point of view of English poetic tradition. I beg leave to suggest that we stop talking of this or that Welsh 'influence' and treat him for what he is, an Anglo-Welsh poet who found his birthright when he came to Wales ('always for me', he said, 'a mother of Muses') and was only prevented from committing himself to her conversion by his prior commitment to have no allegiances except to Christ and the Society of Jesus.

Clearly, what happened to his poetry when he left Wales is another story, and we have no time to detail it here. Both metrically and in the stance he adopted for his poetry it is likely he moved towards a more English position. His later sonnets are perhaps comparable with Donne's. But the tension that exists between his later work and the demands of his profession is also much greater. The tradition of Taliesin, if only he could have found an audience that knew what he was doing, would have answered his needs much better than the constipated English expressionism of his later years – however powerful the sonnets are as bursts of energy in the prevailing emotional aridity of his life.

# 7

## David Jones and the ironic epic

~

### In Parenthesis

David Jones is one of the great modernists – T. S. Eliot recognized that he belonged with Joyce, Pound and himself. As an Anglo-Welsh representative of that international movement he deserves a separate chapter of our history. It is true that he liked to discuss his work in quasi-geological terms – he talks frequently of 'deposits' of lore, and he quotes Nennius at the opening of the Preface to *The Anathemata*, 'I have made a heap of all that I could find'. In a way, he belongs more with writers who found buried treasure in the *traddodiad* than with those who, like Dylan Thomas, in the name of modernism rejected *buchedd* values in the thirties and forties. But, while he does encourage this approach (and certainly gets it from academic scholars who subscribe to his cult) it seems to me more profitable to start with *In Parenthesis* as an ironic epic, comparable as a work of fiction, for example, to Kafka's *Trial*.

Northrop Frye[1] makes a useful distinction between literary fictions according to the status of the hero. In myth, the hero is a god, superior in kind to both humanity and nature. In romance, he is superior in degree to other men and to nature, so that his actions are marvellous though he is still accepted as human. In the 'high mimetic' mode of most epic and tragedy, he is superior in degree to other men but shares the same natural environment. Then fourth, in the 'low mimetic' mode of most comedy and realistic fiction, he is equal to us, and faced with the same environment. Prof. Frye then describes the fifth mode:

---

[1] Northrop Frye, *Anatomy of Criticism* (New Jersey: Princeton University Press, 1957), 33–4, 40–3. 'Irony' is used as a formal attribute here, not primarily as a description of style.

If inferior in power or intelligence to ourselves, so that we have the sense of looking down on a scene of bondage, frustration or absurdity, the hero belongs to the ironic mode. This is still true when the reader feels that he is or might be in the same situation, as the situation is being judged by the norms of a greater freedom.

Ironic tragedy occurs when all elements of the special case are eliminated. There is no reason why this man should suffer or die rather than that. The victim is no more and no less deserving of what happens to him than anyone else. He is caught in a tragic pattern where who he is or what he has done is of very little relevance to what he suffers.

*In Parenthesis* traces a progression from the low mimetic of its opening through the ironic tragedy of its denouement to the reappearance of myth in its close. This is what we might have expected, according to Northrop Frye – he does not refer to David Jones but to Kafka, Joyce and Henry James:

> Irony descends from the low mimetic: it begins in realism and dispassionate observation. But as it does so, it moves steadily towards myth, and dim outlines of sacrificial rituals and dying gods begin to appear in it. Our five modes evidently go around in a circle.

Much of the strangeness of *In Parenthesis* is explained by this analysis. Is it a prose work or a poem? Is it a 'realistic' war book? If it is, what is the place in it of such obviously unrealistic fantasias as Dai's boast in Part 4 or the activities of the Queen of the Woods in Part 7? Why does the work begin in prose and gradually 'disintegrate' into verse? Why, above all, is no moral judgement implied on the war, as it is in all the other war poets, from Rupert Brook to Wilfred Owen?

When one reads the first part of *In Parenthesis*, 'The many men so beautiful', it seems at first a realistic description of a battalion being paraded before it embarks overseas. A certain stylization is present, true, but military parades are stylized anyway. There is even a suggestion, in the person of Private Ball, late and improperly dressed for parade, of a hero or focal point we can identify with, as in a comic or realistic novel. The book begins like this:

> '49 Wyatt, 01549 Wyatt.
> Coming sergeant.
> Pick 'em up, pick 'em up – I'll stalk within yer chamber.
> Private Leg . . . sick.

> Private Ball . . . absent.
> '01 Ball, '01 Ball, Ball of No. 1.
> Where's Ball, 25201 Ball – you corporal,
> Ball of your section.

The build-up to Private Ball's appearance is what we're first aware of. First Wyatt, then Leg, are discarded as centres of interest, to make way for our real hero, Ball. It's the sort of technique that we recognize from school stories, for example. But then certain features disturb this pattern. The sergeant quotes from a famous poem by a sixteenth-century namesake of Private Wyatt:

> They flee from me, that sometime did me seek
> With naked foot, stalking in my chamber.

The way this intimate metaphor (for Wyatt is talking of his past girlfriends as pet falcons) is accommodated to the tone of the parade ground is very typical of David Jones's use of quotations. They both draw attention to themselves as incognito and they preclude realistic comment – it would be absurd to have a note on how learned this particular sergeant was in the byways of English literature. The quotation in fact jams our low mimetic expectations almost from the start. As Northrop Frye says, 'the situation is being judged by the norms of a greater freedom'. In Joyce, this technique often leads to actual punning and misspelling of words to suggest a many-layered apprehension; in David Jones it is more often a tonal ambiguity, as when a musician uses a chord that belongs to two different keys at once. A more powerful example occurs on the next page when Private Ball's worries about being improperly dressed are interrupted by the commanding officer calling his battalion by name:

> His imaginings as to the precise relationship of this general indictment from the book to his own naked mess-tin were with suddenness and most imperatively impinged upon, as when an animal hunted, stopping in some ill-chosen covert to consider the wickedness of man, is started into fresh effort by the cry and breath of dogs dangerously and newly near. For the chief huntsman is winding his horn, the officer commanding is calling his Battalion by name – whose own the sheep are.

The use of a full-blown Homeric simile about a wrongly packed mess-tin is itself ironic, of course: whereas epic poets usually use the extended simile to compare great things with small, such as the emergence of a town's defenders with bees coming from a hive, David Jones compares small things with great. We note in passing that it is not usual, outside C. S. Lewis's Narnia, to describe animals as 'stopping to consider the wickedness of man'. But it is the last five words of the passage that release the authentic David Jones ironic imagination in all its moving complexity. The quotation is from Christ's parable of the good shepherd: 'He calleth his own sheep by name, and leadeth them out' (John, 10:3). The identification of the huntsman with the shepherd is a violent twist to the imagery, itself ironic; but to identify the commanding officer with Christ is startling. Yes, we can allow the officer's devotion to his men, his determination to preserve them, as having a lot in common with Christ's care for his people. David Jones knew how decent and humane many officers were. But even so, they were not leading their men to safety like the good shepherd but into the most murderous battle-front history has ever known. All this – the admiration, compassion even, for the officer as well as the terror of the implied blasphemy – is implied in those five words. Lightly, be it said, for we are still in the near-comedy of an embarkation parade. But the hunter and the shepherd are one, and it is his own sheep he is leading to slaughter.

The comparison between military and sacred is a constant one, of course, throughout the book. In this first part we have already had Lance-Corporal Lewis who 'had somewhere in his Welsh depths a remembrance of the nature of man, of how a lance-corporal's stripe is but held vicariously, and from on high, is of one texture with an eternal economy'. The opening of Part 3 opens with the rubric from the Good Friday liturgy as the men go to the front line; and 'the liturgy of their going-up assumed a primitive creativeness, an apostolic actuality . . .' And so on. It is important to keep the sense of simile: religious and military order are like each other, but not the same. The irony is preserved. This is true whether or no René Hague is right in saying that David Jones enjoyed the army – indeed, it is clear on one level that he did. He had companionship, order and purpose given to him, and in a sense the rest of his life was an attempt to recover those things. But of course fighting in the war was terrifying. He lost many companions, he was often very frightened, in acute discomfort, wounded. It was indeed a way of the cross. But what you don't find in David Jones – indeed, in one of his letters[2] he repudiates the idea as blasphemous – is the sense

2 René Hague (ed.), *Dai Greatcoat: A Self-portrait of David Jones in his Letters*, (London: Faber, 1980), 245-6.

that Christ himself was suffering with the soldiers, was himself a common soldier, seen on the battlefield. You find that in the other war poets: Sassoon and Owen and so on were the heirs of the Romantics, and kept a more or less 'low-mimetic' view of both the war and Jesus. They satirized the generals for their folly and demanded that the war should be ended, because they still had the sense, which Wordsworth had had in the revolutionary France of 1792-3, that it might be possible to lead, or at any rate influence, the actions of their fellow men. The fundamental axiom of the 'low mimetic' is that the hero – including Christ – is a man like you. He is a common man who because of his situation and character takes a leading as opposed to a subordinate role. David Jones had no such confidence. Theologically of course he knew that Christ was man as well as God; but the relation between high and low, leader and led, in his work is a sacramental one, an acceptance together of a common sign – whether army insignia or the breaking of bread in the mass – rather than a social contract agreed more or less between equals. The fact that Sassoon and Owen were officers whereas David Jones was a private symbolizes a deeper helplessness, a heroism that is without personal responsibility or power.

Up to the end of Part 2 of *In Parenthesis*, despite the stylization and the odd 'poetic' phrase, you could still be reading a realistic account of John Ball's war experiences. Indeed, this element never quite disappears – it is what gives form to the book as a whole, and differentiates it sharply from the later books and fragments, where the poet has somehow to give shape to the 'heap of all that I could find'. But after the soldiers experience their first shell-burst at the end of Part 2, the contained realistic narrative tends to give way to separable voices. The changes of tone get more rapid and ironic. Whole sections can be read as poems in themselves, as with the lyric about the rat of no man's land that ends Part 3:

> You can hear the silence of it:
> you can hear the rat of no-man's-land
> rut-out intricacies,
> weasel-out his patient workings,
> scrut, scrut, scrut,
> harrow-out earthly, trowel his cunning paw;
> redeem the time of our uncharity, to sap his own amphibious paradise.
>     You can hear his carrying-parties rustle our corruptions through
> the night-weeds – contest the choicest morsels in his tiny conduits, bead-
> eyed feast on us; by a rule of his nature, at night-feast on the broken of us.

Those broad-pinioned;
blue-burnished, or brindle-back;
whose proud eyes watched
            the broken emblems
droop and drag dust,
suffer with us this metamorphosis.

These too have shed their fine feathers; these too have slimed their
dark-bright coats; these too have condescended to dig in.
The white-tailed eagle at the battle ebb, where the sea wars against
the rivere
the speckled kite of Maldon
and the crow
have naturally selected to be un-winged;
to go on the belly, to
sap sap sap
with festered spines, arched under the moon; furrit with whiskered
snouts the secret parts of us.
When it's all quiet you can hear them:
scrut scrut scrut
when it's as quiet as this is.
It's so very still.
Your body fits the crevice of the bay in the most comfortable
fashion imaginable.
It's cushy enough.

So cushy indeed that John Ball is found by his mate napping on sentry-
duty! But what we have to notice is the way the rats are not merely the
heirs of the eagles, kites and crows that feed on the dead in heroic poetry;
the rats parody the 'metamorphosis' of the soldiers themselves –
'carrying-parties', and so on. But they also 'redeem the time of
our uncharity' by using the dead bodies as food: the rat 'saps his own
amphibious paradise' – saps, of course, in the military sense, 'to make
trenches'. Rats at least know what they're doing, they don't just obey
orders. They have 'condescended to dig in'.

Then, in Part 4, Dai 'articulates his English with an alien care' in a
boast that rapidly loses all contact with realistic narrative in what
is surely the first prefiguring of the technique of *The Anathemata* and
the later 'fragments':

I was with Abel when his brother found him,
under the green tree.
I built a shit-house for Artaxerxes.
I was the spear in Balin's hand that made waste King Pellam's land . . .

97

It is an awkward moment in the conduct of the narrative: it is not easy to modulate from soldierly realism to the bitterly ironical, literary and yet oracular speech of Dai's boast, echoing, as the author's note reminds us, the boasts of Taliesin and Glewlwyd the porter of Arthur in Welsh, and Widsith in Old English.

The boast is linguistically split – very unevenly – in two. The first six lines appear to be indeed Dai's articulation of an alien English:

> My fathers were with the Black Prinse of Wales
> at the passion of
> the blind Bohemian king.
> They served in these fields,
> it is in the histories that you can read it, Corporal – boys
> Gower, they were – it is writ down – yes.

Dai does sound like a man thinking in Welsh and translating as he goes along. It is also a very different kind of boast to the rest – it is literally true that men from Gower served in France with the Black Prince. Dai's mates react with deflating Cockney humour: 'Wot about Methuselum, Taffy?' And after that we hear no more Welsh accent, neither does the boast refer to the historical deeds of Dai's ancestors. Instead, an 'I' who speaks literary English with an RP accent claims to have been personally present at various times of strife from the Revolt of the Angels onward. One has to ask, is it Dai's boast at all, or is it the poet himself interpolating a different kind of utterance entirely? True, his messmates respond with the same Cockney humour, this time of ironic astonishment: 'Cripes-a-mighty-strike-me-stone-cold, you don't say'. But the boast is not smuggled in, like the sergeant saying to Private Wyatt, 'I'll stalk within yer chamber'. It is blatant myth-making, without any real-life analogue in what happened in the trenches. On the other hand, Paul Fussell's description of it seems overly low-mimetic and simple:

> [Dai] delivers what amounts to a history of wars and soldiers based on personal testimony through multiple incarnations . . . The reader comes away from this persuaded that the state of the soldier is universal throughout history. But the problem is, if soldiering is universal, what's wrong with it? And if there's nothing in the special conditions of the Great War to alter cases drastically, what's so terrible about it? Why the shock? But Jones's commitment to his ritual-and-romance machinery impels him to keep hinting that this war is like others. (Paul Fussell, *The Great War and Modern Memory* (New York and London: Oxford University Press, 1975), 150)

There are several non-sequiturs here. A thing may be universal, for instance, and yet wrong. We are all of us sinners. Nor does the fact that the Great War was uniquely drastic prevent it from being similar in some respects to every other war. In low-mimetic poetry, metaphor is generally more valued than simile, because you are aiming at imaginative fusion, a kind of chemical change where two things come together and make a third. Fussell thinks that because David Jones constantly refers to ritual and romance, therefore he is asserting the identity of the Great War with the rituals of the Church and the romance of Malory. But David Jones is a profoundly ironic writer – and not just at some points and in some respects: the whole shape of his work depends on an ironic viewpoint. Irony favours simile rather than metaphor, because much of the tension in irony comes from a perception of huge difference coexisting with similarity.

David Jones's irony reaches right round the corner into myth, but even at its most tender (as in the Queen of the Woods episode in Part 7) it remains ironic myth. That is to say, the hero, even while he is present at the ritual of the gods – assisting, as they say of people at Mass – is still 'inferior in power to ourselves, so that we have the sense of looking down on a scene of bondage, frustration or absurdity'. John Ball is wounded, trying to make up his mind to dump his rifle and try to reach some kind of shelter before the stretcher-bearers come. His mind, despite or because of the pain, slips in and out of a dream-like state, half nightmare, half revelation. So do wounded men cry out like children for their mothers. You could hardly suffer more bondage, frustration or absurdity and still preserve a human imagination:

> It [the rifle] is not to be hidden under your failing body.
> Slung so, it troubles your painful crawling like a fugitive's irons.

> The trees are very high in the wan signal-beam, for whose slow gyration their wounded boughs seem as malignant limbs, manoeuvring for advantage.
> The trees of the wood beware each other
> and under each a man sitting;
> their seemly faces as carved in a sardonyx stone; as undiademed princes turn their gracious profiles in a hidden seal, so did these appear, under the changing light . . .

> Hung so about, you make between these your close escape.

> The secret princes between the leaning trees have diadems given them.
> Life the leveller hugs her impudent equality – she may proceed at once to less discriminating zones.

It is, of course, not realistic narrative, but the mind remembering, looking back, finding language and symbols for what was felt and apprehended and suffered on that day – experience almost behind experience – in the broken woods of Mametz. The vision of the dead soldiers – German and British – as princes, as gods, is close to the basis of mystery religions everywhere, whether in Eleusis, among the Red Indians of the Plains, or in the Christian mass. Life may level us down to slaves, prisoners, wounded privates – but that is her 'impudence' in the face of this vision. John Ball, however, is still alive – he must himself 'proceed to less discriminating zones'.

The astonishing poetry of the Queen of the Woods passage now unfolds itself:

> These knew her influential eyes. Her awarding hands can pluck for each their fragile prize . . .

But the poem (for by this time *In Parenthesis* has surely become that) does not end there, but in a scatter of thoughts – about his rifle, about post-war tours of the devastated areas, about Blighty, about the stretcher-bearers. The German – Emil who had a curious crown of saxifrage, Ulrich smiling for his myrtle wand, as we have just seen them under the Queen's 'influential eye' – becomes Jerry again: 'Lie still under the oak', Ball tells himself:

> next to the Jerry
> and Sergeant Jerry Coke.

The unconscious pun on the name is a fit symbol of 'Life's impudent equality', ironic to the last.

### The 'Attempted writing'

While he was finishing *In Parenthesis* in 1933–4, David Jones had a nervous breakdown and was taken on a Mediterranean trip to help him convalesce, to Jerusalem. There, in the bazaars surrounded by bargaining Arabs, he 'caught sight of a figure who carried me back a couple of decades or thereabouts'; or chanced to come upon a couple off duty: 'Gotta gasper, mate? . . . Christ, what a sod of a place.' 'It might', he wrote to Saunders Lewis, 'have been a rain-soaked Givenchy duck-board trackway instead of a sweltering Hierosolyma by-street.' But sometimes he saw a squad of these British soldiers, and the unfamiliarity of their tropical parade rig, short-sleeved shirts and shorts, 'evoked not the familiar things of less than two decades back, but rather of two millennia close on . . . so they were a section from the Antonia, up for duties in Hierosolyma after all!'

After the war he had become a Catholic: and this experience in Jerusalem, where two decades and two millennia ago seemingly coexisted, took him into an imaginative world where Christ was offering himself as a sacrifice at the Last Supper – round the corner, as it were – while David Jones, veteran of the Royal Welch Fusiliers, identified with the soldiers who had been detailed to crucify Him.

It was a heady mixture. Apart from the transitional and unfinished 'Book of Balaam's Ass', almost everything he wrote subsequently was an exploraton of the meaning of those moments in a Jerusalem street in 1934. Let us look at some of the cross-relationships involved. First of all, the wholly ironic one of the soldiers to the Cross: to them it was just an unpleasant fatigue-duty, one of many in this 'sod of a place'. It was by a series of accidents and coincidences that they were the ones to do it. The end of 'The fatigue' traces these coincidences:

> from where an high administration deals in world-routine, down
> through the departmental meander
>> winding the necessities and accidents
>>> the ball rolls slowly
>>> but it rolls
> and on it your name and number.

Going through a whole page and a half of accidental or necessary circumstances, whether the inner cabinet meets before or after noon, whether there's an r in the month, and so on, the ball with your name and number on it rolls:

>> By your place on a sergeant's roster
>> by where you stand in y'r section
>> by *when* you fall in
>> by if they check you from left or right
>> by a chance numbering-off
>>> by a corporal's whim
>> you will furnish
>>> that Fatigue.

Secondly, there is the ironic relationship of the soldiers to Rome. David Jones imagines them drawn from all parts of the Empire, very much as his own regiment was mixed, partly genuine Taffies from Wales, partly, like himself, Londoners – the two poles of his Britain. David Jones does not challenge Empire – he knows it is another name for robbery, but he nowhere urges revolution against it. The sergeant in 'The fatigue' says to the unfortunate private: 'It's whoresons like you as can't keep those swivel eyes to front one short *vigilia* through as are diriment to our unific and expanding order.' 'The narrows' begins with two soldiers talking:

> No end to these wars, no end, no end
> at all. No end to the world-enrolments
> that extend the war-shape, to police the
> extending *limes*, that's a certainty –

and ends:

> So long, Porrex, we'd best not long
>     be found together twice in one vigilia, or
> they'll suppose we tell together
>     the beads of Comrade Sparticus –

who led the great slave-revolt in 73 BC. The speaker speculates ironically as to how two concepts of revolutionary Marxism will apply after death: the Dialectic whereby social classes generate their opposites and in the struggle progress is made towards a classless society; and the 'withering away' of nation states which is supposed to take place under communism:

> I wonder how the Dialectic
>     works far-side the Styx
> or if blithe Helen toes the Party Line
> and white Iope and the Dog
>     if the withering away
>       is more remarked
> than hereabouts.

Thirdly, as the soldiers came from all over the Roman world, there is the relation of the individual districts and communities to the Empire as a whole. In the ironic mode, the classic expression of this relationship is 'The tribune's visitation', where a visiting staff-officer tries to take the regiment into his confidence and cut through Rome's propaganda to its reality:

> But you are soldiers
> with no need for illusion
> for, willy-nilly
> you must play the appointed part . . .
> Listen! be silent!
> you *shall* understand
> the horror of this thing.

The horror lies in the way all the humanity and naturalness of the 'dear known-sites' is used and squandered and perverted by the demands of the 'world-floor':

> so is the honey-root of known-site
> bitter fruit for world-floor.

The cultural obsequies must be already sung before empire can masquerade a kind of life . . .

> What then?
> Are we the ministers of death?
> of life in death?
> do we but supervise the world-death
> being dead ourselves
> long since?

The tribune has no real answer – which is why his honesty cannot be other than ironic – except to plead that he is a soldier too and partakes of their sacrament, the oath of loyalty to Caesar.

This is the relationship, as we've said, that is close to the underlying tension in the *traddodiad* of Welsh civilization. When David Jones thinks of the 'dear known-sites', Wales is never far from his mind – a Wales that is threatened at every level by the 'world-floor', the mega-culture that is our substitute for Empire.

He usually expresses this relation in mythical terms. In 'The tutelar of the place' (which, as he says, might be seen as a companion piece to 'The tribune's visitation') he invokes the Mother-goddess,[3] Tellus the Earth-Goddess as:

---

[3] For the feminine in David Jones, see the fine essay by Désirée Hirst: 'Fragility and force: a theme in the later poems of David Jones', in Roland Mathias (ed.), *David Jones: Eight Essays on his Work as Writer and Artist*, (Llandysul: Gomer Press, 1976).

> She that loves place, time, demarcation, hearth, kin,
> enclosure, differentiated cult, though she is is but one
> mother of us all . . .

'She's a rare one for locality.' He describes her as an actual mother, playing with her toddler and then:

> Come now it's time to come now for tarry awhile and slow
>             cot's best for yeanlings
>             crib's best for babes
> here's a rush to light you to bed
> here's a fleece to cover your head
> against the world-storm
>             brother by sister
> under one *brethyn*
> kith of the kin . . .

He prays to this Mother, 'Queen of the differentiated sites':

> When they proscribe the diverse uses and impose the rootless uniformities,
>     pray for us.
>             When they sit in *Consilium*
> to liquidate the holy diversities . . .

> In all times of *Gleichschaltung*, in the days of the central economies, set
> up the hedges of illusion round some remnant of us, twine the wattles of
> mist, white-web a Gwydion-hedge
>             like fog on the *bryniau*
>             against the commissioners

> against the assessors bearing the writs of the Ram to square the world-
> floor and number the tribes and write down the secret things and take
> away the diversities by which we are, by which we call on your name, sweet
> Jill of the demarcations.

The fourth relationship involved as the imagination of David Jones contemplated his meeting with British soldiers in Jerusalem in 1934 – soldiers reminding him of the Roman troops detailed to crucify Jesus – was therefore that of the crucified Christ to those various localities – and, in particular, to Britain and to Wales. As this was above all mediated through the Mass, it was not possible to disentangle this fourth relationship, which involves a study of particular histories, from a fifth, the theological relation between the Mass, instituted at the Last Supper, and the Crucifixion of the following day: that is, between Maundy Thursday and Good Friday, or (as David Jones calls them) 'Sherthursdaye and Venus Day'.

The first work that crystallized out of the mass of poetic drafts inspired by his experience in Jerusalem, was *The Anathemata*, which Faber published in 1952 subtitled *Fragments of an Attempted Writing*. More 'fragments' appeared in *The Sleeping Lord* in 1974, and yet more, mostly unauthorized by the poet and including long drafts of the matrices out of which some of the individual pieces were cut, in *The Roman Quarry and Other Sequences*, edited by Harman Grisewood and René Hague in 1981, after the author's death. It looks as though David Jones considered all this work as parts of a huge 'encyclopaedic' structure which he was never able to complete. In fact the publication of the various 'fragments' was in a sense an act of despair, knowing he would never finish it.

The poetry was published in the reverse order to our list of the relationships involved. The material based on the first three, those of the soldiers to the Crucifixion, of the soldiers to Rome and of known-site to world-floor, is mostly found in the various poems of *The Sleeping Lord* of 1974; whereas *The Anathemata* of twelve years earlier explores the fourth and fifth relations, of the Mass to the Island of Britain and of the Mass to the Crucifixion itself. (These are obviously only broad generalizations: the Mass plays a large part, for example, in the actual title-poem of *The Sleeping Lord*.)

*The Anathemata*
*The Anathemata* has a curious ambiguity as a work of art. As a visual object, a book, it looks like a work of scholarship produced by a first-rate academic press. Every page is divided into two – the top being text, the bottom (in smaller type) numbered footnotes which often go into considerable detail. On occasion, there are so many footnotes that the text is suspended for a whole page at a time. Just as scholarly editions are often illustrated by photographs of the original manuscripts, so David Jones's own inscriptions punctuate the book. There is a long 'critical' introduction detailing (amongst other things) the author's procedure in composing both the text and the notes, and why it is called what it is. As a visual work, read with the eyes, it is eminently characteristic of the second phase of our literary history, which we have called the search for buried treasure. It is a poem that is also a work of scholarship; and it exists to bring the past to life.

However, as a spoken thing, it is quite different. Even in *In Parenthesis*, we had the sense of other voices breaking into the narrative, of oral speech-rhythms taking over from written prose. This was one of the factors that led David Jones towards verse in the latter part of the book. The oral nature of what he was doing grew on him – he goes out of his way to insist that his work has to be spoken; a good proportion of his footnotes tell us how to pronounce it. When Douglas Cleverdon produced *The Anathemata* on the BBC as a kind of play for voices, he was not really going against its grain. To hear the 'fragments' read is still the easiest way to come to grips with them, particularly (I find) if one also follows the text with the eyes. He is similar to James Joyce in this respect. When I looked at *Finnegans Wake* for the first time, I was appalled. It was only when I heard the 'Anna Livia' section read aloud that my delight in it made it meaningful.

As an oral work, *The Anathemata* functions as a kind of serious dream. The sudden transitions and frequent changes of tone, the long, seemingly almost meaningless passages of learned chatter, the emergence from them into terrible and moving relevance, the way images – such as the ship, for example – take shape in one century and reappear five pages later in quite another, yet recognizably the same ship: all this is dream-like. Like *Finnegans Wake* it is an epic poem that operates within the confines of a dreaming – or at least day-dreaming – mind. Indeed, David Jones as good as tells us so in his Preface:

> In a sense the fragments that compose this book are about, or around and about, matters of all sorts which, by a sort of quasi-free association, are apt to stir in my mind at any time and as often as not 'in the time of the Mass'.

He describes the effects as 'mental associations, liaisons, meanderings to and fro, "ambivalences," asides, sprawl of the pattern, if pattern there is', and goes on to talk of 'thought-trains . . . set in motion, shunted or buffered into near-sidings or off to far destinations'. Critics have tended to assume that he was doing himself an injustice here, but it seems to me a fairly accurate description of the texture that one hears as it is read aloud.

David Jones seems to have written his 'fragments' fairly quickly at first, and then spent years chipping away at them, condensing, fusing together and separating. The relation between the material – the 'heap of all I could find' – and the form – the 'shape' it had to take – was a good deal more problematic for him than in *In Parenthesis,* where his memory of events gave him both heap and (to some extent at least) shape as well.

Nevertheless, if *In Parenthesis* is a kind of ironic *Iliad*, a song of wrath, *The Anathemata* can be seen as a latter-day *Aeneid*. Just as Virgil's poem tells how Troy's household gods, after the city's destruction, were taken by Aeneas to a reborn Troy in Rome, so *The Anathemata* is about the conveying of holy things (anathemata) from a death in Jerusalem to a rebirth in a New Jerusalem predestined to receive them, that is, for us and for David Jones, the island of Britain. Like all good epics, it begins in the middle, with a priest saying Mass: 'The cult-man stands alone in Pellam's land: more precariously than he knows he guards the *signa* . . .' Pellam is the king of the Wasteland, and so 'in Pellam's land' is a kenning for the modern world, where 'this man, so late in time, curiously surviving', re-enacts the Last Supper:

> In a low voice
> as one who speaks
> where a few are, gathered in high-room
> and one, gone out.

The room has been swept, the feast prepared:

> They make all shipshape
> for she must be trim
> dressed and gaudeous
> all Bristol-fashion here
> for:
> Who d'you think is Master of her?

That is the first introduction we have to the notion of the Church as a ship, with Christ as her captain, bringing the faith from the 'Middle-sea', the Mediterrranean, to the 'Lear-sea' of British waters. It is a good deal more complicated than that, of course; the narrative is slippery as a dream, mediated through other scenes and other voices. Neil Corcoran's book on the poem is called *The Song of Deeds,* but deeds are precisely what we don't find. Memories, speculations, questionings, epiphanies are the stuff of ironic epic, not deeds. We glimpse, sometimes, the effects of deeds, Hector dragged round the walls of Troy; or Arthur's queen in her finery attending the Christmas Mass. Eventually we come back to the beginning, to the institution of the Mass at the Last Supper and its relation to the unique sacrifice on the cross:

He does what is done in many places
what he does other
          he does after the mode
of what has always been done.
What did he do other
          recumbent at the garnished supper?
What did he do yet other
          riding the Axile tree?

# PART III

## 8

## *The advent of modernism*

~

We have seen how David Jones was a great modernist on the international arena. He was widely recognized by his peers. For T. S. Eliot, he ranked with Joyce, Pound and Eliot himself. There is a sense in which he should only be judged by the criteria appropriate to international modernism, as a poet of what Northrop Fry calls 'ironic' epic. But of course his work (like Eliot's) has also been valued by readers and scholars who are not particularly modernist in outlook: they have responded to his Catholicism, for example, or to his recalling of traditional pieties and 'connectiveness'; or, sometimes, to his yearning towards a realization of Welshness.

All the same, we can look at David Jones as a truly Welsh phenomenon, in an 'insider' way, not just as someone looking for roots; and then his work illustrates another kind of modernism altogether. He belongs, in effect, with Sir John Morris-Jones, T. Gwynn Jones and Ifor Williams, the scholars and poets who, in reviving the old Wales of the *traddodiad*, created a leverage against the dullness and compromise of *buchedd* culture; even if, like Hopkins, he does so at second or third hand, without benefit of the community of Welsh life. The scholar in this world is king. As we've seen, *The Anathemata* as a visual object looks like a work of scholarship. Of course, the other great modernists also built vast edifices of erudition, *Ulysses*, *The Cantos*, 'The waste land'. But Pound's relation to Provence or Cathay, or Joyce's relation to ancient Greece, is not relevant to those cultures directly, as David Jones's relation to the Welsh *traddodiad* was relevant to Wales. Pound's grandfather was not a native speaker of Provençal or Mandarin Chinese, whereas David Jones was the grandson of a Welsh-speaking Welshman from Treffynnon (Holywell) in Flintshire. And even Joyce, though he commented on the national struggle in Ireland, did nothing to further it as David Jones tried to further Welshness.

There were almost as many varieties of modernism as there were authors. Artistic revolutions succeeded each other with bewildering speed. Even the insistence on the absolute necessity of being modern did not preclude a preoccupation, even an obsession, with the past, as the work of Pound and David Jones amply illustrates. Sometimes modernism implied little more than a new fashion, a different style to what has gone before – though of course stylistic change can have profound consequences: Plato once remarked that when you change the music, the walls of the city crumble. Quite often, however, the transformations were fundamental. In painting representation gave way to abstraction, in music tonality was ousted by serialism. Artistic dogmas were toppled, and in the process the way we view history, the way we look at ourselves, were irreversibly changed.

Modernism in Wales tended ineluctably to be hostile to *buchedd* consensus values. This is true even of authors like Saunders Lewis (1893–1985) in Welsh or Davies Aberpennar (Pennar Davies) in his early poems in English, who actively sought to propagate an awareness of the Welsh inheritance. Modernism in Welsh is a topic that would require more time and knowledge than I possess to evaluate, but clearly a poem like Saunders Lewis's 'Golygfa mewn caffe' ('Scene in a café') has some relation to modernist techniques as well as to the right-wing anti-Semitism of Pound and Eliot:

> . . . Ymhlith y sgerbydau llafar, y lludw rhodiannus,
> Ymwthiasom drwy ddrysau'r caffe
> Gan guddio'n penglogau gweigion tu ôl i'n ffigysddail,
> A chipio cornel o ffwrdd rhag byddin Babel,
> A gweiddi uwchben yr esgyrn a'r dysglau te
> Ar forwyn gerllaw.
>
> Fuaned oedd gweini'r forwyn –
> Dug inni wystrys a finegr Kosher a'r gwasanaeth claddu ar dost.
> Cwympodd y glaw fel parasiwt ar y stryd,
> Ond safodd gwarchodlu dinesig y cistiau lludw
> Fel plismyn yn rhes ger eu tai.
>
> (. . . Among the loquacious skeletons, the walking ash,
> We squeezed through the café doors
> Hiding behind fig-leaves our empty skulls
> And snatched from the host of Babel a table corner
> And over the bones and tea-things shouted
> To a nearby maid.

How swift was the maid's attendance –
She brought us oysters and Kosher vinegar and the burial service on
                                               toast.
Rain fell like a parachute on the street,
But the civic guard of ashbins
Stood by their houses like policemen in a row.)

The up-to-date mixed with the biblical ('parachute' with 'fig-leaves') and the constant changes of register, together with serious despair masquerading as surrealist comedy, represent a degree of difficulty and an extremism of expression that puts it immediately outside *buchedd* consensus poetry. The poem ends with a picture of Wales as an old hag, scavenging from dustbins and eventually hanging herself on a handy lamp-post:

A gwybuom wrth ei menyg gwynion a'u hoglau camffor
Yr hanfu o'r hen wlad.

(And by her white gloves smelling of camphor we knew
She was from the old country.)

Thus *buchedd* respectability ends up, 'her shanks turning in the rain'.

Modernism in Welsh was often connected with the new nationalism, and usually resulted in a poetry of commitment. Sometimes, though, as in the work of Euros Bowen, it achieved a detachment of aesthetic response that reminds one of Mallarmé or Jiménez; but with this difference, that Euros Bowen's (1904–88) aestheticism is rooted in Anglican Christianity – is in fact sacramentalist in intention.

Writers in English, however, once they had shaken off the dust of *buchedd* loyalty, had nowhere they could gravitate towards except London. They either stayed in Wales and festered in isolation, or they offered themselves as international or colonial recruits to the London intelligentsia. Nationalism was hardly an option for most of them, except in the vaguest or most sentimental sense. Anglo-Welsh modernists, therefore, tended to attack the *buchedd* from a position of would-be rootlessness. The short stories of *My People* (1915) by Caradoc Evans achieved a notoriety in this respect that made him the best-hated man in Wales.

Caradoc Evans is usually taken to be the founding father of the Anglo-Welsh movement. In a strict sense, of course, this is nonsense: there were novelists like 'Allen Raine' (Anna Puddicombe *née* Evans),

dramatists like J. O. Francis (1882–1956) and poets like Ernest Rhys and
W. H. Davies a long time before *My People* appeared. M. Wynn Thomas
has made out a case for Francis's play *Change* (1912) as a key work in
Anglo-Welsh literature, in which the strains within *buchedd* society, the
end of consensus and the dominance of conflict ('strife') were sensitively
dramatized.[1]

However, Caradoc's stories were certainly the beginning of Anglo-
Welsh modernism, and that is a significant element in the offence they
caused in Wales. He invented a grotesque dialect, part translated from
Welsh idiom, part biblical, part pure linguistic fantasy, and used it with
considerable animus to describe the turpitude of peasant life in his native
Cardiganshire:

> Now the day the Big Man chastened him he drank much ale, and,
> unaware of what he was doing, he sinned against his daughter Matilda. In
> the morning he perceived what he had done, and was fearful lest his wife
> Hannah should revile him and speak aloud his wickedness. So, having laid
> a cunning snare for her, and finding that the women did not know
> anything, he spoke to her harshly and without cause. This is what he said:
> 'Filthier you are than a cow.'
> 'Evan, indeed to goodness,' Hannah replied, 'iobish you talk. Sober
> dear, do I not work to the bone?' With a knife she scraped through the
> refuse on her arm and displayed to him the thinness to which she ref-
> erred. Then in her anger she spoke: 'Slack you are, Evan Rhiw. Your little
> land you drink in the tavern of Mistress Shames. Are not the people
> mouthing your foolish ways on the tramping road and in Shop Rhys?'
> Matilda entered the kitchen and threw these words at him: 'Dull and
> whorish you are, son of the Bad Spirit. Serious me, clean your smelly
> flesh in the pond.'
> Hannah interpreted the meaning of Matilda's words, and she
> reproached him bitterly.
> But Evan answered none of the women. He went to the inn, and in his
> muddle he sorrowed: 'Five over twenty years have I been wedded. When I
> took Hannah the servant of Bensha to my bed, rich was I. Did I not have
> six pairs of drawers, and six pairs of stockings, and six pairs of shirts of
> white linen? And three pairs of rib trousers? There's rib, people bach.
> Ninepence over half a crown a yard it cost in the Shop of the Bridge in
> Castellybryn. Not a shirt of linen do I possess this day. Wasteful has
> Hannah been with mine. Sad is my lot. Disorderly is the female, and
> Matilda says this and that about me to my discredit.'

---

[1] M. Wynn Thomas, *Internal Difference* (Cardiff: University of Wales Press, 1992),
12–16.

He brayed his woe also in the narrow Roman road which takes you past the Schoolhouse and in the path that cuts over Gorse Penparc into the field wherein stands Rhiw. At an early hour in the morning Matilda said to her mother: 'Mam now, the cows fach are lowing to be milked', and receiving no answer she looked into Hannah's face and examined her body, and she saw that the woman was cold dead, whereupon she went out and into the stable, in the loft of which Evan slept, and cried up to him: 'Father bach, do you stir yourself. Old mam has gone to wear a White Shirt.' ('Lamentations' from *My People*, 1915)

The stories concern hypocrisy, ruthless materialism tempered only by superstition, and heartlessness and savage cruelty, particularly towards women. In this story, for instance, Evan's daughter is blamed for his incest and, literally, displays her nakedness in the streets before being led at the end of a rope to the lunatic asylum at Carmarthen:

After that Evan did not sin any more; his belongings increased, and he had ten milching cows and five horses, and he hired a man servant and a maid servant, and he rented twenty-five acres of land over and beyond the land that was his, and his house remained religious as long as he lived.

The animus against the chapel culture of the *buchedd* is everywhere manifest, and is echoed in the grotesquerie of the language. Indeed, modernism in Wales is most at home with the grotesque. It is there that modernism characteristically shows itself, in Saunders Lewis as much as in Caradoc Evans or Dylan Thomas. The nightmare of monstrosity underlies the middle-class rejection of the *buchedd*, the sense of being suffocated by its hypocrisy and narrowness.

However, Welsh modernism is not simply home-grown. It is part of an international climate. David Jones may be discounted as a special case, only belonging to Wales through a conscious identification with the land of his father. But other Anglo-Welsh modernists were affiliated to a wide variety of sources: the art of Dylan Thomas, the chief of them, was derived principally through Eliot from French symbolism and Elizabethan drama. This judgement will seem strange at first, because critics have not often seen him in that tradition. They have tried to emphasize his Welshness or his relation to the Romantics. In my view, Dylan's Welshness is largely a negative thing – he is not English; and the very last epithet we should apply to his work is Romantic. I think the often-mentioned influence of Hopkins is a red herring, a piece of special pleading to demonstrate his continuity with Welsh bardism. Swinburne and Francis

Thompson were possibly more relevant – Dylan said they were, anyhow – as further links with symbolism and the Elizabethans.

Of the other Anglo-Welsh poets of the time, Lynette Roberts (1909–95) was influenced by American modernists, Hart Crane amongst others, but also by the *In Parenthesis* of David Jones, acclaimed in her husband's magazine *Wales* as a masterpiece almost from the start. Glyn Jones was spellbound by D. H. Lawrence and later tried to learn from the Welsh tradition. The other two important poets of the movement seem a good deal less centrally modernist: but Vernon Watkins was a translator from the German Romantics, and Alun Lewis found inspiration and a sort of fellowship in war in the poetry of Edward Thomas.

Dylan Thomas is a modernist in the symbolist tradition. That is, he looks to an international horizon that began (more or less) in France in the third quarter of the nineteenth century. The Romanticism of the early part of that century had revolved round an alternation of joyous freedom and sterile dejection. In this respect it had similarities to the psychotic illness called manic-depression. Symbolism and the various modernist movements descended from it, on the other hand, have a far more schizoid sensibility, in which the ego semi-deliberately withdraws from complete involvement and views life with an ironic detachment that conceals and numbs the uncertainty of the suffering self.

In a way, all modernism is a critique of the Romantic's sense of the uniqueness of the individual. A Marxist would say that this uniqueness is a legal fiction anyway, derived from the laws of property. Of course, in any society one person differs from another. In a purely numerical sense, his or her tastes, perceptions, biography, don't occur to anyone else. Such differences are acknowledged: the question is how important they are. In most societies – and we in Wales cannot but be conscious of this in relation to our own history – success or failure has not been a matter of 'being true to oneself', as we say, but of performing roles that are assigned to you by custom or circumstances. You work in the fields, you fight in battle, you tell stories in the men's house, you look after your sister. You may be successful in one role but a failure in others.

But now, suppose I own a piece of land, say, not to use it myself (the tribe might let me do that) or because I inherited it (as in the feudal system), but simply because I bought it. In law, my uniqueness in relation to this land is quite distinct from any role I happen to play. Whatever I do – unless I sell it or give it to someone else – it belongs to me. The question 'Who am I?' thus becomes divorced from 'What do I do?' or 'What is my relationship to other people?' Who I am becomes an absolute, a uniqueness whose continued existence is guaranteed by the continuity of ownership. Once this individual consciousness is born, however, it uses the model of ownership which created it to preserve itself in areas where the model does not apply. I assert my uniqueness by the generation of a personal point of view and the adoption of a continuous life-style. 'To thine own self be true', says Polonius, and therefore be impatient of traditional roles and customs which stop you doing this.

But by the end of the nineteenth century, we can see property beginning to devour its child. A man who owns a business can very easily equate his success or failure with its profit or loss: bankruptcy is a great cause of suicide. But capitalism now is not really a matter of that kind of individual business any more. It has invented a new kind of toy to play with, the Public Limited Company – Co. Ltd or PLC. 'Limited' stands for 'limited liability', that is, you can own shares in a company without being totally liable for it if it fails. In fact, mostly, if you invest in such a company and it goes bust, all you lose is the money you put into it in the first place. Before this useful invention, if you owned a share in an enterprise, you were totally responsible for your share of its debts.

Limited liability is the clue to the modern world, as feudalism was to the twelfth century or the alliance between the bourgeoisie and the monarch to the Elizabethans. It is easy to see how, with limited liability, property ceases to stabilize the ego and begins to undermine it: who owns ICI or General Motors? Great individual moguls are still found, of course, but they are often tragic figures, our modern Tamburlaines, revealed as incompetent crooks as they plunge to their individualist doom. The average director of a firm is as faceless as anyone else.

Except at a petty-bourgeois level, to own property no longer confers individuality. What it does do, is exert pressure on you to indulge in higher consumption, mainly of goods that are not meant to last. To be a consumer seems to guarantee your uniqueness and stabilize your ego; but only for a while. 'Things fall apart; the centre cannot hold.' The identity of the company is what counts, if anything does, not that of the man or woman who owns or manages it, let alone the consumer of its products. Symbolic letters like ICI or BP, or symbolic names like SHELL or ROVER or BIRD'S EYE, replace both personal names – J. Morris and Son – and descriptive titles – The Afon Wen Laundry. Our ordinary language is full of such new words, the clutter of pure symbolism in action.

In psychological terms, every culture that is based on inequality tends towards one or other of the neuroses or psychotic illnesses. In feudalism, for example, success depends on attracting the attention of your superior to how much you need his support: so feudal culture tends to hysteria, a condition where your subconscious manufactures a reason why you ought to be pitied – for example, you become ill. It is typically a cry for help, usually displaced from the immediate lord and addressed to God or the Virgin, or the lady in Courtly Love.

The Tudor settlement meant tension between the bourgeoisie and the monarch they depended on for protection: the sixteenth-century neurosis was melancholia, or a form of withdrawal founded on self-hate. The queen was the cynosure, the source of all grace and favour; and yet she favoured your unworthy rivals and not you. You hated yourself because you were as yet incapable of breaking from her.

During the Romantic and early Victorian period, when the individual's compulsion to capitalize on what he owned (and therefore on what he was) was at its most intense, the culture, as we say, seems manic-depressive, alternating between joyous freedom ('blessed' is the typical epithet) and incapacitating dejection:

> But, as it sometimes chanceth, from the might
> Of joy in minds that can no further go,
> As high as we have mounted in delight
> In our dejection do we sink as low,
> To me that morning did it happen so;
> And fears and fancies thick upon me came;
> Dim sadness – and blind thoughts, I knew not, nor could name.

Wordsworth's 'Resolution and independence' is interesting because he actually points the problem in undisplaced economic terms – how can he expect, the poet asks:

> that others should
> Build for him, sow for him, and at his call
> Love him, who for himself will take no heed at all?

But the pressure is usually more indirect: a good many Romantic poems ('The ancient mariner', the 'Ode to a nightingale', even *The Prelude* and 'Hyperion') are attempts to break the fatal cycle of unballasted joy and 'blind' dejection.

The beginning of the modern age is marked by a change to schizoid sensibility – of which, indeed, 'limited liability' is a fair enough description. It first surfaces as a cultural fashion in France, perhaps because the banks and the big financiers had achieved a hegemony there that in Britain they did not have over the manufacturers until much later. France in 1848 was already governed by the banks; whereas 1840–60 was the golden age of industrial competition in England. In the visual arts particularly, but also in the music of Debussy and the poetry of the symbolists, French innovations of the period 1870–1914 have dominated the consciousness of the West ever since. They have provided, at a highbrow level, much of the theory and most of the prototypes for all subsequent innovation in the arts. (Dylan Thomas was called the 'Rimbaud of Cwmdonkin Drive'.) Their direct influence is ubiquitous in decoration and advertising. Neither is pop culture exempt, as a glance at the lyrics of sixties singers like the Beatles or Bob Dylan will show. Indeed, the milieu of adolescence is where modernism seems most naturally at home in our time.

There were almost as many movements and 'isms' in France as there were artists, but very roughly the two polarities were impressionism and symbolism, one a devotion to the moment as absolute, the other, equally absolute, a devotion to the eternal, the impersonal nature of things contemplated in icon and symbol. One corresponds to the attitude of the consumer, the other to the abasement of the personal before the symbols of the great firm, the mystic OM that is greater than we. They only seem irreconcilable opposites; really they are two sides of the same thing, the debasement of the person under modern capitalism.

Of course, the symbolists were not writing propaganda for big business, but they could not help conceiving the universe in terms of the complexity and mysterious oneness of the great firm offering for sale the bewildering multitude of its products – an ideal corporation, in fact, with the artist as its PRO and sales representative. At the end of his greatest work, *Les Illuminations*, in the section called 'Solde' ('Clearance sale') Rimbaud makes the comparison explicit:

> For sale what the Jews have not sold, what neither noble birth nor crime have tasted, what accursed love and the infernal integrity of the masses know nothing of; what neither time nor learning need recognize;
>
> The voices reconstituted; the fraternal awakening of all choral and orchestral energies and their immediate application; the opportunity, unique, of freeing our senses.

For sale anarchy for the masses; irrepressible satisfaction for connoisseurs; frightful death for the faithful and for lovers!

For sale dwelling-places and migrations, sports, perfect magic and perfect comfort, and the noise, the movement, and the future they create . . .

For sale bodies, voices, the immense unquestionable opulence, that which will never be sold. The firm is not at the end of its clearance stock! Our travellers won't have to turn in their accounts for a long time yet! (trans. Oliver Bernard)

It is not really surprising that the symbolist's dislocations of time and place, language and meaning, should have become part of the advertiser's stock-in-trade; or that Rimbaud himself should have abandoned the implicit imperialism of his art and tried his hand – unsuccessfully as it happened – at the reality of selling rifles in Abyssinia.

No poetry is so dominated by the ego; and yet symbolist poetry is not personal. The I is someone else, 'JE est un autre',[2] as Rimbaud said. In a typical symbolist poem, the I appears out of nowhere, having no history. Its only function is to experience vision. In order to speak with this non-historic I, the poet must jettison his individuality. Rimbaud talks of making himself a *voyant*, a seer, by a long, immense and systematic disordering of all the senses – a kind of ascetism of total debauchery. Time makes everything easier, of course. Now *voyant*-hood is two-a-penny, and the I achieves being someone else by nothing more arduous than switching on a TV.

Much of the peculiarity of Dylan Thomas as a poet is explicable in terms of the modernism he derives from. It is often said that he distrusted and feared people asking him about his poetry; but this does not seem to be true. He was quite prepared, certainly as a young man, to expound at length on his writing methods:

A poem by Cameron *needs* no more than one image; it moves around one idea, from one logical point to another, making a full circle. A poem by myself *needs* a host of images, because its centre is a host of images. I make one image – though 'make' is not the word, I let, perhaps, an image be made emotionally in me and then apply to it what intellectual and critical forces I possess – let it breed another, let that image

---

[2] Lettre à Paul Demeny, Charleville, 15 mai 1871.

contradict the first, make, out of the third image bred out of the other two together, a fourth contradictory image, and let them all, within my imposed formal limits, conflict. Each image holds within it the seed of its own destruction, and my dialectical method, as I understand it, is a constant building up and breaking down of the images that come out of the central seed, which is itself destructive and constructive at the same time. (Letter to Henry Treece, 23 March 1938)

English critics and biographers are reluctant to take this seriously: Constantine FitzGibbon calls it 'a smoke-screen of semi-abstract verbiage'. On the contrary, it seems to me a very lucid description of how one would write *18 Poems*, as accurate as one has any right to expect from a practitioner. The whole correspondence with Vernon Watkins, moreover, is a discussion of particular poetic effects in particular poems.

What Dylan's critical theory demands is that we totally forsake representational or (in painterly terms) impressionist prejudices. Much as a cubist painting rejects perspective and insists on itself as a creation of the picture surface, so Dylan's poems offer poem-surfaces. They live only as poems – or at least that is what he spent hours, weeks, years trying to achieve. All his statements on poetry insist on this – for example, he says somewhere that a poem's main object is to reach its last line. He talks of the 'momentary peace that is a poem'. Even when he acknowledges a debt to his own biography – as in his later poems he obviously does – this becomes a further technical problem (and seemingly a very difficult one): to express his own personal feelings – if we mean by that the finding of exact words for the empirical situation he was in – is quite clearly not what he was trying to do.

To ask an abstract expressionist what his painting is about is boring or irritating to the artist because he doesn't think in those terms. We have plenty of evidence that Dylan Thomas hated and feared this kind of inquisition – nit-picking was one of his words for it – which academics were always liable to foist on him. His biographer Constantine FitzGibbon quotes Caitlin:

> He had the same dislike, amounting to superstitious horror, of philosophy, psychology, analysis, criticism . . . but most of all, of the gentle art of discussing poetry; not that I was likely to do that. We had a mutual agreement to keep off that touchy subject; and, if wellmeaning friends started an abstruse, intense interpretation of some of Dylan's most obscure lines, which he had long ago forgotten the meaning of himself, it was not long before Dylan was on the floor wrapped up in the carpet,

scratching himself, like a flea-bitten hyena, in paroxysms of acute
boredom, ending, happily for him, in snoring amnesia. (*The Life of
Dylan Thomas* (London: Dent, 1965), 224)

One has to be careful here, because Dylan always insisted that every line
in his poetry meant something and that he meant it to be understood.
But understanding his poetry meant, for him, preserving the poem-
surface. One is reminded of his often quoted but seemingly impossible
remark on the 'Altarwise by owl-light' sonnets, that he wanted the
reader to take them literally. In answer to a questionnaire in *New Verse*
he wrote: 'The writing of a poem is, to me, the physical and mental task
of constructing a formally watertight compartment of words, preferably
with a main moving column (i.e. narrative) to hold a little of the real
causes of the creative brain and body' (ibid., 151). The making of such a
construct does not of course mean that the poem that results has no
relation to the poet or to the external world. He is emphatic that 'the
causes and forces are always there, and always need a concrete expression';
and that his poetry is 'useful' to himself and to his readers as a record of
'my individual struggle from darkness to some measure of light'. But (as
I interpret him) it is the whole poem, as a thing in itself, a made, 'watertight' object, that is the concrete expression and the record of struggle;
not what the poem is about, but what it is. A poem is far more like a
prehistoric standing stone in a field than it is like a photograph or a map.

In the next chapter, I hope to show how Dylan Thomas dramatized
the symbolist *voyant*, the I that is someone else; and how he refurbished,
probably under Eliot's influence, the tragic soliloquy of Marlowe and
Shakespeare to do so.

# 9

## 'I saw time murder me':
## Dylan Thomas and the tragic soliloquy

~

The chronology of Dylan Thomas's poems is strangely topsy-turvy. He wrote something like two hundred poems into his famous notebooks before he left Swansea in 1934 – possibly more because at least one notebook is lost. He was then twenty years old. His first book, *18 Poems*, appeared in the same year. All but one or two of the eighteen were new, written into the last of the extant notebooks or after it was filled up. The achievement of *18 Poems* is thus all of a piece. It shows a new-found maturity, a sense of unity and purpose that (for various reasons) none of his subsequent books show.

His second volume, *Twenty-five Poems*, is a curious compilation. It begins and ends with new work, 'I in my intricate image', which is an *18 Poems* piece that he wrote too late for that book, and the sonnet sequence, 'Altarwise by owl-light', the culmination of his early style; but all but five or six of the others are (in varying degrees) revisions of notebook poems that preceded those of *18 Poems*. The same is true of his third book, *The Map of Love*, a combination of stories and poems: most of the latter are revisions of early notebook pieces. Revision, of course, is not a simple process: some poems are changed only in detail, whereas others are thoroughly rewritten. Even so, one must distinguish revisions from cases where a new poem takes off from a couple of lines or a bare idea in an old one: 'After the funeral' in *The Map of Love* is really a new poem, and an important one, though it opens with one line from a notebook piece, continues for a few more as a revision, and is obviously inspired by the same occasion, the death of his aunt. But the remnants of the early poem embedded in the new one are no more than fossils: Dylan himself was uneasy about their presence. He thought they were a fault in the poem – and it is difficult to disagree; but he did nothing to remove them.

*Twenty-five Poems* and *The Map of Love* are hard to judge as new developments out of *18 Poems* because of the preponderance of early work they contain. The next book, *Deaths and Entrances,* is more complex: there are still a few revisions from the notebooks – among them the popular 'Hunchback in the park' – but the main problem now is the sudden achievement of a new style and a recovery of relative fluency in the output of 1944–5. This means that the book splits into two groups, though they are carefully muddled together: those in the transitional style from 1939–41 continuing on from *The Map of Love* and those in the much more flowing and nostalgic manner of 1944–5.[1]

The notebooks are mostly very dull and, with notable exceptions like the Hunchback poem, revisions from them do not usually add up to very much. But if they are read as leading up to *18 Poems* and 'Altarwise to owl-light', one can see something of where the poet's instinct is taking him: for instance, an interest in dramatic soliloquy. Here is one fragment that found its way into *Twenty-five Poems*:

> Out of the sighs a little comes,
> But not of grief, for I have knocked down that
> Before the agony; the spirit grows,
> Forgets and cries;
> A little comes, is tasted and found good;
> All could not disappoint;
> There must, be praised, some certainty,
> If not of loving well, then not,
> And that is true after perpetual defeat.

After that fine, tragic opening, the poem loses itself in the usual notebooks jargon of wounds, spilt words and acrid blood. When he came to revise it he joined the fragment to another, ending on a fine rhetorical flourish –

> For all there is to give I offer:
> Crumbs, barn and halter

---

[1] It is this latter group that includes some of the most popular poetry of the twentieth century, 'A refusal to mourn', 'Poem in October', 'This side of the truth', 'A winter's tale', 'In my craft or sullen art' and 'Fern Hill' – the pieces that constitute what most people think of as Dylan Thomas's best poetry, along with a very few ('Especially when the October wind', 'The hand that signed the paper', 'And death shall have no dominion', 'After the funeral', and the 'Hunchback in the park') that are earlier, and 'Do not go gentle', 'Over Sir John's Hill' and 'Lament' from the later work.

– but the new material does not seem altogether apposite and is certainly less impressive than his opening.

Marlowe in *Tamburlaine* and *Faustus*, and particularly Shakespeare in *Hamlet* and *Macbeth*, had made the soliloquy a new kind of poetic form. Earlier dramatists used the soliloquy as a dramatic convenience – dialogue without the other person, as it were – to convey information to the audience that only one character knows. It was an extension of the aside. But Tamburlaine's 'What is beauty, saith my sufferings then' or Hamlet's 'To be or not to be' give only a very small amount of new information about the action. They are poems opening out the action of the play on to interior vistas: in a way they are comparable to the great choruses of Greek tragedy or the use of dance in Noh plays. We see the world of the play from inside, we don't just look at what's happening on the stage. Hamlet's speech is an existentialist poem about suicide; but it is also a poem about the play-world of *The Tragedy of Hamlet* – almost we can hear Shakespeare himself commenting on the relation between his creation and the 'real world' outside it. Psychologically, and I suppose this is how critics usually justify it, it reveals Hamlet's mind – what kind of man he is, what he's thinking or feeling: but actually we know that already, it seems to me, and it is because we know it that the soliloquy works, rather than the other way round.

The invention of the soliloquy as a poetic form was not very often developed by subsequent poets. The so-called dramatic monologue of Browning (which has forerunners in Ovid, where mythical heroines write or talk to their lovers; in Pope's imitation of Ovid, 'Eloisa to Abelard'; and in Wordsworth's *Lyrical Ballads*) is not the same thing at all, but a form of first-person fiction. The obvious problem about using the soliloquy, the dramatic I-poem, is that it seems to require a play to grow out of.

However, as we've said, in the schizoid modernism that followed the symbolists, the 'I' has no history. He just appears out of nowhere, a naked *voyant* whose only function is to see and suffer. In this sense, the whole of 'The waste land' is what Tiresias sees, not just the scene 'enacted on this same divan or bed'. 'The waste land' can be seen as a huge, dislocated soliloquy, like 'Gerontion' only more so. Eliot solved the problem of the play-less soliloquy, as Mallarmé had in his 'eclogue', 'L'Aprés-midi d'un faune', by confusing the boundaries between dream and reality, so that the schizoid 'I' has access to all times and all places, like a dreamer, and yet as a man confronts the world we know with wakeful eyes.

Now the trouble with 'Out of the sighs' as a soliloquy is precisely that it seems to require a play to grow out of; and Dylan Thomas, who was only in his late teens, did not yet have the poetic resources to write such a drama. The poem fizzles out. However, in *18 Poems*, the schizoid 'I' is firmly in place – a very different place from Gerontion's or Mallarmé's, a young 'I' looking out on the varied scene from Cwmdonkin Drive. Instead of the vague, sleepy rhythms we tend to find in Mallarmé or Eliot, this 'I' harangues us with considerable lyrical force. His stanzas move with contained energy. They ask questions. Sometimes they talk to us as if we were in a lover's quarrel. Sometimes they revolve round refrain-like phrases with a grave sardonic beauty.

> If I were tickled by the rub of love,
> A rooking girl who stole me for her side,
> Broke through her straws, breaking my bandaged string,
> If the red tickle as the cattle calve
> Still set to scratch a laughter from my lung,
> I would not fear the apple nor the flood
> Nor the bad blood of spring.
>
> Shall it be male or female? say the cells,
> And drop the plum like fire from the flesh.
> If I were tickled by the hatching hair,
> The winging bone that sprouted in the heels,
> The itch of man upon the baby's thigh,
> I would not fear the gallows nor the axe
> Nor the crossed sticks of war.
>
> Shall it be male or female? say the fingers
> That chalk the walls with green girls and their men.
> I would not fear the muscling-in of love
> If I were tickled by the urchin hungers
> Rehearsing heat upon a raw-edged nerve.
> I would not fear the devil in the loin
> Nor the outspoken grave.
>
> If I were tickled by the lovers' rub
> That wipes away not crow's-foot nor the lock
> Of sick old manhood on the fallen jaws,
> Time and the crabs and the sweethearting crib
> Would leave me cold as butter for the flies,
> The sea of scums could drown me as it broke
> Dead on the sweethearts' toes.

This world is half the devil's and my own,
Daft with the drug that's smoking in a girl
And curling round the bud that forks her eye.
An old man's shank one-marrowed with my bone,
And all the herrings smelling in the sea,
I sit and watch the worm beneath my nail
Wearing the quick away.

And that's the rub, the only rub that tickles.
The knobbly ape that swings along his sex
From damp love-darkness and the nurse's twist
Can never raise the midnight of a chuckle,
Nor when he finds a beauty in the breast
Of lover, mother, lovers, or his six
Feet in the rubbing dust.

And what's the rub? Death's feather on the nerve?
Your mouth, my love, the thistle in the kiss?
My Jack of Christ born thorny on the tree?
The words of death are dryer than his stiff,
My wordy wounds are printed with your hair.
I would be tickled by the rub that is:
Man be my metaphor.

It is a great pity that Dylan Thomas did not record more readings from *18 Poems* on disc. His recordings from his later books are numerous and well known; but from *18 Poems* only two survive, this one and 'Light breaks where no sun shines', plus the first of the 'Altarwise by owl-light' sonnets which belong to the same phase of his art. His reading of 'If I were tickled by the rub of love', at any rate, is sharply distinguished from the rather booming, lyrical note he struck in his later verse – though it must be said that the more one studies these readings the more one is impressed, in general, by their variety and intelligence. In 'If I were tickled', he uses his voice like a Shakespearean tragic actor, dramatic, rapid and sardonic. The repeated phrases emerge as gear-changes in a helter-skelter ride to damnation, culminating in the bitter questions of the last stanza. Only in the last couplet does Dylan open his voice in something like the affirmation we are used to.

It is the repeated phrases, used like musical motifs, that both shape the poem and resolve it: 'If I were tickled by the rub' or its variations occurs as a conditional clause in each of the first four stanzas: in stanzas 1 and 4 as the first line and in stanzas 2 and 3 as medial lines. A variation on it, 'If the red tickle' etc., is also used medially in the first stanza to insist on the 'key' – the conditional mood. 'I would not fear' occurs as the climax in the last couplet of the first three stanzas; and a variation, 'would leave me cold as butter for the flies', forms the coda of the fourth.

The opening four stanzas, then, insist on a single grammatical structure and a single grammatical mood: 'If I were . . . I would not . . .' One is reminded of Marvell's 'Coy Mistress': 'Had we but world enough . . .' Marvell follows his subjunctive with 'but' and the indicative, 'But at my back I always hear . . .' Thomas similarly modulates into the simple present for a marvellously expressive middle stanza about his predicament as a sexual young adult fearful of old age and death:

> This world is half the devil's and my own,
> Daft with the drug that's smoking in a girl
> And curling round the bud that forks her eye.
> An old man's shank one-marrowed with my bone,
> And all the herrings smelling in the sea,
> I sit and watch the worm beneath my nail
> Wearing the quick away.

It is the sudden release both from the 'if' structure and the phrasing – 'tickle' and 'rub' and all the rest – that gives this stanza its 'kick-start' as it were. The imagery is complex, but not inchoate. The 'bud that forks her eye' involves both the burgeoning of spring and the pitchforks of the devil, but 'eye' can be used as a horticultural term in the operation called 'budding', a form of grafting used in rose-cultivation. You take out an 'eye' or undeveloped bud on the stock and replace it with a new bud from the scion you want to graft. In fact you 'fork its eye'. (A bud on a potato is also called an 'eye'.) The sense of grafting is sardonically echoed in the next line, 'An old man's shank one-marrowed with my bone', where, in addition to the obvious meaning, there may be a hint of 'marrow' meaning 'mate' as in northern dialect, when the bone becomes the 'rib', that is, the woman. Even as he copulates (or imagines he copulates) with his 'bone', that is, he is aware of the old man's shank taking over his limbs. Then 'all the herrings smelling in the sea' – most of us have forgotten the sheer multitude of smelly death when the herring boats came to port. I remember the fisher-girls in their rubber aprons on the quay in Port St Mary in Man, gutting the fish till the seawater was crimson, putting them in barrels ready to pickle or make kippers. Everywhere the gulls wheeled, the chains creaked, the smell was monstrous. As an image of pullulating death it has stayed with me all my life: one imagines the poet must have experienced such a scene in the fishing ports of south Carmarthenshire where he visited as a boy.

> To dye to sleepe,
> To sleepe, perchance to Dreame; I, there's the rub,

says Hamlet, that is, there's the point where difficulty arises. But a rubbing collar, for example, tickles. The rub of love is both negative – an impediment to freedom – and a kind of pleasure, a titillation that 'tickles'. If the various rubs of sex, love, procreation really did 'tickle' – amuse or entertain him – then he would not fear the various terrors of life – the apple of original sin, the flood of God's judgement, the gallows and the axe of justice and the crossed sticks ('crossed Styx', the river in hell) of war; nor would he fear concupiscence, the 'devil in the loin' nor the blatant nightmare of death, the 'outspoken grave'. Above all he would not fear old age, even if it drowned him in 'a sea of scums'. But nothing really tickles except the

> worm beneath my nail
> Wearing the quick away.

The sixth stanza does not seem to be as decisive or accurate as the rest of the poem: it succumbs to Dylanesque cliché, perhaps, or it may simply be my inability to see what is happening. We have to remember sometimes even in the greatest of *18 Poems* that Dylan Thomas was only twenty when he wrote them. On the whole it is remarkable how controlled they are. Certainly 'If I were tickled' shows a formal magnificence that is only faulted, if at all, momentarily at this point. Considering the huge range of imagery and verbal effects involved, tragic utterance is matched as nowhere else in modern English by formal control and the achievement of a great music.

The last stanza recovers itself. 'The worm beneath my nail' leads to a very different kind of nail and prepares us for 'My Jack of Christ born thorny on the tree'. The extraordinary range of the poem – death's feather on the nerve, the mouth of his lover, 'the thistle in the kiss', the Christ born (in both senses) in him, the words of the poet 'dryer than his stiff', and yet 'wordy wounds' printed with his love's hair – all these come together in a kind of counterpoint, a pedal-point where one note – the question, 'And what's the rub?' – is held in the bass while the other voices join and resolve above it. And then the final affirmation:

> I would be tickled by the rub that is:
> Man be my metaphor.

It is not as simple as it sounds: for one thing it returns to the conditional or subjunctive of the four opening stanzas – and in this context we simply don't know whether it is conditional (If I were, I would be . . .) or the subjunctive of wish or intention (I want to be or I intend to be . . .). The meanings don't differ all that much, but the grammatical uncertainty seems to underline the difficulty of the final cadence: 'Man be my metaphor'. Metaphor for what? Every reader has to propose his or her own answer, I suggest. In fact, the picture-surface which seemed about to refer us to the world outside itself, as in representational art, at the last minute refuses to do so. The schizoid principle of 'limited liability' is preserved, in spite of the sound and fury, the control and the visionary range.

This reluctance to come clean is not a fault of *18 Poems* but a condition of their being:

> The force that through the green fuse drives the flower
> Drives my green age; that blasts the roots of trees
> Is my destroyer.
> And I am dumb to tell the crooked rose
> My youth is bent by the same wintry fever.

The main image here is that of a man detonating an explosion. You put the explosive, with a fuse, where you want it, then lay a long wire to a hiding place where you have a box with a handle on it. If you 'drive' the handle in, electricity ('force') is generated and travels down the wire, causing a spark in the fuse which then ignites the explosive. It is a cliché image of the cinema, made familiar by countless acts of sabotage as well as mining, e.g. for gold.

As Dylan uses it, the flower is the sudden explosion that results when the electricity reaches the 'green fuse', that is, the bud. The poet says that his 'green age' – his youth – is driven by the same energy, the hand (of God?) pushing the handle of the generator down to create an explosion. This explosive quality of life also brings destruction – it 'blasts the roots of trees', and it will also destroy the poet himself.

Three possible meanings could attach to the recurring phrase 'And I am dumb to tell': the obvious meaning (at least the one that occurs to me first), 'I am dumb or in some way unable to tell', may not be right. For one thing it seems unidiomatic to use 'dumb' in this way. Another possibility is 'the reason I am dumb is in order to tell' (in this case) the crooked rose that my youth is bent too: that is, that the rose and he are both wrecked by the same explosion, 'wintry fever' as opposed to the spring implied in the first line. A third possibility, as Walford Davies points out, is that he is using the slang meaning of 'dumb' – that is, foolish. One must also allow for the possibility that all three meanings are implied, either simultaneously or at different times in the poem. Clearly what is conveyed by all three meanings is a lack of communication with the natural world in spite of the poet being himself shaped by natural forces.

If the first stanza deals with the explosive force of life and death, the second deals with a life and death governed by the availability of water. The main image here is 'mouthing' – spouting out like a fountain, but also speaking:

> The force that drives the water through the rocks
> Drives my red blood; that dries the mouthing streams
> Turns mine to wax.
> And I am dumb to mouth unto my veins
> How at the mountain spring the same mouth sucks.

And so on. Critics have been misled by the repetition of the pattern into thinking that each stanza is a simple variation on the first, and the whole poem four statements of Thomas's general philosophy of process. On the contrary, each stanza is a new departure, returning all the time to the ambiguity of the 'I am dumb' refrain, the schizoid inability to feel or express anything beyond the *voyant*'s outsider viewpoint. Yes, it is about Dylan Thomas's identification of himself with the processes of physics and biology; and yes, it is also about the failure of that identification to reach anything outside itself. 'JE est un autre.' Out of the two things he makes a grave and restrained passacaglia, a piece of music that is also tragic poetry.

Time and again, reading these extraordinary poems, one is driven to talk in terms of musical – indeed symphonic – form. Dylan Thomas was not known particularly for his love of music, but his best friend at this time was a composer, a future symphonist, Daniel Jones. Preoccupations rub off from one artist to another; and particularly on to such a receptive mind as Dylan Thomas – receptive to ideas, vocabulary, idioms, structures. Before booze and personal inadequacy took their toll on his sensibility, there was no poet more open to the raw materials of tragic poetry. One is driven to reach for Shakespearean comparisons. Think of the use of 'eye' in 'the bud that forks her eye'. How many poets would have heard some old gardener mutter about his roses, and then months later have used it in a poem about a girl? And this kind of verbal receptiveness and fluidity of imagination is normal in *18 Poems*. So the musical influence from his friend is not somehow beyond the pale of critical discourse. It is to be expected and welcomed into our appreciation.

There are of course precedents in poetry for this use of repetition and near-repetition. In his correspondence with Henry Treece over the latter's pioneering book on his poetry, Dylan is very non-committal about the influence of Hopkins, which Treece – like many subsequent critics – have seen in his work.[2] He had read Hopkins, of course, but he feels that he owed much more obvious debts to rather less fashionable writers like Swinburne and Francis Thompson, particularly Thompson's 'The hound of heaven' which, he says, is baying in quite a few of his poems. It seems to me, once again, that the poet is correct in what he says about his poetry and that Hopkins's influence is largely a red herring for his critics. Both Swinburne and Thompson used refrain-like phrases to organize the musical shape of their poems. (So, of course, does T. S. Eliot in 'The hollow men' and 'Ash Wednesday', but his practice does not seem to have much in common with *18 Poems*.) If we want to ignore the evenings making 'music' with Daniel Jones (see his *My Friend Dylan Thomas*, 22–5) we can; but we should remember what a large part 'Warmley' (the Joneses' household) played in his poetic education, improvising and discussing poetry together. Music and 'broadcasting' were all part of the fun that had serious implications later.

Young grandmasters are rarer in poetry than in chess or mathematics. We are suspicious of them. R. S. Thomas put it like this:

> For the first twenty years you are still growing,
> Bodily that is: as a poet, of course,
> You are not born yet.

> ('To a young poet')

So a poet who is 'born' – and not merely born, a great warrior of poetry – at twenty is shocking, a prodigy and a danger to established habits of thought. In myth we have the infant Taliesin coming out of nowhere and challenging the king's bards as false poets. But in real life too, the young grandmasters rouse in us a mixture of intense passions. Think of Christopher Marlowe, or Chatterton, the marvellous boy; or Keats, or

---

[2] Paul Ferris (ed.), *Collected Letters* (London: Dent, 1985), 296–7.

that prodigy of nineteenth-century drama, Georg Büchner, the author of *Woyzeck* who was dead before he was twenty-four; or Rimbaud himself, shattering nineteenth-century sensibility and dragging the modern world to birth before he was twenty. We both love them, these *enfants terribles* of the imagination – for they do what we feel young poets ought to do, challenge and entrance us – and they exasperate or alarm us. There is always something grotesque about them, a sullenness maybe; though they are (mostly) supremely intelligent artists, who could beat us at our own game if they chose (think of 'The hand that signed the paper'), they shamble along their own disastrous ways, rude, exhibitionist, violent, even a bit mad.

So it is with Dylan Thomas. Critics often seem to react to his work with considerable animus. They abjure it, in the name of psychological or moral wholeness. David Holbrook reads it as a casebook of a neurotic. Roland Mathias, if I take him right, thinks Dylan concocted his poems to achieve fame with the avant-garde. He has been used as an object-lesson, almost a bogyman.

However, it is no use just treating these poems as a psychological case-book. Of course they're schizoid – they're meant to be. That's what modernist art is. Though it may be that Dylan was himself a schizoid personality and this goes some way to account for the deadness and monotonous obscurity of his worst work, it does not explain the fact that his triumphs, his best poems, are also profoundly schizoid in feeling. We can sometimes see him, as he revises a poem, making it more schizoid, more convoluted and obscure, because of some criterion he has of what his poetry should be doing. Walford Davies and Ralph Maud in their notes to the Everyman *Collected Poems 1934–1953* (p. 245) print a war-time draft:

Lie still, you must sleep

> Lie still, you must sleep, sufferer with the wound
> In the throat, burning and turning. All night afloat
> On the silent sea we have heard the sound
> That came from your wound. Your wound is a throat.
> Under the mile off moon we trembled listening
> To music pouring like blood from the loud wound
> And when the bandages broke in a burst of singing
> It was to us the music of all the drowned.
> Open a pathway through the sails, open
> Wide the gates of the wandering boat

> For my journey to the end of the wound.
> The voices cried when the bandages were broken.
> Lie still, you must sleep, hide the night from your throat,
> Or we shall obey, and ride with you through the drowned.

It seems to me, as it stands, a most moving and beautiful poem, maybe (as the editors suggest) to his father who had suffered from curable throat cancer in the thirties. Sore throats might mean the cancer had come back, with all the danger that involved, inspiring the poet with memories of the original operation. Or (less likely, I feel) the poem might be to someone actually wounded in the blitz.

The piece is urgent dramatic utterance: the repeated injunctions, 'lie still, you must sleep', give us a sense of occasion, of a patient actually lying in hospital, 'turning and burning'. The image of the wound itself as a throat pouring forth music is grotesque, but grotesque like experience itself. We listen on the 'silent sea' (cf. 'The ancient mariner':

> We were the first that ever burst
> Into that silent sea)

for signs of hope, feeling all the time apprehension and compassion for the patient in a concentration that is like someone listening deeply to music. Daniel Jones is snooty (probably with reason) about his friend's appreciation of music, but this poem surely indicates that Dylan knew what music could do – its concentration, its pain, its ability to lead us into an Otherworld – the burst of singing that 'was to us the music of all the drowned'.

The beginning of the sestet is more problematic:

> Open a pathway through the sails, open
> Wide the gates of the wandering boat
> For my journey to the end of the wound.

It seems like the imagery of his own 'Ballad of the long-legged bait', written three years earlier. There is a strange sense that the bandages round the wound are the sails of the boat where we sail in the 'silent sea' listening to the unearthly music. But the dominant feeling is of imaginative metamorphosis typical of such poems as 'The hunchback in the park', 'Poem in October' and 'A winter's tale', which belonged to the same burst of creativity in the middle forties. It reminds us of Blake's telling us to see not with the eye but through the eye. The pathway is *through* the sails, opening the 'gates of the wandering boat', for the journey is not to a place that can be reached by sea but to 'the end of the wound' – a bit like the end of the rainbow, isn't it? And then the haunting resolution of all these images in the final three lines, where the patient is told to lie still because otherwise we shall obey 'the voices' and 'ride with you through the drowned'.

It is a wonderful poem, but one can see why the poet was uneasy with it. The personal fear lies too close to the surface for such a shy man to accommodate. He might have felt that some phrases are too bare – 'Your wound is a throat', or even too derivative as they stand. But mainly, I think, he revised it because it wasn't schizoid enough to suit where his inspiration was leading him. At all events he made a great hash of it, and turned a moving and dramatic poem into a piece of sub-Dylanesque mixed metaphor and poetic trifling:

Lie still, sleep becalmed

Lie still, sleep becalmed, sufferer with the wound
In the throat, burning and turning. All night afloat
On the silent sea we have heard the sound
That came from the wound wrapped in the salt sheet.

Under the mile off moon we trembled listening
To the sea sound flowing like blood from the loud wound
And when the salt sheet broke in a storm of singing
The voices of all the drowned swam on the wind.

Open a pathway through the slow sad sail,
Throw wide to the wind the gates of the wandering boat
For my voyage to begin to the end of my wound.
We heard the sea sound sing, we saw the salt sheet tell.
Lie still, sleep becalmed, hide the mouth in the throat,
Or we shall obey, and ride with you through the drowned.

A salt sheet presumably refers both to a sail (but as such it is a misnomer, for a sheet in nautical terms is not a sail but a rope that regulates the tension of a sail – you can't wrap anything in it) and to the bedding or dressings (salt with sweat?) the wound is wrapped in; but since sailors are buried at sea wrapped in a sail, there may be a bit of that in it too. At all events, the pun is merely confusing. By substituting 'salt sheet' for the more accurate but unpoetic 'bandages', he does nothing but hide the meaning in a web of nonsense. What the hell, one may ask, is a 'slow sad sail'? The whole richness of metaphorical significance of 'music' in the original, directing our attention so urgently to the concentration of the watchers round the patient, has been expunged. At every point, it seems to me, the revision weakens the poem with cliché and gratuitous lyricism.

The really disastrous change, however, is to throw the attention away from the 'sufferer with the wound' on to the poet himself. In line 11, for example: 'For my journey to the end of the wound' becomes 'For my journey to begin to the end of *my* wound' (my italics): the journey has stopped being one of hope for the sufferer's recovery and become a self-centred pilgrimage of grief. Nor is it clear, in the revision, what 'we shall obey' for the 'voices' have changed to 'sea sound' and you don't, except in Masefield lyrics, obey the sound of the sea.

Dylan Thomas is often praised for his painstaking craftsmanship. He spent months, we are told, revising and polishing a poem. On the contrary, he seems to me a poet who relied almost totally on instinct – on inspiration, if you like. Inspiration can be a very slow business; it doesn't have to be quick as a flash. I think his celebrated work sheets, Roget's *Thesaurus* numbers and everything, are really a form of hanging around until the line came right. When it didn't come right, or when (as with 'Lie still, you must sleep') the result for some reason dissatisfied or frightened him, the craftsmanship he had to fall back on was clumsy and ill-focused. That is why he needed Vernon Watkins's help so often and so urgently. It is ironic in view of Vernon's dislike of critics, that Caitlin (Dylan's wife) saw him primarily in that capacity:

> His real strength was his criticism; he had all the understanding of technique to have become a major critic, if he had applied himself to it. I think Dylan recognised that quality in him, although sometimes he found it irksome.
>
> Whenever we went to their house, the point would always come when Vernon would invite Dylan into his study to talk about poetry. Dylan

found it something of an ordeal, and when the invitation came his eyes would roll skywards and he would give me a quick, fleeting glance before the study door closed behind them. Sometimes they would be gone for four or five hours, and Dylan would reappear almost squashed to the ground.

As she says, Dylan would hardly listen to other poets in the same kind of way. She saw her husband as a magical person, not an analytic one like Vernon: 'Dylan had a very strange sense of his own ability. He knew that with him words would suddenly spurt out without him having any idea where they came from. Like most highly analytical people, Vernon lacked that magical quality' (*Caitlin: A Warring Absence*, by Caitlin Thomas with George Tremlett, 42–3). But Caitlin tended to see the relationship as hero-worship on Vernon's part and a mixture of gratitude and cultural benefit on Dylan's. Because she never discussed poetry with her husband, she almost certainly had no conception of how useful to him Vernon's craftsmanship actually was.

The problems Thomas had with 'Lie still, you must sleep' are part of a wider bafflement he experienced in the late thirties and early forties. The flow of poems almost dried up after the amazing creativity he had experienced in 1933 and 1934. He was reduced to concocting 'new' poems by treating the notebooks (particularly those prior to the main body of *18 Poems*) as a quarry. Old poems had to be made credible as pieces by the great modernist he had recently become. This is sometimes explained as a by-product of leaving Swansea and succumbing to the 'capital punishment' of Bohemian London. It is true that he always wrote much more poetry in Wales than in England; and that London was bad for him. The change of locale might have had something to do with his inability to start again after the vein of *18 Poems* was exhausted.

But even in *18 Poems*, there are signs of the poetry going to seed. If we except 'When, like a running grave', which is one of the best in the book (Dylan considered it so, along with 'I see the boys of summer'), the later pieces included do not have the dramatic immediacy of 'If I were tickled by the rub of love' or 'The force that through the green fuse'. Narrative seems to be replacing tragic utterance. It is difficult to feel any dramatic presence in lines like

> Half of the fellow father as he doubles
> His sea-sucked Adam in the hollow hulk,
> Half of the fellow mother as she dabbles

> To-morrow's diver in her horny milk,
> Bisected shadows on the thunder's bone
> Bolt for the salt unborn . . .
>
> ('My world is pyramid')[3]

And in 'I, in my intricate image' (composed too late for *18 Poems* but included as the first piece in its sequel) the sense of intellectual exposition rather than drama is overwhelming:

> Beginning with doom in the ghost, and the springing marvels,
> Image of images, my metal phantom
> Forcing forth through the harebell,
> My man of leaves and the bronze root, mortal, unmortal,
> I, in my fusion of rose and male motion,
> Create this twin miracle.
>
> This is the fortune of manhood: the natural peril,
> A steeplejack tower, bonerailed and masterless,
> No death more natural;
> Thus the shadowless man or ox, and the pictured devil,
> In seizure of silence commit the dead nuisance:
> The natural parallel.

But as narrative or intellectual exposition, the style of *18 Poems* is decidedly a ham-fisted instrument. Though you can certainly derive pleasure from deciphering the poet's meaning, it seems a trivial thing compared with the dramatic expression that it replaces.

You have to see the 'drying up' in perspective. Some veins of poetry, once struck, go on yielding poems for a long time – even a lifetime. Once Philip Larkin had written *The Less Deceived*, he continued to capitalize on it for many years – though even that vein eventually gave out on him. Poets used to refer to this potential as 'mileage' – there's a lot of mileage there, they'd say. But some great poems have very little mileage to them. What do you do if you've just written Gray's 'Elegy' or 'The waste land'? Coming to a dead halt is embarrassing, but it may be a risk inherent in the sort of poetry you're trying to write. There may be nothing for you to do except wait for a new beginning – if it ever comes. Eliot was fortunate: his new-found religious vision allowed him to go on from the stalemate of 1922 to 'Ash Wednesday' and *Four Quartets*.

Of all forms, perhaps, the schizoid soliloquy of the *voyant*, cut off as it is from all the variety given by history and circumstance, was at once

---

[3] The second half of the poem, it is true, is more dramatic – in fact, its sudden recollection of the milieu of Wilfred Owen and Sassoon's war poetry is, as we shall see, an important clue to the meaning of *18 Poems* as a whole.

the greediest of mileage and the one likeliest to produce great poetry in the first half of the twentieth century. T. S. Eliot's 'Gerontion' is the most familiar example in English. Compared with 'Gerontion', which seems to me quite final of its kind, 'The waste land' is literally a heap of fragments 'shored against his ruin', and requiring the ministrations of a 'miglior fabbro', in the shape of Ezra Pound, to fabricate a satisfying shape for it.

What to do? There is perhaps a temptation to regard Dylan's predicament as a judgement on him for rejecting academic education. Had he gone to university, would he have found a way out? But had he gone to university he would never have written *18 Poems* in the first place: the experience of being an undergraduate is perhaps the most destructive of creativity that a young poet normally suffers. A college education might eventually have helped him intellectualize or 'empiricize' his talent – turned him into a minor Auden or Norman Nicholson – but what had it to offer a tragic *voyant* soliloquizing outside circumstance about what it meant to be alive and afraid in 1934?

For that is, finally, what these extraordinary pieces are about: a sensibility, a 'naked thinking heart', caught between two wars, stripped of all the comforts of received ideology and waiting to be ground into Flanders mud or Coventry blitz. Remember what was happening in 1933–4. The socialist revolution had failed in the West; in Russia communism was poisoned by Stalin. Mussolini and Hitler were on the move. Britain and America were in the grip of economic depression. *18 Poems* expresses a world where the only certain things were bodily existence and its answering state of mind, the creativity of a poet; and they were both threatened by the insanity of modern war. When war did break out, Dylan's main preoccupation was to avoid being killed or called up. It is arguable that the war nevertheless was the most significant event in his adult life.

It is generally not in the nature of *18 Poems* to talk about war directly. He is not a Wilfred Owen or an Alun Lewis. However, in 'My world is pyramid', a piece which as a whole I don't understand,[4] as very often in

---

[4] Elder Olson (*The Poetry of Dylan Thomas* (Chicago: University of Chicago Press, 1954), 36) says it is 'a strange meditation on the physical child and "the secret child," and resolves the problem of death in these terms, through the discovery that "the secret child" survives'. This leaves me as confused as ever. Is it some sort of confirmation of Holbrook's theory (*Dylan Thomas: The Code of Night* (London: Athlone Press, 1972)) that the poet's mother, even as she bore him, was mourning the loss of another baby that died; and that this was one of the dominant facts in his psychological make-up?

*18 Poems* a stanza suddenly looms out of the murk and speaks to me
very directly indeed:

> My world is cypress, and an English valley.
> I piece my flesh that rattled on the yards
> Red in an Austrian volley.
> I hear, through dead men's drums, the riddled lads,
> Strewing their bowels from a hill of bones,
> Cry Eloi to the guns.

This is the world of the 1914–18 war – the pastoralism, the nightmare,
the identification of the common soldier with Christ – 'Eloi (or Eli) lama
sabachthani' – the cry from the cross, 'My God, my God, why hast thou
forsaken me?'

The achievement of *18 Poems*, as we say, was precarious. Dylan
Thomas could not repeat it; and there is a lot of evidence that he
abandoned the style with relief. In a letter to Glyn Jones thanking him
for a review of *Twenty-Five Poems*, he says: 'You're the only reviewer, I
think, who *has* commented on my attempts to get away from those
rhythmic and thematic dead ends, that physical blank wall, those wombs,
and full-stop worms, by all sorts of methods – so many unsuccessful'
(*Collected Letters*, 243). In the same letter he says that he considers
'Then was my neophyte' the best of these attempts, 'clearer and more
definite', and 'holding more possibilities of progress than anything else
I've done'. Detailed consideration of this poem would not be to the
purpose; but it is true that its texture does suddenly clarify in the last
stanza. 'Who kills my history?' And then, 'Time kills me terribly', and 'I
saw time murder me'.

This sudden confrontation between the schizoid *voyant*, the 'I who is
someone else', and the 'me' who has a history to be killed and therefore
also relationships with other real people, is crucial to Dylan Thomas's
middle-period attempts to escape from the impasse of *18 Poems*. As
Walford Davies puts it, 'he saw the impasse unequivocally as a failure of
human commitment' (*Dylan Thomas*, 37). From then on, 'history' and
autobiography enter more and more into the subject-matter of his poetry;
or rather, re-enter, for of course the *voyant* did not come from nowhere.
The notebook poems are as full as we would expect of Dylan Thomas
as a Swansea adolescent trying to express himself – in fact they're often
a good deal more circumstantial than any poetry he wrote later – and
perhaps his largely tactical return to the early notebooks for new 'copy'
had some part to play in the direction he was to take.

At all events, he tried to involve the *voyant* 'I' in the 'me' of his own life. Long poems, 'exhausters', about his relationship with Caitlin or his approaching fatherhood – even in one famous case the death of his aunt – began to be interspersed with 'opussums' (little opuses) about his own childhood or about his poetic vocation or about anything else that took his fancy. The trouble was, the tragic rhetoric of a soliloquizing *voyant* is fundamentally unsuited to biography. A condition of its being is that I is someone else. The gap between language ('I') and subject matter ('me') is always threatening to swallow him up. All these poems have a willed feeling about them. As Walford Davies puts it, poems to Caitlin such as 'Not from this anger', 'I make this in a warring absence' and 'Into her lying down head', show a critical disproportion between their manner and their matter – like using three stones to kill one bird. A good many of the 'opussums', certainly, seem close to doodles; and not done with much grace either. The poet's kaleidoscopic imagination is always in danger of merely offering crossword-puzzle satisfactions.

For all our suspicions of its schizoid egotism and its hints of masturbatory sex, however, in the best of *18 Poems*, the tragic utterance *was* a human thing. It did not need to be 'humanized'. It expressed as no other poetry of the period – not even Auden's – what it felt like to be alive and afraid in the thirties, between two wars and naked of ideological covering. Dylan Thomas's new concerns seem trivial by comparison. In retrospect the title of his third book, *The Map of Love*, seems only too accurate. He was making a map of where he wanted to go, rather than letting poetry (in Keats's words) come naturally as leaves to a tree.

Gradually, under this pressure, the tragic utterance of the *voyant* changed into something else – elegy, affirmation and something I shall call 'metamorphosis' – the use of dream or day-dream, often in narrative form, to make coexistent two different orders of experience: for example, the hunchback's miserable existence and the woman 'straight as a young elm' he made from his crooked bones ('The hunchback in the park'), or the poet's thirtieth birthday with his childhood ('Poem in October'). The presence of two orders of experience is not usually presented as memory or act of imagination but as something occurring in the 'real world' of the poems. In 'Poem in October' it was the weather that turned around, not his mind:

> There could I marvel
> My birthday
> Away but the weather turned around.

> It turned away from the blithe country
> And down the other air and the blue altered sky
> Streamed again with a wonder of summer . . .

In 'A winter's tale' the messenger from the past is a she-bird 'rayed like a burning bride'. The co-presence of past and present is dwelt on in the language of a real resurrection:

> Listen. The minstrels sing
> In the departed villages. The nightingale,
> Dust in the buried wood, flies on the grains of her wings . . .

This, it could be said, is wish-fulfilment with a vengeance. The poet, worn out with worry and personal failure, is imagining a world where ifs and ans *are* pots and pans and wishes are *really* horses. But that doesn't quite answer to our experience of the poetry. We apprehend both worlds as reality: one does not cancel the other out, as it would if it were simply wish-fulfilment. Though one cannot, obviously, discount altogether that element, is it not fairer to remember that the poetry of *Deaths and Entrances* was contemporary with T. S. Eliot's *Four Quartets*?:

> Time past and time future
> What might have been and what has been
> Point to one end, which is always present.

> ('Burnt Norton')

> We die with the dying:
> See, they depart, and we go with them.
> We are born with the dead:
> See, they return, and bring us with them.
> The moment of the rose and the moment of the yew-tree
> Are of equal duration.

> ('Little Gidding')

It seems to me that 'A winter's tale', in particular, shows clear influence of *Four Quartets* – 'the minstrels sing in the departed villages' and the whole atmosphere of rustic revelry:

> Look. And the dancers move
> On the departed, snow bushed green . . .

is surely not innocent of 'East Coker'; and the repeated injunctions to the reader to 'listen' and 'look' are quite in Eliot's manner.

To return to 1939, and the poems to Caitlin. In 'I make this in a warring absence' the old splendour of tragic utterance is still fitfully present. In the midst of a lot of turgid word-spinning you suddenly come upon a stanza like:

> I make a weapon of an ass's skeleton
> And walk the warring sands by the dead town,
> Cudgel great air, wreck east, and topple sundown,
> Storm her sped heart, hang with beheaded veins
> Its wringing shell, and let her eyelids fasten.
> Destruction, picked by birds, brays through the jaw-bone
>
> And for that murder's sake, dark with contagion,
> Like an approaching wave I sprawl to ruin.

But the end of the poem shows a different kind of strength, a poetry of affirmation that already foreshadows the 'natural piety' of 'Poem in October' and 'Fern Hill', and a rhetoric that associates fulfilment with the 'song's truth' of childhood:

> Now in the cloud's big breast lie quiet counties,
> Delivered seas my love from her proud place
> Walks with no wound, nor lightning in her face,
> A calm wind blows that raised the trees like hair
> Once where the soft snow's blood was turned to ice.
> And though my love pulls the pale, nippled air,
> Prides of tomorrow suckling in her eyes,
> Yet this I make in a forgiving presence.

There are some tactical confusions here – the punctuation is deliberately vague, does 'my love' in line six refer to him or to her? – but the basic metaphor is that of a baby calmed by being given the breast. The affirmation is not yet the mature instrument it was to become, but the mode is already in place. If he did learn from Eliot that the moment of the rose and the moment of the yew-tree coexist, it was because his own poetry was ready to receive that knowledge, caught as it was between 'I' and 'me', tragic soliloquy that had nowhere to go and a personal life once full of promise and now at every turn looking failure in the face.

# 10

## *A lonely path:*
## *the early poetry of Glyn Jones*

~

In the chapter on Idris Davies we remarked on the fact that in the Anglo-Welsh poetry of the inter-war period we are essentially dealing with a new language. English in the families of Vernon Watkins, Glyn Jones, Dylan Thomas and Idris Davies was no more than a generation or two old. Before that, people no doubt spoke it, but it was a foreign speech to them. And this is true in spite of the fact that all four writers used English as their first language, and the two from Swansea spoke no Welsh at all. One effect of this newness, if I may quote myself, is that in matters of vocabulary

> the actual words are often without the *patina* that English writers would instinctively give them. The big words – 'father' or 'love' or 'death' – when an English writer uses them are worn like stone steps in a cathedral. They are fitted into the intimacies of the language, they gather nuances. Trace elements of pathos, irony or snob-value control their usefulness. In Dylan Thomas's poetry nothing is half-said, words are sounded at full power. Not since the Elizabethan dramatists has English verse been able to strut like that. The English culture of the Thomas family was 'all in the head', as Lawrence would say. It hadn't had time to be natural.

It is not only the 'big' words that have this nakedness. In Dylan Thomas and particularly in Glyn Jones's early poetry, the vocabulary often seems almost sufficient reason for writing. Glyn Jones's world is a sensuous one – all five senses tingle with awareness – but the overall impression is not that of a man trying to chart sensation but of one in love with words:

> Now it begins, though God knows why.
> *– Beneath my blind a rich blue sky –*

Shamed and sick, my soothed heart knows
The sweet, soft, explosions of the rose.

*– Today floats molten, its gold froth chars*
*The oblong, set with three stone stars*
*And looped with a new moon's silver wire –*
My null flesh torches forgotten fire.

*– Three from the dawn, three blazing swans*
*Flash it off their migrant bronze –*
I hold this moment *– the sun's afloat! –*
My murderous life, God, by the throat!

('Morning')

That's an early poem, of course. I am not sure what it's about, but what is clear is how beautifully words are used. I once tried to write a French poem, and it turned out fifth-rate Verlaine simply because Verlaine writes French poetry as my English ear hears the way French poetry 'ought' to sound: this is not a judgement on him of course, but on the way a foreigner falls in love with a language not his own. Glyn Jones gives words a pebble-like clarity of outline, a beauty which English certainly has, but an English poet would tend to soften and make less naked, just as a French poet would rarely give free rein to the impressionist softness I was imitating in Verlaine.

Glyn Jones stands somewhat apart from the other Anglo-Welsh poets who started to write in the thirties and forties. Though he thought of himself as primarily a poet, it is clear, at least until he finished the last of his novels in 1965 and *The Dragon has Two Tongues* in 1969, that he put most of his fundamental brainwork and creative 'poke' into his prose – fiction and autobiographical and critical writings. Many of his early poems read like fragments of story, and very often the meaning only seems to clarify when the fiction emerges as primary, often under the influence of D. H. Lawrence. 'Esyllt', for example:

As he climbs down our hill my kestrel rises,
Steering in silence up from five empty fields,
A smooth sun brushed brown across his shoulders,
Floating in wide circles, his warm wings stiff.
Their shadows cut; in new soft orange hunting boots
My lover crashes through the snapping bracken.

The still gorse-hissing hill burns, brags gold broom's
Outcropping quartz; each touched bush spills dew.
Strangely last moment's parting was never sad

But unreal, like my promised years; less felt
Than this intense and silver snail calligraphy
Scrawled here in the sun across these stones.

Why have I often wanted to cry out
More against his going when he has left my flesh
Only for the night? When he has gone out
Hot from my mother's kitchen, and my combs
Were on the table under the lamp, and the wind
Was banging the doors of the shed in the yard.

Many small touches tend to baffle the reader at first. It is not immediately clear who 'he' is in the first line – is it really the kestrel? 'As he climbs down our hill my kestrel rises' – true, one climbs down, the other rises, steering up. But the poem is full of oxymorons – a 'smooth' sun 'brushes', the 'still' 'gorse-hissing' hill 'burns' (if 'still' is an adjective, which we've no means of telling), 'last moment's' parting was 'never' sad. Even when we've realized that 'he' and the kestrel are the same, however, we've still the puzzle of why 'he' is described as 'my' kestrel. Is the speaker a falconer? No, falconers don't usually leave their hawks to fly by themselves. And yet the man is in his 'new soft orange hunting boots', so perhaps they have had a row when they were out hawking and she was so upset she left the kestrel to its own devices; or maybe, for the parting was 'unreal', she continued her hunting with the bird after her lover had gone. Again, 'my' may be just a term denoting affection and familiarity. 'My kestrel' may be the one that lives round the farm, one I've got to know and be fond of. It is very unclear what precisely is happening, except that some connection is felt between the kestrel and the lover – their shadows cut, they are both hunters. A male kestrel is described in the literature as 'rufous' which is ornithological English for a browny orange. Lawrentian symbolism is clearly being suggested. (It is just possible that some half-suppressed reference is being made to kestrel courtship behaviour, when the male circles above the female on the ground. In which case it is her kestrel because it is courting her!)

Who is Esyllt? Her name is the Welsh form of Tristan's lady, Iseult or Isolde. But the whole milieu of the poem is uncourtly. A lord does not leave his lady from her mother's kitchen, nor would a lady hunt with a kestrel – a low kind of hawk compared with peregrines or merlins. This girl is clearly a small farmer's daughter, or something of that sort. But something must be meant by giving her such a name.

The first two stanzas, then, present us with a series of puzzles. A girl is watching her lover leave her in the morning (there's still dew about). It seems unreal to her. At the same time the sensory imagery is insisted on, to consciously incongruous effect: the 'new soft orange hunting boots' crashing through snapping bracken – she imagines them, feels them ('soft') across five empty fields. Again, as he goes, she imagines (or is she experiencing it herself?) 'each touched bush' spill dew. His leaving her is less felt:

> Than this intense and silver snail calligraphy
> Scrawled here in the sun across these stones.

The effect is strange. Her sensations are so vivid that they are always on the point of relegating her feelings (which is what the poem is ostensibly about) to inconsequence. The poem is breaking apart under the strain, it seems to me, coupled with the fact that so many details are puzzling and we have to guess what they mean.

In the 'Sketch of the Author' which Glyn Jones characteristically appended to the back of his first book, *Poems*, he acknowledges his debt to Lawrence:

> I did not begin writing poetry until I was twenty-four, and I started off powerfully under the influence of D. H. Lawrence. By this I mean (is it necessary to say it?) that the *vocabulary* and *imagery* of Lawrence affected me deeply when I first encountered them, but that I remained entirely indifferent to the Lawrence doctrine. I was delighted with the brilliance of his colouring, with the richly sensuous texture of his verse and so on, and like most young poets I tried to reproduce in my own early poetry the effects I admired.

The trouble is, Lawrence's imagery, the brilliance of his colouring and so on, are organic to his whole sensibilty as it fashions the 'doctrine' for itself. That is not to say that Lawrence does not sometimes apply doctrine from the outside, often in a hectoring and unpleasant way; but surely not in his successful poems, the ones Glyn Jones would have admired. To detach imagery and colouring like this, from such a deeply committed writer as Lawrence, is to risk the arbitrariness of pastiche. However beautiful or striking the images are, and those in 'Esyllt' are certainly that, they become distracting the moment the reader starts to lose confidence in the wholeness of the fiction.

However, the problems we have with the first two stanzas of 'Esyllt' would almost certainly not have arisen in prose. The author, because of the concision demanded of poetry, has failed to articulate his narrative.

It is a fiction, a scene from a story; but it is also a poem, full of brilliant observation and imagery. The two things interfere with each other.

That is, in the first two stanzas. In the third they don't because he lets the fiction have its due. We realize that her lover has stayed the night with her for the first time. The poem is about the unreality of satisfaction compared with the customary sharpness of unfulfilled desire – the combs out of her hair and him hot, but the wind banging the door in the yard. The situation, the fiction and the imagery come together. If the mode is still Lawrentian, it is at least whole cloth, not just appliqué work.

The inclination to create and discuss poems as if they were a matter of 'brilliance of colouring' and 'richly sensuous texture' was (and remained throughout his life) one pole of Glyn Jones's inspiration. It is clearly derivable from his early experience, coming to English poetry as a relative foreigner, delighting in its wonder world, and at the same time separated from everything that gave it social relevance. He has described how isolated he was as a young writer in Cardiff: 'There was no stimulus, no other writers to talk to, no literary atmosphere to prompt one to write, nowhere to send one's work if one *had* written anything' (*Setting Out: A Memoir of Literary Life in Wales*, 8). It was a 'literary wilderness', in which the greatest need for a writer was proof of his own existence, through meeting other writers and finding they respected what he was doing. Glyn Jones *could* have stayed put as an old-fashioned *buchedd* poet. There were such people around, even in English – he mentions W. H. Davies, Huw Menai and A. G. Prys-Jones as writers he knew about even then. But 'they were unlikely to be much of a spur . . . to someone so determined to be modern as I was':

> In this vast cultural moonscape of nothing and nobody, whose boundaries seemed to be co-extensive with those of Wales, where was one to turn? No wonder that about that time I wrote a long poem called 'Maelog the Eremite', which was about a dotty hermit who came from Merthyr.

But there was another side to Glyn Jones. He has described how he chose to go to a teachers' training college at Cheltenham – a decision he bitterly regretted, it was so cold and alien – rather than follow his mother's wishes and go to art school, 'the usual bolt-hole for people in my situation', as he describes it. Following this he taught in a Cardiff slum. There was a puritan and even a socialist polarity to him, as well as an aesthetic. He wanted to serve the people – at a time, moreover, when the Depression made such service more than usually hard. There were no jobs; apathy and near-starvation were everywhere. In 'Sketch of the Author' in *Poems*, he says,

> My ambition when I began to tire of reproducing endlessly the effects of another man's verse, was to achieve a body of workers' poetry. By this I didn't mean at all an imitation of the public-school-communist verse which was fashionable at the time and which used to amuse me by its naive earnestness and its exotic air when viewed from the stand-point of working-class life and institutions, but rather poems which the workers themselves could read, understand and appreciate.

That is, he tried to become a folk poet, a writer in the tradition of the *hen benillion* or stanzas to the harp. 'Rain' is an example:

> Though night comes on and drizzle
>     Begins to fall,
> He halts me when we near
>     This dry-built wall.
>
> Here in the dripping darkness
>     Under the trees,
> My cheeks might not be burning
>     For all he sees.
>
> And now rain like the darkness
>     Take my part,
> Come, drown this painful beating
>     Of my heart.

True, the final stanza does have something of the emotional snap that *hen benillion* often end with:

> Mynd i'r ardd i dorri pwysi,
> Pasio'r lafant, pasio'r lili,
> Pasio'r pincs a'r rhosys cochion.
> Torri pwysi o ddanadl poethion.
>
> (Went to the garden to pick a posy,
> Passed the lavender, passed the lily,
> Passed the pinks and the red roses,
> Picked a posy of stinging nettles.)
>
> Dod dy law, on'd wyt yn coelio,
> Dan fy mron, a gwylia 'mriwio;

> Ti gei glywed, os grandewi,
> Swn y galon fach yn torri.
>
> (Put your hand, if you believe me,
> On my breast, and take care not to hurt me;
> You shall hear, if you listen,
> The sound of the little heart breaking.)

But even if one ignores the Lawrentian overtones implicit in the scene – Gerald kissing Gudrun under the bridge is surely not very far away – the language has the wrong kind of self-consciousness for folk poetry: 'he halts me', for example, or 'this dry-built wall', or the whole emphasis on the this-ness or here-ness of the situation. Despite his attempt to write with actual working-class people in mind, Glyn Jones failed as a folk poet. He says: 'But the workers work eight hours, have had a three R's education, and care nothing for poetry.' We can certainly sympathize with his attempt, but at the same time recognize that he was trying to short-circuit a traditional process from the outside, almost as much as the public-school poets he mocks.

He tells us that about this time he started to study Welsh seriously. He had almost stopped being able to speak the language and realized with shame that he knew very little of the enormous wealth of Welsh poetry. From this point on, imitations of Welsh poetry in various ways consciously influenced his own.

Indeed, his knowledge of the Welsh tradition – where he came from – is one of the things that sets him apart from other Anglo-Welsh writers of his time. It gave him a vantage point from which to discuss what he and other writers were doing. In fact it gave him the chance to write criticism, properly so called, not just the subjective notes of approval or distaste that is all other Anglo-Welsh writers could articulate. (It is still very noticeable that Anglo-Welsh critics of any stature either have a knowledge of the Welsh-language tradition directly – Bobi Jones, Tony Bianchi, Wynn Thomas – or have some other purchase on it, such as the historical scholarship of Roland Mathias (1915– ). The only apparent exception I can think of is Jeremy Hooker, who of course approaches Anglo-Welsh writing from the firm ground of his English roots – i.e., from the other side.)

Glyn Jones is almost the first self-consciously Anglo-Welsh poet to concern us. The critical positions he pioneered in *The Dragon has Two Tongues* (1968) have become orthodoxy. They focused on the loss of the language, the feeling of being Welsh with little to show for it, the background ('genius belt' as he calls it) of Welsh-speaking radical non-conformity. At the same time Glyn Jones defended individualist vision against the community-based attacks of Welsh-language critics:

> The Welsh accuse them [the Anglo-Welsh] of falsity, of giving a hopelessly distorted picture of Wales in their writings, of not portraying or interpreting Wales truly and adequately to the world. The true Wales, the Welsh say, is nothing like the Wales of Caradoc Evans or Rhys Davies. I have myself, as a young Anglo-Welsh writer, been subject to this sort of criticism, and the first time I encountered it I was bewildered by its complete irrelevance to anything I had thought or attempted. The idea of undertaking anything so portentous as an interpretation of Wales to the world had never entered my head. All I wanted to do as a young writer was to express what had moved me to delight, or horror, or laughter, or pity; to make my own statement about the Wales I knew; to impose some sort of pattern, acceptable to myself at least, upon the shoals of impressions pouring in upon me. (*The Dragon has Two Tongues*, 44-5)

The knowledge of Welsh poetry that he was acquiring in the thirties was an ambivalent gift: on the one side it was a desperate attempt by a loneliness-haunted writer to realize his roots. Welsh poetry is a very socially oriented art, it arises out of actual communities in place and time, it presupposes besides these another community – that of poets throughout Wales and throughout time – who know and value each other, certainly because of their work but also as friends and personal acquaintances meeting, for example, at eisteddfodau country-wide. To an extent Glyn Jones has been accepted by this community. I met him once on the *maes* of the National Eisteddfod when he had just been inaugurated into one of the bardic orders for his services to Welsh literature. It was for me a strange situation in which to find an Anglo-Welsh poet, and I found myself wanting to joke about it; but Glyn, though he understood my embarrassment, obviously took it quite seriously. After all, he had by then written a great deal of Welsh prose and this ceremony was a traditional acknowledgement of its value.

On the other hand, Welsh poetry as it can be translated and imitated in English tends to present a shimmering verbal surface of imagery and consciously wrought phrasing, heavily alliterated and 'poetic', and a long way from what English people would think of as the accents of a man speaking to men. In a kind of appendix to his second book, *The Dream of Jake Hopkins*, Glyn Jones prints three translations from Dafydd ap Gwilym, three ways of translating *cywyddau* which remarkably prefigure the methods respectively of Gwyn Williams, myself and (almost) Joseph Clancy. It is clear he had thought it all out a long time before any of us got to work! 'The seagull', translated into free verse, is the only one he kept in the *Selected Poems*:

> Gracing the tide-warmth, this seagull,
> The snow-semblanced, moon-matcher,
> The sun-shard and sea-gauntlet
> Floating, the immaculate loveliness.
> The feathered one, fishfed, the swift-proud,
> Is buoyant, breasting the combers.
> Sea-lily, fly to this anchor to me,
> Perch your webs on my hand.
> You nun among ripples, habited
> Brilliant as paper-work, come.

It seems worthwhile to compare this with the original, not to pick holes in the translation but to see what aspects of Dafydd's poetry Glyn Jones was able to assimilate into his own. Of course this is only the opening *dyfalu* or description of the seagull – the poem is actually a love-poem in which Dafydd asks the bird to go to his girl-friend and tell her how much he loves her:

> Yr wylan deg ar lanw dioer
> Unlliw ag eiry nag wenlloer,
> Dilwch yw dy degwch di,
> Darn fel haul, dyrnfol heli.
> Ysgafn ar don eigion wyd,
> Esgudfalch edn bysgodfwyd.
> Yngo'r aud wrth yr angor
> Lawlaw â mi, lili môr.
> Llythr unwaith llathr ei annwyd,
> Lleian ym mrig llanw môr wyd.

More or less literally, this translates as:

> Fair seagull[1] on a flowing tide, in truth
> One colour with snow or the white moon,
> Immaculate your beauty,

---

[1] 'The fair seagull' or 'O fair seagull' are both possible; but the context shows it is meant as an address.

> A piece like a sun, gauntlet of brine,
> You [float] lightly on an ocean wave,
> Swift-proud fish-food bird,
> Yonder you'd go at anchor,
> Hand in hand with me, sea lily,
> Like a letter, bright of its nature,
> A nun on top of a tide you are.

The first thing to notice about the Dafydd is the form. The *cywydd* was a new form, in one way, when he used it – he may have actually invented it as we know it today; but in another way, of course, it was very familiar indeed. The *cynghanedd* would have immediately put it into a definite category of utterance, not indeed used in conversation or legal codes or scholarship, but still a socially acceptable and welcomed kind of speech called poetry. The man who was able to handle this decorated speech was both honoured and conferred honour. The nearest thing I can think of is the use of heroic couplets in eighteenth-century England or the type of verse – the type of language – used in folk-song. Glyn Jones (or any other translator) cannot rely on an English form giving him this kind of social acceptability. His free verse certainly does not: by using it, he has to emphasize his own verbal sophistication – for example, 'the snow-semblanced, moon-matcher' instead of 'one colour with snow or the white moon'.

The translation is a good deal more abstract than the original. Dafydd's language can be ornate and difficult enough, God knows, but on the whole he uses fairly simple words, however artfully put together. What is more, he is primarily addressing the bird, not describing it. The translator, though, does not move into the second person until the seventh line, when it seems a slightly odd thing to do. Again, the word *llythr* (letter) is paraphrased as 'habited brilliant as paperwork' – not without excuse from the scholars who think that's what it means! But Dafydd is seeing the seagull – certainly because it is white and smooth and shining (*llathr*) – as a letter, and therefore sendable to his love. In 'The thrush' he sends the bird with a letter ('ei lythr gwarant'), but in 'The seagull' he goes one better and sends the gull as a letter in itself. Similarly, *lleian*, a nun, is not just a poetic description: nuns and clerics have surely always been used by lovers as go-betweens or confidants. Think of Shakespeare's Friar Lawrence. They have easy access to young girls, because of their holiness and status as honorary eunuchs.

The translation (to put it harshly) substitutes a web of fine phrases for a socially relevant set of invocations. The *llatai* or love-messenger in medieval Welsh is perhaps chosen arbitrarily; but the fun is to make it relevant to the courtly code. Glyn Jones simply sees it as description.

His knowledge of Welsh poetry, then, once he had abandoned his plan to be a folk poet, tended to shift him still further towards the aesthetic, phrase-savouring pole of his art. But the other thing that happened to him as a thirties poet, his meeting with Dylan Thomas, rather unexpectedly seems to have had the opposite effect – though to say so goes against his own judgement in the matter:

> Just as I was beginning to see how hopeless and visionary my scheme was [viz. to write poetry for the workers] I met a famous young poet, a countryman of mine. His verse seemed to me entirely to disregard the reader, or the potential reader, of whose existence, because of my socialist theories, I had always been acutely aware. But paradoxically this poet who appeared completely unconcerned with the social or communal aspect of poetry, was also the one for whose work, difficult and even perverse as it was, I felt the greatest admiration at the time. We argued, and partly in a sort of despair, partly in relief at escaping their cramping invigilation, I dismissed the figures of the young collier and the engine-driver and the coal-trimmers from my mind . . . Now my poetry became less ambitious – I was content to communicate with myself, to indulge my love of those words and phrases which I had suppressed to a large extent before the scrutiny of my workers, and to ignore the limitations of an audience. ('Sketch of the Author' from *Poems)*

And yet the poems he actually wrote under the influence of Dylan Thomas – was he Dylan's first disciple? – show him as never before expressing the angst and social distress of his time:

> Some dread a sudden death, the busy hand
> Convulsing like burnt paper round
> The bitten bread; some dole-queues, sitting slain
> On public seats, staring the pansies down;
> And some a loneliness, a hooting arctic's edge . . .
>
> ('Wounds')

He cannot quite sustain this tragic utterance, but there are passages in the sequence poem, 'Biography', that seem almost to prefigure Allen Ginsberg's 'Howl':

> his bored
> Eventful body, beleagured in angel-smell and flame of its
> Paradisal defender, passed like a sundering leprosy . . .

                                          In that erect
        Slab of sweetwater he encountered flying Europe,
        Seeing the prison faces staring out like fire and lions

together with at least one line that Dylan Thomas surely remembered –
the influence was not all one-way: 'The golden hawk above the gallows-
dangle of the corpse'.


After the rich experimentation and promise of his first book, *Poems*
(undated but published in 1939), his second, *The Dream of Jake Hopkins*
(1954), is clearly transitional. It is dominated by two longish poems in
which Glyn Jones attempts, whether by precept or example, to discipline
his poetic language; but both of them point to prose fiction as the way
forward rather than poetry. The title poem, like R. S. Thomas's 'The
minister', was one of the first batch of 'radio odes', commissioned by
Aneirin Talfan of the Welsh Region of the BBC. Poets were given half an
hour's radio time and four or five actors – 'voices' – and had to compose
an original poem suitable for broadcasting. Perhaps the intention was to
find a successor to *Under Milk Wood* or at least exploit the rich field
that Dylan Thomas had opened up. The series continued well into the
seventies, but more as a gesture towards sponsorship of poetry than with
any hope of contributing to the art of radio. That in itself had a
deadening effect on the form; but at the start, Aneirin Talfan's initiative
and the example of Dylan striking gold did force poets into a real
confrontation with the new medium.
   Glyn Jones characteristically sets out the reasoning behind 'The dream
of Jake Hopkins' in a concluding note. He rightly says that aural poetry
has to have different criteria to written. He draws attention to early heroic
verse, such as the Llywarch Hen poems, and he defines its characteristics
as 'directness, repetition, contrast and absence of ambiguity'. He also says
that there is a similar directness in Chaucer, Dafydd ap Gwilym and
Villon: 'Poetry written before the invention of printing was poetry written
for the ear. It was in fact radio poetry.' This seems to me to beg any
number of questions. For a start, the reciter of early poetry was present
to his hearers as a live person, in the same way as an actor is in a theatre.
Adrenalin flowed between them. Radio poetry (or even more, poetry on
a record) is in this respect far more like reading from a book than being
present at a live reading. It is true that we are not trained to listen – to
read with our ears, as it were; but this is not a particularly difficult skill
to acquire. Once you have it, poetry read with the eyes and poetry 'read'

with the ears certainly do differ in the satisfactions they offer. (I wonder, if I could follow braille with my fingers, whether touched poetry would be different as well.) One difference is that heard poetry is more personalized. The voice of the reciter will never go away as the handwriting of the writer is lost in the impersonality of print. However, there are still three terms, not two: poetry read with the eyes, poetry listened to – 'read' – with the ears, and poetry where the reciter is personally present and part of a group that includes you.

Then again, the recordings of poetry that I go back to over and over again, almost like music, are not necessarily, or even mainly, the most direct. They include Siobhan McKenna reading 'Anna Livia Plurabelle' – pure poetry, even if written in prose – from *Finnegans Wake*, T. S. Eliot reading 'The waste land' and *Four Quartets,* Ralph Richardson reading Blake, David Jones reading 'The hunt' and Dylan Thomas 'If I were tickled by the rub of love'. Some of these I had previously found impenetrable on the page, but 'understood' immediately (in the sense that one understands any work of art) when I heard them. I still prefer to listen to them rather than reading them with the eyes.

I know this is being wise after the event. In the early fifties the idea of radio poetry was new and unexplored. The position was further complicated by the four or five 'voices' you were given. If the poets had had much sense of living drama (as Dylan Thomas clearly did) it might have led to a rash of one-act verse plays; as it was, the adaptation of prose fiction for radio proved a compulsive model for almost everyone.[2]

Glyn Jones says that he decided that his poem 'must be immediately intelligible, it must be clear, straightforward, to be grasped at one hearing. It was not to be more difficult to follow than the ordinary dialogue of a play.' What play? one is tempted to ask. *King Lear*? Or one of Terence Rattigan's? Glyn Jones seems to me to have surrendered all too quickly to what we would now call Radio 4 orthodoxy. But if radio wants poetry, then it should be on poetry's terms – as music is. No one expects all music to be immediately intelligible or grasped at one hearing by any Tom, Dick or Harry who happens to be listening. Wordsworth said long ago that, with a poet:

> you must love him, ere to you
> He will seem worthy of your love.

---

[2] I wonder, by the way, why no one seemed to use that other successful radio form, comedy series like *Itma* or the Goons. The half-hour *Goon Show* would seem on the face of it very close to what the poets were asked to provide.

That is as true of a radio poet as any other kind. One is not denying that radio poetry is possible; merely that there is no reason why it has to conform to reach-me-down standards of what good radio consists of. To deny radio poetry the possibility of being repeated, for instance – to say it must always be a one-off like a political discussion or a quiz programme – is to deny it as poetry and therefore as good radio also.

One can discern behind all this Glyn Jones's old desire to write poetry for the people – *hen benillion* for modern workers; and behind that again, the root ideology of the *buchedd*, the idea that culture must not be divisive or difficult. That's probably the negative side; but in terms of Glyn Jones's own development as a writer, 'The dream of Jake Hopkins' carries us forward into the world of the novels he was about to write. I don't just mean *The Learning Lark* which shares much of its subject matter with the poem. 'The dream of Jake Hopkins' is a poem essentially conceived by the prose imagination. It would require a novel fully to explore the situation of Jake the schoolteacher. Indeed, parts of the poem, like the visit of HM inspector of schools, read as though they should be sections of a comic narrative.

Glyn Jones's second requirement for his radio poem was that it ought to be in rhyme and metre:

> Against much of the free verse I have heard over the air I say nothing as poetry; but as *radio* poetry it has often sounded boneless and shapeless. It is a truism now that poets threw away aids very valuable to themselves and to their readers when they discarded rhyme and metre.

Well, it may be a truism, but it is not obvious to me for example, that Whitman's 'Out of the cradle endlessly rocking' or Christopher Smart's 'For I will consider my cat Jeoffrey' (neither of them using metre or rhyme) are boneless or shapeless on the radio. Are they inherently inferior as heard poetry to the near-doggerel into which 'The dream of Jake Hopkins' is in constant danger of slipping?

> Here hops my boss like a voluble vulture
> Trying to talk with the accents of culture
> To a person with French hands, and eyes always darting,
> And hair split in two in a beautiful parting.

But the determination to rhyme foundered against the clock: to finish his poem in time for the broadcast Glyn Jones had to jettison rhyme for most of the central section, where the Voices of Memory tempt Jake to despair.

Glyn Jones says that he was persuaded to publish 'The dream of Jake Hopkins' against his better judgement, because it was never intended for the eye of a reader. Indeed, whatever it may have sounded like on the wireless, on the page it suggests a rather truculent capitulation to middlebrow tastes. It is possibly the most unmodernist piece he ever produced.

If 'The dream of Jake Hopkins' leads into the novel, the other longish poem in the book, 'Merthyr', seems at first to point to the kind of 'autobiographical' literary criticism one finds in *The Dragon has Two Tongues*' (London: Dent, 1968). 'Merthyr' has been popular with south-Walian critics for obvious reasons; but I see it as a piece of stylistic self-criticism rather than a topographical poem about his *bro*. It takes the form of a prayer to God about where he wants to die. At first he begs the Almighty to let it be in the Brecon Beacons behind Merthyr:

> Upon some great green roof, some Beacon slope
> Those monstrous clouds of childhood slid their soap
> Snouts over, into the valley . . .

He imagines his funeral:

> Lay me, lead-loaded, below the mourning satin
> Of some burnt-out oak; the skylark's chirpy Latin
> Be my '*Daeth yr awr*'; gather the black
> Flocks for bleaters – sweet grass their ham – upon the back
> Of lonely Fan Gihirich; let night's branchy tree
> Glow with silver-coated planets over me.

But this mixture of verbal magnificence and grotesquerie he tells God he finds suspect in himself:

> my gift for logopoeic dance
> Brothers, I know, a certain arrogance
> Of spirit, a love of grandeur, style and dash,
> Even vain-glory, the gaudiest *panache*,
> Which might impel to great rascality
> A heedless heart.

'Sir', he says to God, 'that death I sought was pure effrontery.' Nature would simply tempt him to unreality, so he now prays to die *inside* Merthyr:

> An object has significance or meaning
> Only to the extent that human feeling
> And intellect bestow them . . .
>
> But far more than the scene, the legendary
> Walkers and actors of it, the memory
> Of neighbours, worthies, relatives,
> Their free tripudiation,[3] is what gives
> That lump of coal that Shelley talks about
> Oftenest a puff before it quite goes out.

What this skeleton plan of the poem fails to give, of course, is the physical detailing of his early life in Merthyr that inspired him to write. But, taking that as read, compare the passage from *The Dragon has Two Tongues* (pp. 44-5) that we have already quoted:

> All I wanted to do as a young writer was to express what had moved me to delight, or horror, or laughter, or pity; to make my own statement about the world I knew; to impose some sort of pattern, acceptable to myself at least, upon the shoals of impressions pouring in on me. In short I was a writer whose impulse was primarily lyrical.

The poem clearly arises from a similar sort of thinking as the prose passage – in fact it is a comic exaggeration, almost a burlesque, based on the same idea. The impulse in both is basically a critical one: to defend 'Merthyr' as a subject matter, to stress his own roots, and to clear his mind of any pretensions to anything more high-falutin.

As with the critical book, the poem frequently seems to involve great long lists. Almost every other page of *The Dragon has Two Tongues* involves us in lists of writers who illustrate something or other that Glyn Jones wants us to know. To pick an example at random we are told on p. 53: 'The two Anglo-Welsh magazines, *Wales* and *The Welsh Review*, together with *Life and Letters Today*, published stories by, among others, Dylan Thomas, Caradoc Evans, Nigel Heseltine, George Ewart Evans, Rhys Davies, Geraint Goodwin, Llywelyn Wyn Griffith, Gwyn Jones and Margiad Evans.' Perhaps as belated protection against the loneliness and isolation he felt as a young writer in Cardiff, he obsessively keeps on listing his fellow authors; but it is also characteristic of his style in general – as though the 'shoals of impressions' pour in upon him so fast that he just ticks them off, not having the time to deal with all of them individually.

---

[3] A dance of joy.

'Merthyr' is largely made up of lists and certainly climaxes on one:

> My undersized great granny, that devout
> Calvinist, with mind and tongue like knives;
> The tall boys from Incline Top, and those boys' wives;
> The tailor we believed a Mexican,
> A rider of the prairies; Dr. Pan
> Jones (he it was who gave my father
> The snowy barn-owl) Bishop – *soi-disant* rather;
> Refined Miss Rees; Miss Thomas ditto; Evan
> Davies and the Williamses from Cefn.

So did Widsith in Anglo-Saxon unlock his word-hoard in a great catalogue of the stories that he knew.

It is not impossible that Glyn Jones made some of these characters into subjects of later poems. However, they and people like them are surely more obvious material for prose fiction: the sheer multitude would defeat a lyric poet, even a list-maker like Glyn Jones. Both 'The dream of Jake Hopkins' and 'Merthyr', therefore, show his mind turning more and more to things that prose fiction does better than poetry and presage the long poetic silence of 1954–67 when he turned his attention to novels and prose autobiography and criticism.

'Jake Hopkins' is about his job as a teacher, 'Merthyr' about his *bro*, his native district. The third important poem in this collection, 'Cwmcelyn', is about his roots in rural west Wales, perhaps some sort of answer to Dylan Thomas's 'Fern Hill' which deals with the same area.[4] However, the piece which looks forward most clearly to Glyn Jones's mature preoccupations as a poet is none of these, but one called 'Easter' on p. 24:

> Morning in the honey-months, the star
> Of annunciation still lit in the sky,
> Upon me fell the heavy unpinned hair
> Of apple, perfumed almond, pear,
> With dawn-chorus, dewfall, and the incarnate
> Promise of the primrose flesh in bloom.
> Leaving the morning garden, I sought the room
> The bedside of a woman winsome to me
> Once, though old, clean in her white cap, comely
> In candle-light, or the green shine of stars.

---

[4] Lynette Roberts's heroic poem, 'Gods with stainless ears', was also originally titled 'Cwmcelyn' and located in the same valley.

In death's stink now, with tears I watch her, old
And hideous in her dying – bitterly
She moans, her face death-dark, her tangled hair
Tortured behind her little rolling head.
She wakes a moment, calming our kindling room,
Opens untroubled eyes and lifting up
Bone arms like glistening sticks, prays for the droll
Child of her weeping sailor. Anguish returns;
Again she moans – it is the grave-bound flesh
That grieves – but soon now must remission come
Upon the agony of this endured embrace,
Soon must the flesh rot in its stony bed.

Now, with a burning in the east, the breeze
Curves across the young cheek of the day;
Soon shall the thrush be at his crowing point,
Frailer than filigree the stems begin to bud;
Soon over grooved fields shall grow the soft
Plush-pile of the grass-like wheat, the green
Velvety nap of springing corn burst forth –
Soon, soon, the door of every grave shall open
And the light of dawn shall shine upon the dead.

The four parts of the poem, four phases of the moon, define succinctly Glyn Jones's universe. First of all, the delight in nature, the words enacting ripe pleasure in its variety and charm. Perhaps it was this side of him that loved D. H. Lawrence. The fruit trees' blossom is 'heavy unpinned hair' – Glyn Jones has an enormous sensitivity to human faces in all their moods, beauties and disfigurements. There's something of the old Celtic head-worshipper about him! He sees the primroses as young flesh, like Mary's at the Annunciation, full of incarnate promise.

This is a garden scene: the garden where Christ rose from the tomb – Mary Magdelen thought he was a gardener – but also redolent of the gardens, real or suggested, in Glyn Jones's later poems – the azaleas in 'Nant Ceri', the gold of 'Spring bush'. Even wild flowers, wild fuchsias, bindweed, seem to be appreciated as a gardener would appreciate them.

The poet leaves the garden to visit an old lady 'a woman winsome to me once, though old'. The poet's technique which in the garden had relied mainly on metaphor, now picks its words for their sound: alliteration – woman, winsome, once, white – cap, clean, comely, candle; internal rhyme – clean, green – white, light; Irish rhyme – tó me, comely; assonance – garden, stars – morning, sought – bedside, white, (light), shine – cap, candle. It is an astonishingly complex tracery of what Hopkins called 'lettering', a kind of English pattern-work akin to *cynghanedd* in Welsh. What the words pick out is the winsomeness of the old woman, and her old-fashioned ('comely') neatness and charm. Again and again in the later poems Glyn Jones remembers his friends, their civilized ways, what he calls their 'blessedness' and what he has owed to them.

The change to the third paragraph is brutal, and the shock is partly registered by the vocabulary – stink, hideous – but also by the clogging ugliness of the sound – 'In death's stink now'. Glyn is in tears, overcome with grief for the hideous trick that dying is playing upon his friend. Again, this territory of old age, dying, physical incontinence, senile decay, will be very familiar in the later poems, as will the choking grief that it inspires. I do not feel that Glyn Jones at this stage in his development has quite the measure of it: vivid touches like 'bone arms like glistening sticks' give way to tired abstractions 'anguish returns' and 'grave-bound flesh that grieves': the poet is stylistically uncertain in a way that misses the terrible plangency and yet poise of his later poems:

> Nightly for years Miss Mari Ann,
> The middle one, proclaimed her lonely presence
> By her lighted candle in their crumbling villa,
> Alone, unwashed, her stockings down, unfed,
> Old early and neglected in the stink and solace of
> Her twenty cats, her rows of whisky bottles.
>
> About these three, to whom I gave such
> Boyish devotion, this I heard years later from
> My wise superior Mam, who understood, well,
> The perils of all sweet superiority.

('Superior')

Lastly, we return to the open air – typically portrayed once again in terms of the human head:

> Now, with a burning in the east, the breeze
> Curves across the young cheek of the day.

But the Resurrection theme is introduced too suddenly, in too willed a way after the nightmare of the dying woman. It doesn't really answer the problems posed by her anguish:

> Soon over grooved fields shall grow the soft
> Plush-pile of the grass-like wheat, the green
> Velvety nap of springing corn burst open –
> Soon, soon, the doors of every grave shall open
> And the light of dawn shall shine upon the dead.

The weakness of the final couplet makes one suspect an ironic intent, but there doesn't seem to be any. Resurrection in the later poetry is treated a good deal more circumspectly, though it is often present as an idea or a colouring. 'Bethania' for instance tells how the poet takes for a walk a terminally ill old workman, bringing him like Lazarus as if from the dead – hence the title because Lazarus came from Bethany:

> I bring the wrinkled workman, risen from the dead,
> To park gates, he wearing cap and muffler, winter
> Overcoat; dumb there he stands, staring, at peace;
> Out of the tomb came lacerated belly, bandaged pipe
> And pipe-cough, and long and gluttonous
> Engulphing stare . . .
>
> Death was not yet, grave-linens, face-cloth,
> Death's stink not yet to be; beside him, at the warm
> Black bars I watch and share tranquillity,
> A visionary peace possesses him, a brooding joy,
> His chrism of tears and quietness, between grey gate-stones
> And the iron bars.

If I have sometimes criticized these early poems harshly or taken issue with Glyn Jones's position in them, it is not out of disrespect. Glyn has had much honour amongst us in Wales, and there is no one who deserves more. In the creative isolation of his years as a young teacher, he struggled with almost every problem that afflicts Anglo-Welsh poetry – its relation to the economic decline of Wales, to the poverty and aimlessness of the Depression; to the tradition of Welsh poetry, to the new media, to nationalism. How to be modern, how to remember Zion in a strange land. And he did not, like so many, behave as a know-all, a cultural bully wearing his talent like an inferiority complex. He knew that the sort of poet he was had dangers:

the gaudiest panache,
Which might impel to great rascality
A heedless heart.[5]

Rather, he worked quietly at his writing, made mistakes, kept notes, told anyone who wanted to know where he'd been and what he was doing. And why he was doing it that way. In fact he kept open house, made himself a permanent master-class for Anglo-Welsh poets, so that others could come and take comfort from his steadiness of aim and his integrity.

Finally one returns to Glyn Jones as a great poet of old age, still plagued as I think by divided loyalty and indecision about what a poem is meant to be – beautiful phrasing or moralised fiction – but producing, in spite of it, work with a plangency and expressive power that goes back to Llywarch the Old or Guto'r Glyn. More than that, even, work instinct with the terrible pity of a novelist faced with a subject matter when it has ceased to be capable of anything except pain, imbecility, impotence and death – ceased in fact to be material for novels.

---

[5] If you want a commentary on those lines, look at his most famous poem, 'The common path', which describes how he avoided a woman in trouble, affronted by her suffering.

Because fortune, sunlight, meaningless success,
Comforted an instant what must not be comforted.

# 11

## *Lynette Roberts*

~

Lynette Roberts died at Ferryside on 26 September 1995. She was the last to go of the so-called 'First Flowering' of Anglo-Welsh poetry – David Jones, Dylan Thomas, Idris Davies, Vernon Watkins, Alun Lewis, Glyn Jones – that extraordinarily varied assembly of talent that Keidrych Rhys gathered round his magazine *Wales* in the late thirties and early forties. She only narrowly survived Glyn Jones, who died earlier that year. The giant race before the flood passes into legend.

Of them all, Lynette Roberts's story was the most extraordinary. The details must wait until John Pikoulis publishes his edition; but she was born of partly Welsh parents and educated in an Argentine convent and an English boarding school. She attended classes in woodcarving and textile studies, but eventually trained as a florist and set up her own studio in a London attic. She knew many of the writers and poets of the time, including David Jones, T. S. Eliot, Robert Graves, Edith Sitwell and Dylan Thomas. She was already writing poetry, though she had no formal training in literature; and her work began to find acceptance in magazines.

In 1940 she married Keidrych Rhys, the editor of *Wales*. From being a rather idiosyncratic groupie on the fringes of London literary society, she was whisked off to a poverty-stricken cottage in Llanybri in rural Carmarthenshire, where she immersed herself in Welsh life – it did not stop the locals accusing her of being a German spy! It was here, during the middle years of the war, that she wrote most of the poetry in her two published volumes, and also a prose book, *Village Dialect*. They represent only a fraction of her work, some of which – parts of an autobiography and her correspondence with Robert Graves while she was helping him gather materials for *The White Goddess* – appeared in a special edition of *Poetry Wales* in 1983. Her two books of poetry *Poems* (1944) and *Gods with Stainless Ears* (1951) were published by Faber and Faber. T. S. Eliot admired her work but no subsequent volumes appeared. The fifties were antipathetic to her kind of passion and experiment. Her marriage broke up, and after a few years apparently trying to find a niche in London, she became a Jehovah's Witness, returned to live in Carmarthen, and gave up writing poetry.

In Wales she was the only poet of comparable stature not to benefit from the revival of interest in Anglo-Welsh poetry, the 'Second Flowering' of the sixties and seventies. It was as if during those years Lynette Roberts was seen largely as an adjunct to Keidrych Rhys (a much less interesting poet), and given purely token representation in our anthologies. She had virtually become a one-poem writer – her invitation to Alun Lewis to visit her in Llanybri (a fine piece, but not her only one) was duly trotted out whenever editors had to remember her. Anglo-Welsh critics and anthologists often disliked Keidrych also, as a person, but they could hardly ignore him as they could his erstwhile wife.

I met Lynette only once, in her caravan in Hertfordshire in the early fifties. In fact she was the first poet I ever met. She talked about using African drum rhythms and birdsong in poetry – I carried away from our meeting the importance of experiment, of not bowing to dead convention, and the sense that poetry was a sister art to music and painting, and didn't necessarily have to be like 'writing a book'. A sense too that poetry was interpersonal, between real people.

For many years I seemed to be the only person who was reading Lynette Roberts. That is, apart from 'Poem from Llanybri' which our anthologies printed, in a token way, to represent a writer who was obviously an important literary figure, the wife of the editor of *Wales*, Keidrych Rhys, and a friend of Robert Graves, David Jones, Alun Lewis and Dylan Thomas. But it was not until John Pikoulis, as a by-product of his work on Alun Lewis, visited her in Carmarthen and began to be excited by her poetry, that I really felt the clouds were lifting. Cary Archard, the then editor of *Poetry Wales*, also became an enthusiast and in 1983 produced a splendid special issue on her work, with one of her paintings on the cover, containing long extracts from her autobiography, her complete correspondence with Robert Graves, several of her poems, and essays by Pikoulis on her relationship with Alun Lewis, and myself on her lyrical poems. It was the widest exposure her writing had had since the forties. In 1993 John Pikoulis gave a lecture on her at Gregynog, and he is now engaged on a collection of her work with a biographical introduction to be published by Seren Books. Even more astonishingly, a detailed article by Nigel Wheale has appeared in the English magazine, *Critical Quarterly*, mainly about her long poem *Gods with Stainless Ears* but also dealing with the problem of why she has been so neglected.[1]

One becomes over-protective of one's enthusiasms until they are shared; or sometimes too deprecating in a defensive way. Faced with so much new information and with other people's notices of her work – not least that of Robert Graves in his letters – I now feel that much of what I wrote in earlier essays (including the one in *Poetry Wales*) was inadequate and even misleading. Any consideration of Lynette Roberts's achievement before Pikoulis's edition appears must in the nature of the case be provisional. However, her work is an important element in the mix of Anglo-Welsh poetry, raises feminist and aesthetic issues, as well as the question of the nature of war poetry in our time. It ought to be read, publicized and discussed.

Her fellow writer Brenda Chamberlain (1912–71) is a different case: Brenda's work as a painter, her prose books (notably *Tide Race* about her life on Ynys Enlli, Bardsey Island) and the way our Anglo-Welsh anthologies usually include several of her poems, have kept her name before the public. As a poet she shared much of Lynette's milieu, including friendship and collaboration with Alun Lewis: she edited (not very accurately) his correspondence with her in *Alun Lewis and the Making of the Caseg Broadsheets* (1970).

Lynette Roberts and Brenda Chamberlain constitute the heroic generation of Anglo-Welsh women poets. They ought to be joined by Margiad Evans (Peggy Whistler) the novelist and poet who, born in England, yet identified herself as Anglo-Welsh. All three have this sort of problematic relation to Wales, all three are visual artists as well as writers, and all three are 'primitives' in the sense that we use the word of painters – poets without a training in literature, whose work therefore involves problems in appreciation. In particular, the clear boundaries most poets with literary training make between private and public worlds are frequently transgressed. This is not simply a matter of using private emotions – all lyric poets do that – but of using phrases or words which mean very precise things to them but which are often not totally intelligible without explanation. As with other primitives (John Clare, Emily Dickinson) these poets' viewpoint is eccentric to their culture's

---

[1] Nigel Wheale, 'Lynette Roberts: legend and form in the 1940's', *Critical Quarterly*, 36, 3 (1994).

literary norm, though perhaps derivable from it. The primitives' isolation is in a sense a reflection of the isolation of all modernist art. That is perhaps why Henri Rousseau lived happily beside the cubists. But it is not necessarily the same thing as modernism, though most 'primitives' would certainly claim to be 'modern'. Modernists create an environment where 'primitives' can come to the fore; so much so that 'primitive' and modernist can often be regarded as two sides of the same cultural upheaval.

To call these writers 'primitives' will doubtless cause confusion. Lynette Roberts, for instance, was certainly not ignorant of what other poets were doing. In her own way, she had considerable learning. Other poets were reading her work – after all, it was published by Faber – as she was reading theirs. Nor, in the final analysis, is her work to be judged as anything but poetry, as Emily Dickinson's is judged. She has nowhere near the quantity of work or the metaphysical insights of the American poet, but she does offer her own quirky and passionate satisfactions.

One thing I do not imply by 'primitive' is a value judgement. Nor (it should not be necessary to say) am I calling them primitive because they are women. Contemporary women poets like Gillian Clarke or Shenagh Pugh are not at all in this category. The latter denies – and with good reason in her case – that gender has much to do with what sort of poet she is. They may or may not write from a woman's point of view or about female subjects; but they do so in a public mode of discourse that they very largely share with their male fellow poets. Nor do earlier women writers usually qualify for the epithet. There is nothing 'primitive' about Elizabeth Barrett or Christina Rossetti.

'Primitives' in our sense seem to arise when cultures are in turmoil. There are new and revolutionary ways of thinking about art; there is also a churning of people in the fathom-rake of the winds of change. The possibility of making significant art seems suddenly available to those who are neither trained as artists nor of the 'correct' social group. They may be peasants, like John Clare; or women caught between cultures, like our three poets. There is indeed a 'primitive' element in most Anglo-Welsh poetry before the 1960s. It is one of the sources both of its difficulty and of its power. Consistently the poets have the air of going where angels fear to tread. In the case of Lynette Roberts, Brenda Chamberlain and (to an extent) Margiad Evans this was intensified by their gender; by their being expatriate and exotic in their chosen culture; and by the pain and even tragedy it cost them to be artists and poets against the odds.

Lynette Roberts was, I think, the most accomplished poet of the three. Chamberlain was primarily a painter, though she passionately wanted to be a poet; and Margiad Evans was a better novelist and prose-writer. But Lynette, during those fierce few years when she operated as a maker, was a poet or she was nothing. This period – roughly from 1939 to the early fifties – was only one part of an extraordinary life. It included her marriage to Keidrych Rhys, the editor of *Wales*; the birth of her two children; and the breakup of her marriage. For much of the time she was living in a damp little cottage in Llanybri in Carmarthenshire, isolated and lonely, while Keidrych was away as a soldier and being unfaithful to her.

In his fine article John Pikoulis characterizes her style as individual: 'a spare syntax, light but pointed use of mythology and history, a compressed, flashingly vivid vocabulary and a sculptural sense of form, tightly controlled, only hinting at emotion. The central thrust was visual.' He analyses her prose poem on the bombing of Swansea and concludes:

> The scholarly dazzle of 'The New Perception of Colour' is wholly typical, as impressive as it is chilly, surprising and, finally, warm. The poet watches, her heart feels, and the greater she feels, the more she watches, containing and cryptifying the emotion. It is the habit of a woman who has given more emotion than she has received, whose fireside repose, so resplendently comforting, has been taken from her more than once. ('Lynette Roberts and Alun Lewis', *Poetry Wales*, 19, 2,[2] pp. 9-12)

We are not dealing, therefore, with a poet who uses poetry as an extension of an intimate journal, as I often feel we are in the case of Margiad Evans. Lynette's poems are primary: they stand in their own space, they can dominate (as so few poems can) a page of prose in which they occur. The pleasure one has in them is to a considerable extent a formal pleasure: they move in such angular yet spacious ways, their cadences are so accurate and forceful, their repetitions so controlled.

And yet it seems to me that they are better read in a context of prose – journal or autobiography or what not. The poem about the blitz on King's Bench in London, 'Crossed and uncrossed', seems a much more accessible piece given as part of her autobiography on pp. 49–50 of the *Poetry Wales* issue, than it does in her *Poems*. There is a stupid preju-dice against poets explaining their work in print – they are allowed and even encouraged to do so in speech, in poetry readings or interviews. But in print nothing must come between the poem and its reader. Not all the

---

[2] From now on referred to as *Poetry Wales*.

difficulties of Lynette Roberts's work are dispelled by knowing its biographical context; but at least the reader does not have to guess.[3]

In her autobiography she tells of two experiences of the London blitz, one of which concerns us:

> I missed Keidrych dreadfully. I joined him in Yarmouth and had to pass through London so went to Celia Buckmaster's home at King's Bench Walk. I was astonished to find the results of a raid were still pending after days. The firemen were pinned to the bleached bricks trying to put out the fires. The library books were in heaps on the ground. The Round Church had had a direct hit. The coloured windows were blown out and in brilliant pieces on the ground. Pegasus had melted and fallen. There remained a plane tree, some lily of the valley. It was Celia's mother who executed such bravery. The gentlemen assigned to be there had missed duty. (*Poetry Wales*, 49)

This was the subject of 'Crossed and uncrossed', one of her best poems and perhaps the finest poem on the blitz by any poet in English, lacking completely both the empty rhetoric that afflicted Dylan Thomas's or Edith Sitwell's war poetry and the commonplace pathos or self-pity that lesser poets usually expressed. The title refers to the way crusaders were buried: 'Their shock . . . causes the crusaders to uncross their legs and through burning they turn into Tang shapes'.

### Crossed and uncrossed

Heard the steam rising from the chill blue bricks,
Heard the books sob and the buildings' huge groan
As the hard crackle of flames leapt on firemen
    and paled the red walls.

Bled their hands in anguish to check the fury
Knowing fire had raged for week and a day;
Clung to buildings like swallows flat and exhausted
    under the storm.

---

[3] There are several kinds of literary work that successfully mix prose and poetry: from the Irish epic, *Táin bó Cuailnge* to *Alice in Wonderland*, from Dante's *Vita Nuova* in Italian to Basho's *Journey to the Deep North* in Japanese. The fact that such possibilities are not felt to be open to modern poets in English has always seemed a pity to me, a sort of own goal which our culture is always scoring against itself.

Fled the sky: fragments of the Law, kettles and glass:
Lamb's ghost screamed: Pegasus melted and fell
Meteor of shining light on to a stone court
    and only wing grave.

Round Church built in a Round Age, cold with grief,
Coloured Saints of glass lie buried at your feet:
Crusaders uncross limbs by the green light of flares,
    burn into Tang shapes.

Over firedrake floors the 'Smith' organ pealed
Roared into flames when you proud widow
Ran undaunted: the lead roof dripping red tears
    curving to crash.

Treasure was saved. Your loyalty broke all sight,
Revived the creed of the Templars of old;
Long lost. Others of the Inn escaped duty
    in black hats.

Furniture out, slates ripped off, yet persistently
Hoovering the remaining carpet, living as we all do
Blanketed each night, with torch, keys, emergency basket
    close by your side.

From paper window we gaze at the catacomb of books,
You, unflinching, stern of spirit, ready to
Gather charred sticks to fight no gas where gas was
    everywhere escaping.

Through thin library walls where 'Valley' still grows,
From Pump Room to dry bank of rubble titanic monsters
Roll up from the Thames, to drown the 'storm' should it
    dare come again.

Still water silences death: fills night with curious light,
Brings green peace and birds to top of Plane tree,
Fills Magnolia with grail thoughts: while you of King's Bench
    Walk, cherish those you most love.

The first thing to notice is that it is a praise-poem, a Horatian ode imitating very well the effect of the Sapphic metre: she acknowledges in the notes her debt to Prof. George Thomson's analysis of the third and extended line of the Sapphic stanza. It is a poem in praise of the mother of Celia Buckmaster, the friend she was staying with in London. Like the vast majority of her poems, it is totally rooted in her immediate experience. She knows what she's talking about, at first hand; and if we don't always catch on, that's a risk she is prepared to take. Even in the context given by her autobiography there are still two phrases I'm not sure about: 'only wing grave' in stanza 3 and 'to fight no gas' in stanza 8. I can make intelligent guesses what they mean and they don't matter much, any more than an undecipherable printing mistake in a Shakespeare play. In fact, the lacunae are almost part of the texture. I am quite sure, however, that the poet herself knew clearly what she meant.

The poem contrives to be both a public praise-poem and an expression of intimacy. It is a dangerous combination that not many English poets would risk. Take, for instance, what is potentially the most bathetic stanza in the poem, and the one most likely to be rejected by sophisticated readers of modern verse:

> Treasure was saved. Your loyalty broke all sight,
> Revived the creed of the Templars of old;
> Long lost. Others of the Inn escaped duty
> in black hats.

The vocabulary may be a bit dated, though I think it would not have seemed so to expatriate middle-class women of the time. (I can imagine my mother coming back from India using 'treasure', 'loyalty', 'duty' – but probably not 'of old' which belongs to a slightly different register – in this straightforward, unironical way.) But the stanza is set in such magnificently concrete surroundings, and the rhythms (and even the idioms – 'broke all sight') have a strangeness to them, and such self-confidence, that it makes natural and spontaneous what in other contexts would be corny and second-hand. There is even a touch of bizarre humour in the notion of escaping duty in black hats – I take it she means the black tin-hats of air-raid wardens.

But what above all gives the stanza life, I think, is the sense we have in it of a real person being spoken to and praised. Lynette Roberts is that rare thing in modern poetry, a writer of odes, *carmina*, in the sense that Horace or Marvell would have used the term, lyrics addressed to specific persons (or sometimes specific places) in specific situations. Her poems characteristically give form and significance to others, not just to herself or to the third-person scene. Consider such lines as:

> You must come – start this pilgrimage
> Can you come? – send an ode or elegy
> In the old way and raise our heritage.
>
> ('Poem from Llanybri')

> My eyes are raw and wide apart
> Stiffened by the salt bar
> That separates us.
> You so far;
> I at ease at the hearth
> Glowing for a welcome
> From your heart.
>
> ('Low tide')

> Hard people, I will wash up now, bake bread and hang
> Washing over the weeping hedge . . .
>
> ('Raw salt on eye')

> To you who walked so proudly down the line . . .
>
> ('Argentine railways')

So with 'Crossed and uncrossed': it praises her friend's mother, but from a background of shared experience. The stanza we have just quoted is immediately followed by lines very physically evoking the life of women getting on with their housework in the intervals between air raids:

> Furniture out, slates ripped off, yet persistently
> Hoovering the remaining carpet, living as we all do
> Blanketed each night, with torch, keys, emergency basket
> close by your side.

It is this sense of shared life that makes this a true poem about the blitz. Lynette's use of quotation marks underlines the sharing: 'Valley' – quite impenetrable till you've read the prose – suggests that this is what the Buckmasters called the lilies of the valley that grew there.

Secondly the formality of the rhythm, the truncated syntax and the beautifully accurate imagery clearly indicate that this poem is a made thing, not just a slice of life. The strong stress that begins so many of the lines, achieved by leaving out pronouns and by the occasional inversion, means that the poetry moves to a kind of grave dance, like a chaconne. The frequency of initial verbs suggests that a Welsh sentence structure (verb-subject-object) may have been at the back of her mind.

171

The verbal effects are very various: the beautiful epic simile of the firemen compared to exhausted swallows, the violence of some of the juxtapositions, the pun on 'pealed' – for the organ does not simply peal like bells, it also 'peels' off the wall in the roaring flames; and then the final wonderful stanza of still water silencing death, of Marvell-like green peace, and the grail thoughts filling the Magnolia tree like its enormous white flowers:

> while you of King's Bench
> Walk, cherish those you most love.

The poetry is so rich it can compress a tradition going back to the Crusades into a tribute to that cherishing, and still etch the present scene under the blitz, 'living as we all do'.

Though she is primarily a war poet, Lynette responded to rural life in west Wales with delight as well as sadness. Her poem 'Rhode Island Red' may stand for this side of her art, a slight but not negligible lyric in which she identifies with a domestic hen – the title is the name of a breed of poultry:

### Rhode Island Red

> Spade jackets and tapping jackdaws on boles of wood,
>  Song of joy I sing.
> Prim-pied under sky full of fresh livelihood,
>  Smile for eye of man.
> Outhouses sweet with air stand whitened by the flood,
>  Of sun blanching spring.
> In plate green meadows sheepdog and farmer brood,
>  On galvanised can.
> Calling cattle from celandine and clover to mood,
>  Song of joy I sing.

We know that Lynette Roberts was reading and imitating Anglo-Saxon poetry. 'Rhode Island Red' reminds one of some of the riddles in the Exeter Book, where the object of the riddle is made to speak and so reveal its life. That may be the reason why she has chosen to make her punctuation purely prosodic – a comma at the end of every odd line and a full-stop at every even one – in imitation of an ancient manuscript. However, it doesn't make understanding any easier, and it seems worth while for the nonce to repunctuate the poem according to modern usage (i.e., to bring out the sense), with the proviso that such a revision calls for decisions which can limit the meaning:

Spade jackets and tapping jackdaws on boles of wood –
    Song of joy I sing,
Prim-pied under sky full of fresh livelihood,
    Smile for eye of man.
Outhouses, sweet with air, stand whitened by the flood
    Of sun-blanching spring.
In plate-green meadows sheepdog and farmer brood.
    On galvanised can,
Calling cattle from celandine and clover to mood,
    Song of joy I sing.

The hen (free-range, of course!) is cackling from the top of an empty petrol can in the farmyard, probably having just laid an egg in one of the outhouses 'sweet with air'. The meadows are plate-green perhaps because the new grass is so short, it is like a plate. I am not sure what 'spade jackets' are. I think they refer to the jackdaws' appearance, a bit like a playing-card spade with the head as the handle and the folded wings as the blade.

Both the struggle to achieve visual exactness and verbal concision, and the experimentation with form and metrical complexity (the elaborate rhyme-scheme – ABACABACAB – assonance and alliteration, along with the sprung rhythm), remind one surprisingly of Hopkins though there doesn't seem to be much direct influence. And consider the word 'mood' in the last line but one. Isn't she thinking of the Anglo-Saxon use in *The Battle of Maldon* where it means something like steadfastness in courage (my dictionary says it is from a Teutonic root meaning grief and the anger that grief causes)?

> Will shall be harder, heart the bolder,
> Mood the more, as our might lessens.
>
> (trans. C. M. Bowra)

The hen is like a heroic lord exhorting her companions to 'mood', but at the same time the poet is seeing the cows *mooing* their way back from the fields to be milked.

The wit in word and texture is typical. If I am right about 'mood' then the presence of the war even in this joyous little lyric is still implied. Her poems of living as a stranger in a Welsh village (and therefore suspect – there were rumours she was a spy!) waiting for her soldier husband to return, are at the centre of her work. Though they are not necessarily the most achieved works of art, the intensity of them informs and explains all the rest.

The undertow of lament in both her books – lament for the war, for the worry and privations of war, and for the waste, particularly the waste of time and love – can be represented at its simplest by a poem like 'Low tide', where she portrays herself, alone in her cottage, separated from Keidrych who has gone as a soldier.

### Low tide

Every waiting moment is a fold of sorrow
Pierced within the heart.
Pieces of mind get torn off emotionally
In large wisps.
Like a waif I lie, stillbound to action:
Each waiting hour I stare and see not,
Hum and hear not, nor care I how long
The lode mood lasts.

My eyes are raw and wide apart
Stiffened by the salt bar
That separates us,
You so far;
I at ease at the hearth
Glowing for a welcome
From your heart.
Each beating moment crosses my dream
So that wise things cannot pass
As we had planned.
Woe for all of us: supporting those
Who like us fail to steel their hearts,
But keep them wound in clocktight rooms,
Ill found. Unused. Obsessed by time.
Each beating hour
*Rings false.*

The abstraction and unreality of worry can rarely have been conveyed so physically:

My eyes are raw and wide apart
Stiffened by the salt bar
That separates us . . .

She's reached a point where she doesn't care how long 'the lode mood lasts' – lode as in lodestone, the magnet that monotonously points always in one direction; but also punning on 'load' as in 'heavy load', the mood – again that word – which is a burden to her. When you first see it on the page, the poem looks spiky and over-emotional; but I hope you will agree that, read aloud, it conveys its true power as lament, as keening against wasted time:

> Every waiting moment is a fold of sorrow
> Pierced within the heart.

Is she thinking of her heart as a kind of linen cupboard, fold on fold of sheets and pillows, all of them 'pierced' – ruined – at the core? Or are there two metaphors here, the folds of sorrow and the piercing of the waiting moments in the heart; almost like making a Christmas decoration, a streamer don't they call it, where folded coloured paper is pierced on a string like a necklace to hang across the room?

'Low tide', as I say, represents the undertow in her work as a war poet; but what strikes one, reading her, is the variety, the different situations and moods she conjures to counterpoint this lament. She is at her most attractive as a poet, witty, precise, colourful and feminine, when she is creating a social role for herself – as in her 'Poem from Llanybri' inviting Alun Lewis to visit her – or when she is using a convention she believes in. She writes of real occasions, real interpersonal motivations, no longer a total outsider but capable of behaviour which has social significance. One of her best poems in this mode is 'Earthbound', about going to the funeral of a villager. It begins with seeing the post office van 'like lipstick' reflected in her mirror as she puts on her make-up; then being told by a neighbour of the man's death, presumably on active service, and making a wreath for him of ivy and the surviving flowers of early winter (and we remember here she had worked as a florist); and then the reaction of the villagers – or lack of reaction, rather – as she and Keidrych offer the gift.

### Earthbound

> I, in my dressing gown,
> At the dressing table with mirror in hand
> Suggest my lips with accustomed air, see
> The reflected van like lipstick enter the village
> When Laura came, and asked me if I knew.
>
> We had known him a little, yet long enough:
> Drinking in all rooms, mild and bitter,
> Laughing and careless under the washing-line tree.

The day so icy when we gathered the moss,
The frame made from our own wire and cane;
Ivy in perfect scale, roped with fruit from the same root:
And from the Pen of Flowers those which had survived the frost.

We made the wreath standing on the white floor;
Bent each to our purpose wire to rose-wire;
Pinning each leaf smooth,
Polishing the outer edge with the warmth of our hands.

The circle finished and note thought out,
We carried the ring through the attentive eyes of the street:
Then slowly drove by Butcher's Van to the 'Union Hall'.

We walked the greaving room alone,
Saw him lying in his upholstered box,
Violet ribbon carefully crossed,
And about his sides bunches of wild thyme.
No-one stirred as we offered the gift. No-one drank there again.

The coming of the red van is like lipstick, a suggestion, a thing of custom, yet it brings news of tragedy. The man's death is already being placed within the normalities of village life; even as an outsider, the poet is drawn into those normalities. She had not known the dead man well, 'yet long enough'. She had been to his house, known him 'laughing and careless under the washing-line tree' – and how delicately that phrase sketches in the feminine context of his male life! Now she and Keidrych make him a wreath, and carry it through the watching street to the butcher's van which served the village as a bus. Arrived at the Union Hall where the corpse is laid out, 'We walked the greaving room alone', she says, making a purely visual pun on 'grieving'. A 'greave' is armour for the legs; so what the pun registers is not merely the grief but also her outsiderness, so that she has to wear armour to walk through the gathered villagers. She and her husband are 'alone'. Nobody else moves or welcomes them.

The theme of the poem is not so much the dead man as the precarious contact made between the villagers and the poet as a result of his death. The wreath becomes a symbol of participation, almost a symbol of the poem that has been made of it. 'Domestic poetry', I've heard someone call it. But Lynette Roberts treats with powerful economy a situation that is not really domestic at all: a tension and a struggle to be accepted, a suspicion of the outsider, the tug of human decencies, the silence with which the gift is received, the summons and the sacrifice.

# PART IV

## 12

### *The end of an era*

~

For a year or so after the end of the Second World War in 1945, Anglo-Welsh poetry of the thirties and forties was still very much in place. True, Alun Lewis had died in action; but Dylan Thomas, Glyn Jones, Vernon Watkins, Idris Davies, Lynette Roberts, Brenda Chamberlain and R. S. Thomas were very much alive and publishing important work. Lynette Roberts's *Poems* and Glyn Jones's *Dream of Jake Hopkins* appeared in 1944, Idris Davies's *Tonypandy* and Vernon Watkins's *The Lamp and the Veil* in 1945, Dylan Thomas's *Deaths and Entrances* and R. S. Thomas's *Stones of the Field* in 1946. The movement had received T. S. Eliot's imprimatur when Keidrych Rhys's anthology, *Modern Welsh Poetry*, was published by Faber in 1944. Of the two Anglo-Welsh magazines, Keidrych Rhys's *Wales* had been revived in 1943, this time published in London, not Carmarthen, and perhaps not so clearly a spearhead of the avant-garde, but still a rallying point; and Gwyn Jones's *Welsh Review* had also reappeared as a quarterly in 1944.

Yet ten years later the scene was in ruins. Idris Davies died in Rhymney in 1953, and later that year Dylan Thomas collapsed in New York. Glyn Jones turned more to prose fiction and hardly surfaced again as a poet till the seventies. Keidrych Rhys's marriage to Lynette Roberts had broken up, and she found it more and more impossible to write poetry or sustain the inspiration of the war years. By the mid-fifties her work as a poet was over. Of the other writers Davies Aberpennar changed to Welsh where he became known as a major poet, Pennar Davies; Emyr Humphreys increasingly turned to the novel, where his great work lies, though he has returned to poetry from time to time to good effect; while two other poets, Leslie Norris and John Ormond, or Ormond Thomas as he called himself then, stopped writing – or at least publishing – until the mid-sixties. After the war years, there was a slump in poetry in Britain generally; but in Wales it was peculiarly severe. Both the literary magazines collapsed. *The Welsh Review* ceased publication in 1948 and *Wales* in 1949, and though Keidrych Rhys revived *Wales* briefly in 1958-60, the soul had gone out of it: it seemed trippery and lacking in punch, certainly compared with what it had been in its heyday.

One reason for the general numbness was certainly the awful vacuum left by Dylan Thomas. The influence particularly of his later poetry was suffocating to any Anglo-Welsh poet born after 1920. But for the obvious lack of creative direction there were social reasons as well. They were years when the tide was turning within Wales: the Depression had ended, true, but the future was no longer in coal. Chapel culture was on its last legs. A newly assertive middle class was about to claim its inheritance and in the process split in two along the linguistic divide. But in 1953 nothing was clear. Exhaustion and poverty and the inevitable dissipation of enterprise by war had done their worst. Politically, the Labour Party which had rushed through Welfare State and nationalization in the post-war years, had shot its bolt. The sense of stasis was overwhelming, after the excitement and dynamism that had characterized the thirties and forties.

Dylan Thomas's *Collected Poems* of 1952 was the most important publishing event in Anglo-Welsh letters of the fifties. His death a year later was greeted as a catastrophe for poetry everywhere. A thick book of elegies for him was published in America. For years London publishers were haunted by his ghost – 'Son of Dylan Thomas' was a common theme in their blurbs for over a decade. In T. Harri Jones's (1921–65) first book, for instance, we are told, 'Wales has a bardic influence, an atmosphere and a Biblical richness of language which has helped to enrich the poetry of such men as Dylan Thomas and T. H. Jones.' That was in 1957. Even R. S. Thomas cashed in on the legend. His first London book, published in 1955, was called *Song at the Year's Turning*, itself a quotation from Dylan's 'Poem in October', and the blurb coyly quotes the Guardian critic: 'This strong and musical poetry is as well rooted in the soil of Wales as is that of more famous contemporaries' – Dylan's technicolour dreamcoat descending like the mantle of Elijah on his successors . . .

But we are not just considering an episode in the history of publicity. Did Dylan Thomas's poetry have any meaningful connection with what came after it? In one way, true, he certainly did influence most of the poets. It was like chicken-pox, an infantile disorder one got free of in a month or two and then never looked back. The symptoms of Dylanitis could not be mistaken for anything else, but in only a very few cases was it fatal or even very serious. Here, for instance, is Harri Jones as a young graduate from Aberystwyth:

> in my green ruins
> I sang like the rain; and the cold dogs
> Of my fathers ran
> Howling in the graveyard of my heart.
> The careless charity of time
> Nailed me with silver to the four, crossed hills;
> A maggot murdered Eden.
> Bird-droppings on the secret withered grass
> Signalled where comfort was.

Or young Dannie Abse (1923– ), in his 'Elegy for Dylan Thomas':

> Stranger, he is laid to rest
> not in the nightingale dark nor in the ambiguous light.
> At the dear last, the yolk broke in his head,
> blood of his soul's egg in a splash of bright
> voices and now he is dead.

But was there anything that connected the later Anglo-Welsh poets to Dylan Thomas other than this verbal disease, Dylanitis?

One thing we can say is that if he did influence other poets creatively – not just with Dylanitis – it happened before the ballyhoo started: that is, before *Collected Poems*, came out in 1952 and before his death in America in 1953. It was a very different Dylan to the rip-roaring, drunken, outrageous bard of the legend; very different too to what his friends called 'Instant Dylan' who turned the charm on at the drop of a hat. Thomas, like so many men who live on their wits, used charm as a burglar uses a jemmy. It got him his bread and butter, it paid for his ale. But before the war so disastrously entangled him with debts to the Inland Revenue, he was simply an intelligent and magical poet, full of ideas that you could argue with, though often a bit like a chameleon. Glyn Jones explains how Dylan rescued him from an impasse in his own poetry. Glyn had been trying, he says, to write verse that the proletariat could enjoy in English as working-class Welsh people had always enjoyed folk poetry – *hen benillion* and so on – in Welsh. 'Just as I was beginning to see how hopeless and visionary my scheme was', he tells us, he met Dylan Thomas. They talked and argued together, and Glyn's admiration made him 'dismiss the figures of the young collier and the engine-driver and the coal-trimmers from my mind and summoned there in substitution the familiar images that had once confronted me from the mirror-maze' (*Collected Poems*, 44).

The Dylan Thomas Glyn admired was of course the poet who had just written *18 Poems* – it was ten years before 'Fern Hill' and the rest of his now popular pieces were published in *Deaths and Entrances* in 1946. Glyn Jones found the experience of reading his poetry 'pure sensation'. It achieved 'the condition of music': 'what I experienced when I first read "Light breaks where no sun shines" seemed to me an almost identical emotion to that aroused by the high strings in the first movement of Eine Kleine Nachtmusik – a sort of transport of ecstasy' (*The Dragon has Two Tongues*, 184). Glyn regarded any attempt to explicate the poetry as doomed to failure. What mattered was the 'thrill, the pure sensation'. But he found the experience a liberating one. It restored him to imaginative vitality by making him go back to himself, and the 'familiar images' of the 'mirror-maze'.

Other Welsh people were not so sure. Indeed, Dylan Thomas divided Welsh opinion more than any other Anglo-Welsh poet before or since. Welsh-speakers, used to the way Welsh poets write out of their community, were bemused by the international success of one who seemed to have no responsibility beyond poetry itself. I think a good many were put off by the 'sex and guts' side of Dylan, suspicious of his spiritual credentials and impatient of what they saw as his failure to grow up. Pennar Davies wrote in *Dock Leaves* comparing Dylan very unfavourably with the much loved Welsh-language poet Kitchener Davies who had also died recently. Pennar Davies writes as one who had responded to the promise he saw in *18 Poems*, but looked in vain for the moral centredness he demanded of a great writer, which Kitchener Davies of course had. 'How can we explain', Pennar Davies asks, 'the fame of this interesting minor poet?' And he concludes:

> The pivotal fact is his adoption by Edith Sitwell as the hero of the reaction against the social verse of Auden, Spender and Day Lewis together with the vogue of Welshness in literary London. A fine voice and a declamatory manner made him a favourite broadcaster. Embracing no causes he made no enemies. Fame is more of a drab than she used to be, and the procuress Publicity is indeed resourceful. He came to be accepted as the New Romantic. (*Dock Leaves*, 15 (Winter 1954), 17)

The division of opinion cut across both language communities, however. On the Welsh side, Aneirin Talfan Davies (he was head of Welsh radio) wrote a book about Dylan as a great religious poet; and Euros Bowen wrote an *englyn* which shows him responding to Dylan's magic:

> Cynaeafodd frig cynefin y gerdd
>    Nes troi'n goch ei ddeufin;
>    Gwirionodd ar y grawnwin
>    Nes syrthio'n feddw. – Gweddw yw'r gwin.

> (He harvested the poem's familiar tip
>    Till his two lips were red;
>    Doted on the grapes till, drunken,
>    He fell dead, widowed the wine.)

(Cerddi, 129)

In English-speaking Wales, besides the enthusiasm of poets like Gwyn Jones, Vernon Watkins, John Ormond and Harri Jones, there was also a considerable body of opinion that really couldn't take Dylan's poetry at all. Harri Webb thought it was all rather nasty and its obsession with sex thoroughly un-Welsh. Harri was a founder member of the Welsh Republican Party, and later the editor of the Plaid Cymru magazine, *The Welsh Nation*. Like so many radical and nationalist idealists, he wanted to purify his country of foreign garbage – lust, as opposed to alcohol, was an Anglo-American import we could do without!

A more interesting case is Roland Mathias, born the year after Dylan Thomas, but lacking completely his astounding precocity as a poet. Mathias is a man who embodies much that is fine in the Nonconformist tradition. His life can be seen as a long struggle against deracination, trying to recover and justify a Welshness he almost lost as a child. Mathias obviously loathed Dylan's early work. He says: 'His poetry was inchoate, suffocatingly romantic and obscure, reflecting very little of what might be called objective life and background experience in the community to which he nominally belonged' (*A Ride through the Wood*, 64-5).

'Romantic' is being used by both Pennar Davies and Mathias as a reach-me-down term of abuse. What does it mean? Presumably, in a literary context, poetry that resembles the work of the Romantic Movement, by writers such as Blake, Wordsworth, Shelley and Keats: writers who made a hero of the individual imagination. It is a poetry alternating between dejection, when your imagination is dead and trapped inside you, and what Wordsworth called 'that serene and blessed mood' when it comes alive and reaches out to the world; just as the Ancient

Mariner alternates between the horror of the dead men on the deck and the heaven-sent release of the blessing of the water-snakes. The great epic is *The Prelude* – the poem on the growth of the poet's mind. Romantic poetry is full of what 'I' felt, what 'I' thought or saw or heard.

And certainly, Dylan's *18 Poems* are full of 'I'. 'If I were tickled by the rub of love' . . . or 'I sent my creature scouting on the globe' . . . or 'As yet ungotten I did suffer'. It is what this 'I' implies that is different. In a typical Romantic lyric, 'The Highland reaper' or the 'Ode to a nightingale', we know where we are. The poet is in a specific place doing or experiencing specific things, walking in the Scottish highlands or sitting in his London garden. The moment of blessing, the moment when the imagination reaches out to the truth in things, exists in the context of history. But in *18 Poems* this is not so. You really have to search hard to find any reference at all to Dylan's actual situation in Swansea. The 'I' seems to have no history, no location in place or time. In Rimbaud's words, 'JE est un autre' – 'I is someone else' – the 'I' of the symbolists, the *voyant* or 'see-er' of Rimbaud and Verlaine. Walford Davies's essay 'The wanton starer'[1] shows how Dylan would often start by setting a poem in a fairly specific locale and then, in revision, make it more abstract and elusive as the 'wanton starer' himself, the 'I' of the poem, became more generalized:

> Am I not father, too, and the ascending boy,
> The boy of woman and the wanton starer . . .
> Am I not all of you by the directed sea?

The great exemplar of this 'I' in English is Tiresias in T. S. Eliot's 'The waste land'. Eliot tells us in his notes that 'what Tiresias *sees*, in fact, is the substance of the poem':

> I Tiresias, though blind, throbbing between two lives,
> Old man with wrinkled female dugs, can see . . .

Tiresias *can* see because he is not bound by history:

> And I Tiresias have foresuffered all
> Enacted on this same divan or bed;
> I who have sat by Thebes below the wall
> And walked among the lowest of the dead.

---

[1] In Walford Davies (ed.), *Dylan Thomas: New Critical Essays* (London: Dent, 1972), 136–65.

One of the things *18 Poems* do, following Eliot's lead, is to take the tragic soliloquy that was one of the great formal discoveries of Elizabethan drama and fill it with this kind of symbolist 'I who is someone else'.

The best of *18 Poems* are tragic poetry such as English had not known since the seventeenth century. But they are tragic in a vacuum. They don't have a play called *The Tragedy of Hamlet Prince of Denmark* to tell us what they're about. They speak out of the I who is someone else. They express a sensibility, caught between two wars, stripped of ideological comforts and waiting to be ground into Flanders mud or Coventry blitz. The only certain things are bodily existence and its answering state of mind, the creativity of a poet; and they are both threatened by the 'gallows and the axe / And the crossed sticks of war'.

*18 Poems* are the least Romantic of modern poetry. But when Dylan Thomas had written them, he had nowhere to go next. There wasn't a tragic theatre that could have used such vision. Slowly and with great awkwardness, he tried to make this tragic poetry of his, his 'mighty line' as we say of Marlowe, into an instrument to express his own feelings. He tried to pretend that this 'I who is someone else' had a history, a biography that coincided at certain points with his own. He tried to write narrative. The result – apart from the wholesale refurbishing of poems he'd written before *18 Poems* – was the turgid verbiage of the poems to Caitlin, poems on his own career as a poet, poems on his childhood – even, I would say, the poems on the London blitz. It wasn't until the middle forties that he achieved anything like the luminous clarity of a great artist again. And once more, it was the example of T. S. Eliot, this time in *Four Quartets*, that pointed the way:

> Sudden in a shaft of sunlight
> Even while the dust moves
> There rises the hidden laughter
> Of children in the foliage
> Quick now, here, now, always –
>
> ('Burnt Norton')

The coinherence of past and present was used by Eliot for visionary ends. In 'East Coker', 'if you do not come too close', you can hear the revelry of long-ago peasants in the fields. For Eliot that was a manifestation of a spiritual economy 'pointing to one end which is always present'. But for Dylan Thomas, coinherence like this was a release from the pressures of the present:

> Listen. The minstrels sing
> In the departed villages. The nightingale,
> Dust in the buried wood, flies on the grains of her wings
> And spells on the winds of the dead his winter's tale.

That is, it released him into fantasy as in 'A winter's tale' or into childhood as in 'Fern Hill'. It led to elegy, but elegy of a very peculiar sort, in which, as in 'Poem in October' the 'weather turns around' and the lost world comes alive again in a kind of bifocal vision. Because the whole process is a metaphor for how he sees the world, it enables him to introduce a certain amount of his own personal biography into his poetry: that is, it solves the technical problem of writing about himself in the style appropriate to the tragic 'I who is someone else'. The price he pays is a slackening of intensity and the softening of tragic vision. Elegy is an easier and less demanding medium than tragedy, and these poems have always been among his most popular.


To get back to the Anglo-Welsh. In the sixties the tide of Dylanism was ebbing fast. A much simpler relation to everyday experience was demanded of poets. The novel, not the tragic drama, dominated literary sensibility. Beginning in the late sixties, our poems often seem no more than fragments of documentary fiction or highbrow journalism. If I may exaggerate a little for the sake of clarity, poets nowadays are like representational painters, they assume that the world of commonsense exists and is the only reality, and their job is to describe the bits of it that have significance for them.

There is no doubt that this plain speaking and 'back to basics' was a release for such major Anglo-Welsh poets as Dannie Abse and John Ormond (1923–90). Neither succumbed to the sterile pseudo-classicism of the 'Movement', but both equally abandoned the high metaphorical style of Dylan Thomas – Abse fairly quickly, John Ormond not till the middle sixties. As the culmination of his early poetry, in 1948–52 Ormond wrote a long sequence 'City in fire and snow', in memory of Swansea destroyed in the blitz. As Randall Jenkins said in *Poetry Wales*,

> This poem is a sort of protracted debate about the moral dilemma posed by the destructive power of the atom bomb. It is written in an elaborately literary style in which the images have so heavy and vague a symbolic load to carry that its narrative development is confused and obscure. (*Poetry Wales*, VIII, 1 (1972), 20)

'City in fire and snow' is the last major attempt by a younger Anglo-Welsh poet to respond to his or her time in the tragic mode of Dylan Thomas. Thomas was still alive, of course; and the poem's style has quite a lot of Dylanism about it. You can exaggerate how much – the traces of Vernon Watkins seem to me just as significant – but there is no doubt of the stance. Jenkins calls it 'elaborately literary', but I would see it as high tragedy;

> She stood with the wings of the cold
> Spread over her, the air antlered
> And hung with the lights of his long
> Love stars, each nailed in its own north.
> She moved as he approached, knelt down
>
> And then in silence
> Lay to lie for me and his love,
> Postured and praising in the white
> Roses of winter's enormous bridals
> Of the children of the ghost
> And the frost of spent stars.

It is beautiful, but as Jenkins implies, it doesn't work. Partly the atom bomb is too big for tragedy; but also John Ormond was not really a tragedian. He had to find himself as a successful journalist and a television director before he could have enough confidence in his vision to become his own man, the poet that he really was.

When the real Ormond emerged in 'Cathedral builders' it was with the satisfaction of a butterfly emerging at last from the constraints of a chrysalis. You remember how the stonemason looks up at the great cathedral he has made, now full of the pomp of bishops who are ignoring him; how he cocks his eye at it and says with defiant pride: 'I bloody did that.' It wasn't only the mason who found his proper place in that remark, it was Ormond himself. 'I bloody did that' is not something you can say in a Dylan Thomas world – not because of the swearword of course but because of the conscious achievement as an end in itself. Tragedy never says, 'I bloody did that.' 'I have done the state some service', says Othello at the end; but what does it matter? He knows it counts for nothing compared with the murdered Desdemona on the bed.

A few months before he died, I wrote to John to congratulate him on his *Selected Poems*. I told him I thought he was the finest love-poet we'd had in Wales since Dafydd ap Gwilym; nor is love-poetry the only thing he has in common with Dafydd. There's a comic bravura, for one thing:

My wife tells me I snore. The night long
(To me it's hearsay, having been elsewhere)
She has played at in-and-out-the-windows
Of her poor sleep's tenement while I all industry
Felled an adjacent forest with my chainsaw.

('Elsewhere')

There's a sense of sadness and loss in the face of mortality, a love of the good life, a strong empathy with other of God's creatures, and a love, also, of human achievements. 'I bloody did that' is not something I can imagine Dafydd ap Gwilym saying, but it seems a lot closer to him than it ever was to Dylan.

It seems fitting, somehow, that the last-written of all the hundreds of elegies to Dylan Thomas should be by John Ormond. He published 'A section of an elegy' – all that ever appeared of it in the special Dylan Thomas number of *Poetry Wales* in Autumn 1973. Perhaps he wrote it for that issue. Twenty years may seem a long time for a poor dead man to wait for his elegy; but poets are like that. Roger Garfitt was still writing his poem for my wedding fourteen years after it happened! Twenty years; but what John Ormond's poem so affectionately exorcizes is not the poet Dylan Thomas, the lyric tragedian who had so greatly influenced his own poetry for so long. Indeed, if you didn't know who it was for, you couldn't swear it was about a poet at all. No, Dylan is transposed into the common, fanciful light of day, essentially the sphere of comedy and fiction. Essentially, also, the sphere of John Ormond's mature imagination. It is Dylan's humanity, not his poetic genius, that is remembered and mourned; and yet it is not quite true that the poet is forgotten. Phrases like 'a cigarette stuck to your lip like a white syllable' or the 'tried thesaurus of laughter' are not innocent: the poet's there all right, but Dylan now is part of John Ormond's creation, not John Ormond part of Dylan's. 'I bloody did that', so to speak.

### Section from an elegy

Dear drinking friend of the public bar,
For twenty years you have been alone
Without a drop in the black parlour.

You slipped away as though to place
A nimble shilling on a certainty
(One of your golden horses with three legs),

Not bothering to return. We loitered
In snug company. Jibbing the slow crawl home,
You went ahead, forgot the bitter barrel.

But you – to whom an hour, a day, a month late
Were the same – would surely reappear
To take up the tall tale where it faltered.

Half your dead lifetime later I still mourned,
Still half-expected you. Any next day, please God,
You would stand in the corner, your glass raised,

Your head flung back, a cigarette stuck
To your lip like a white syllable, removed
Only to quaff or cough or for the defiant

Steeplejack raids into your tried thesaurus
Of laughter; with that badly drawn Rubens hand
(Under the bookie's suit, your shirt-cuff

To your knuckle) yet conduct the concert's
Spendthrift conceits from most improbable
Beginnings to more improbable ends

Which could never come to grief. Yet through
Those broken teeth there could slip, too,
The muttered treacheries against yourself

And the grave misgivings and the murmured
Bad debts of breath. Dear ruinous deserter,
Death, old familiar, wintered in your blood.

Now you have stayed away too long below
At silent paternosters in deep dirt.
We shall not meet again to bend the elbow.

Of course by the time he wrote this elegy – by the time he wrote
'Cathedral builders' – Anglo-Welsh poetry had a new centre of gravity,
as alien to Abse and Ormond as it was to Dylan Thomas himself. For
with the death of Vernon Watkins in 1967 the last of Dylan's peers had
gone. There was no one to dispute the pre-eminence of the Revd R. S.
Thomas as the fashioner of the new Anglo-Welsh sensibility, nationalist,
seeking a rapprochement with Welsh-speaking Wales, disdainful of the
London Welsh and all they stood for. To the more extreme followers of
R.S., Dylan Thomas has often seemed little more than a traitor, or at
best an irrelevance.

# 13

## *The new frontier:*
## *R. S. Thomas*

~

Glyn Jones and Vernon Watkins were close friends of Dylan Thomas and were intimately involved in the movement associated with Keidrych Rhys's magazine, *Wales*. Roland Mathias, though he was published in *Wales* and in Keidrych's Faber anthology, seems more hostile to what it stood for, suspicious alike of the precocious adolescence of Dylan Thomas and the showmanship of Keidrych Rhys. He was more impressed, clearly, with Alun Lewis and Vernon Watkins.

The relation of the fourth and greatest of the 'survivors', R. S. Thomas, to the *Wales* group is more problematic. Keidrych published his first book, *Stones of the Field*, in his Druid Press at Carmarthen. R.S. contributed both criticism and poetry to *Wales* and was of course represented in the anthology. When Hart-Davis published his first comprehensive London collection with John Betjeman's introduction, *Song at the Year's Turning*, it took its title and that of its title-poem, presumably, from Dylan Thomas's 'Poem in October':

> O may my heart's truth
> Still be sung
> On this high hill in a year's turning.

The implications of that quotation have not, as far as I know, been noticed.

There was considerable respect, then, for R. S. Thomas as a new force in Anglo-Welsh poetry; and on his part a readiness to explore his relationship to other Anglo-Welsh poets. He was looking for something to join, a social and cultural base to confirm him in his role as both a passionate Welshman and an English poet. On the other hand, he was an Anglican cleric, a north Walian and not obviously interested in modernism.[1] In all those ways he was a contrast and an object of some bafflement to his free-wheeling, south Walian and would-be modernist confrères. He visited Keidrych and Lynette in September 1945. Lynette's letter to Robert Graves shows her suspicious of him – I don't think she liked him much:

> A young minister & poet has been here. A gloomy sort of person – who like most intelligent ministers today doesn't believe in the church that he preaches. It is the people far more than 'they' who have the conviction – & wish to join in communative praise, or prayer – But *not 'them'* – the yg ministers, who have the courage – guts – to alter & set the old time stage of religion to modern conditions. They are bastards & I am 4 square behind you in this matter. He is R. S. Thomas & has gone to St Davids with Keidrych with the idea of rambling & enjoying the countryside of Pembroke which he does not know. (*Poetry Wales*, 19, 2, p.92)

This vignette of the young R.S. in Keidrych country shows us that Lynette Roberts pin-pointed in him a lack of conviction and a failure to follow through his belief – a criticism which now he would probably endorse himself. When you first read it, it looks as though she's saying that it is the young ministers who have the courage to adapt Christianity to modern life; but that is wrong. It is the people, not 'they', who have the guts, because it is the people who desire communion in worship. The passage is interesting about R. S. Thomas, but it also throws light on Lynette's subsequent conversion to the Jehovah's Witnesses.

Lynette Roberts was right to be on her guard, for with R. S. Thomas the Anglo-Welsh were to be frog-marched on to quite a different frontier. So far we've had Anglo-Welsh of the *buchedd*, the way of life of the peculiar social alliance of nineteenth-century Wales, as it declined and broke up under the hammer blows of industrial strife and economic Depression; and we've had modernism, an assertion of the right of a middle-class English-speaking intelligentsia to express its schizoid and international sensibility in the age of limited liability, regardless of whether *buchedd* culture could comprehend it. The frontier between *buchedd*-sensibility and modernism is of course reflected in Welsh-speaking culture also, for example, in the disputes over 'dark' or obscure poetry that continually haunted eisteddfod adjudications.

---

[1] Though that last point is misleading: probably the poets of the twentieth century who have influenced him most have been Yeats, Eliot, Wallace Stevens and William Carlos Williams, all of them highly regarded by modernists.

That was one Anglo-Welsh frontier: another was between modern, Anglicized, provincial Wales and the old civilization, the *traddodiad* as we've called it, which was *sui generis*, a sister civilization not merely of Irish in the far west but of the Byzantine world and even of our own: all four having arisen out of the fall of Graeco-Roman civilization in the early Dark Ages. This second Anglo-Welsh frontier is also part of a wider area of renaissance within Welsh life as a whole. Hopkins, Ernest Rhys, David Jones and Gwyn Williams the translator are Anglo-Welsh primarily because of this frontier; but in Welsh-speaking Wales you would have to think of poets and scholars like John Morris-Jones, T. Gwynn Jones and Ifor Williams.

The two frontiers of *buchedd* and *traddodiad* are related, as the example of Gwyn Williams the translator shows. Reviving the *traddodiad* was in fact largely an attempt by the new middle class to escape from the claustrophobia of the *buchedd* into something larger and less puritanical. It can be compared to the modernism of Ezra Pound, for example, with its constant search in Provençal, Anglo-Saxon or Chinese traditions for a true poetic escape from the *Golden Treasury* consensus.

With R. S. Thomas a third Anglo-Welsh frontier, that of *iaith* or language, starts to dominate all others. Again, we use the Welsh word as a technical term: for *iaith* stands much more for an ideology than simply a language. Saunders Lewis had set his face against industrialization as the prime destroyer of Wales. Rural Wales, the heartland of the Welsh language, was where Welsh virtue lay; and rural Wales was in ruins, or nearly so. As Tony Bianchi has shown, R. S. Thomas in his early poems was 'the first Anglo-Welsh poet successfully to interpellate his English-speaking readership within the discourse of cultural nationalism', and in so doing earned the respect of the new, relatively powerful and cohesive Welsh-speaking middle class who adopted him as an 'honorary white'. He wrote bitter poetry about Wales:

> There is no present in Wales
> And no future:
> There is only the past,
> Brittle with relics,
> Wind-bitten towers and castles
> With sham ghosts;
> Mouldering quarries and mines;
> And an impotent people,
> Sick with inbreeding,
> Worrying the carcase of an old song.          ('Welsh landcape')

He was ambivalent about Iago Prytherch, his archetypal peasant, both an object of disgust – 'there is something frightening in the vacancy of his mind' – and yet a source of age-old strength and hope for the future:

> Yet this man can teach
> Even as an oak tree when its leaves are shed,
> More in old silence than in youthful song.

('Man and tree')

Above all, perhaps, in his sense of linguistic and cultural deprivation:

> England, what have you done to make the speech
> My fathers used a stranger at my lips –

('The old language')

he was like a photographic negative of what was being felt and expressed time after time in the poetry of Welsh-speaking Wales. Saunders Lewis's lecture on the fate of the language was the catalyst that mobilized this feeling into political action and resistance; but Saunders Lewis was himself too much of an outsider to be its poet. It was Waldo Williams (1904–71), the pacifist from Pembrokeshire – whose first language, ironically, was English, but who had learnt Welsh as a boy and was thoroughly a part of Welsh rural life – who became the laureate of the *iaith*:

### Yr heniaith

> Disglair yw eu coronau yn llewych llysoedd
> A thanynt hwythau. Ond nid harddach na hon
> Sydd yn crwydro gan ymwrando â lleisiau
> A'r ddisberod o'i gwrogaeth hen;
> Ac sydd yn holi pa yfori a fydd,
> Holi yng nghyrn y gorllewinwynt heno –
> Udo gyddfau'r tyllau a'r ogofâu
> Dros y rhai sy'n annheilwng o hon.
>
> Ni sylwem arni. Hi oedd y goleuni, heb liw.
> Ni sylwem arni, yr awyr a ddaliai'r arogl
> I'n ffroenau. Dwfr ein genau, goleuni blas.
> Ni chlywem ei breichiau am ei bro ddi-berygl
> Ond mae tir ni ddring ehedydd yn ol i'w nen,
> Rhyw ddoe dihiraeth a'u gwahanodd.
> Hyn yw gaeaf cenedl, y galon oer
> Heb wybod colli ei phum llawenydd.

Na! dychwel gwanwyn i un a noddai
Ddeffrowyr cenhedloedd cyn eu haf.
Hael y tywalltai ei gwin iddynt.
Codent o'i byrddau dros bob hardd yn hyf.
Nyni, a wêl ei hurddas trwy niwl ei hadfyd,
Codwn, yma yr hen feini annistryw.
Pwy yw'r rhain trwy'r cwmwl a'r haul yn hedfan,
Yn dyfod fel colomennod i'w ffenestri?

(The old language

Their crowns are radiant in the bright courts,
And they beneath them. But no lovelier than she
Who's a wanderer now, listening to voices
That have slipped their old fealty.
She asks herself what tomorrow there'll be,
Asks it in the teeth of the west wind –
In the throats of caves and crevices moaning
Over those unworthy of her.

We never noticed her. She was like light, she had no colour.
We never noticed. She was the air, took smell
To our nostrils. Was water on our lips, the light of taste.
We were not conscious of her arms round the land.
No danger then. Now, it's where larks
Do not climb back to heaven,
Some unwished yesterday has parted them.
This is the winter of the nation, the cold heart
Does not know its five joys are lost.

No! spring will return to her, who fostered
Before their summer, the generation-awakeners.
Generously she poured out her wine for them.
They rose from her tables bold for all beauty.
We that perceive her rank, through the mist of her troubles,
Let's raise here the old, indestructible stones.
Who are these flying through cloud and sun
Like doves to her windows?)

The Welsh language had to be defended against its enemies, because it was the embodiment of the good life:

Fy Nghymru, a bro brawdoliaeth, fy nghri, fy nghrefydd,
Unig falm i fyd, ei chenhadaeth, ei her,
Perl yr anfeidrol awr yn wystl gan amser,
Gobaith yr yrfa faith ar a drofa fer.

Hon oedd fy ffenestr, y cynaeafu a'r cneifio.
Mi welais drefn yn fy mhalas draw.
Mae rhu, mae rhaib drwy'r fforest ddiffenestr.
Cadwn y mur rhag y bwystfil, cadwn y ffynnon rhag y baw.

('Preseli')

(My Wales, brotherhood's country, my cry, my creed,
Only balm to the world, its mission, its challenge,
Pearl of the infinite hour that time gives as pledge,
Hope of the tedious race on the short winding way.

It was my window, the harvest and the shearing.
I glimpsed order in my palace there.
There's a roar, there's a ravening through the windowless forests.
Keep the wall from the brute, keep the spring clear of filth.)

If we go back to R. S. Thomas's early books, the dominant models seem ultimately to have been Wordsworthian – the blank verse visionary descriptions which were included in *The Prelude*, the blank verse narrative such as 'Michael', or the sonnet as a form of social or cultural commentary. I am not referring to the metrical form of the poems, but rather the way one would set about writing them. 'Emotion recollected in tranquillity' – of a sort – is part of the apparatus. (The same models are probably behind a good deal of Alun Lewis's work, particularly the poems he wrote in India.) The models, therefore, are empiricist in origin: they reflect on experience, on sense-experience, with a scientist's faith in his experiment that it is there that the answer lies. Wordsworth devised or refurbished these forms for himself in a period of acute political and psychological crisis, the aftermath of the French Revolution and what that entailed in his biography. The three forms progressively represent three stages, in fact, of cooling down towards the awful dead weight of his later years. Wordsworthian models are a psychological equivalent of the Big Bang theory of cosmology. You start with an explosion so awful it blows you apart; then gradually you start looking around you, the stars condense out of chaos, the planets form, and finally, there you are again, an old man pontificating. But the point is, it is in the looking around you and reflecting on what you see, that poems come. They, quite as much as scientific theories, are part of the cooling process towards knowledge.

It was almost to be expected that Wordsworthian models should be sought by Welshmen writing English poetry at that time. First the breakup of Welsh social patterns in the Depression; then the emergence of loneliness and guilt as the middle class separated out of the *buchedd* culture; and third, the progressive Anglicization of education; when we add the crisis of world war, what we have is a Big Bang comparable at least to that of the French Revolution. What is more, the English poets most studied in Wales at that time were the Romantics, and particularly Wordsworth and Coleridge, who seemed to speak most directly to Welsh experience:

> But Wordsworth, looking in the lake
> of his mind, him I could take.
>
> (Collected Poems (London: Dent, 1993), 284)

Perhaps I should illustrate the sort of poem I refer to as built on Wordsworthian models. The famous introduction to Iago Prytherch, 'A peasant', will do for a start. It begins with what purports to be a straight description of Prytherch at work:

> Docking mangels, chipping the green skin
> From the yellow bones with a half-witted grin . . .

And the poet's bafflement before him – 'There is something frightening in the vacancy of his mind.' This is to be compared with many Wordsworthian descriptions of old men, as in 'Old man travelling' or 'The old Cumberland beggar' or the end of 'Michael' who 'never lifted up a single stone'. The poet's gaze is 'compelled' by such a figure, and he seems to question him eagerly, as Wordsworth did the leech gatherer on the lonely moor, because he feels that there lies the answer. 'This is your prototype', he tells himself, who 'preserves his stock . . .'

> a winner of wars,
> Enduring like a tree under the curious stars.

But R. S. Thomas, fortunately for us, was not allowed simply to endure like a tree. His early work may not be as big a thing as Wordsworth's but his later poetry has nothing in common with the dead weight of that master's last thirty or forty years. He was saved by two things which presented themselves to him as problems: first, by his faith in things that were not susceptible to empirical analysis – God, Christ, goodness and Wales amongst others; and second, by his growing awareness of a crisis in empiricism itself, particularly in scientific thinking.

Let me illustrate the first problem with a poem from *Poetry for Supper* (1958):

### The country clergy

I see them working in old rectories
By the sun's light, by candlelight,
Venerable men, their black cloth
A little dusty, a little green
With holy mildew. And yet their skulls,
Ripening over so many prayers,
Toppled into the same grave
With oafs and yokels. They left no books,
Memorial to their lonely thought
In grey parishes; rather they wrote
On men's hearts and in the minds
Of young children sublime words
Too soon forgotten. God in his time
Or out of time will correct this.

It is surely a very bad poem, because it has not made up its mind what kind of poem it is. It starts as a pure piece of faintly sardonic empiricism – 'I see them . . .' On this empirical level their life is a failure. For all their prayers and learning they topple to the same grave as yokels. Even their one achievement, writing sublime words 'on men's hearts and in the minds of young children' – and it would be interesting to know what R. S. Thomas meant by this dichotomy between adult hearts and children's minds – is 'too soon forgotten'. Surely you don't *forget* things written on the heart – isn't writing a metaphor for 'causing to remember'? The figure of speech is clashing with its own significance. But perhaps 'too soon forgotten' does not refer to the writing, but to the 'sublime words' themselves. The poet has stopped thinking of the country clergy and is indulging himself in a lament over the decay of Christian culture.

These are incidental faults, but the last line and a half must surely be seen, in the empirical logic of the poem, as far more than that, a perfunctory bit of wishful thinking, totally unprepared for, that destroys any integrity the poem might have had. It is no accident that *Poetry for Supper* as a volume is largely concerned with mapping various poetic strategies since, as we see here, the Wordsworthian empiricism and 're-creation' of a situation under the pressure of 'emotion recollected in tranquillity' were quite obviously not coping with what he wanted to say. No amount of searching into the depths of experience will prove the

Trinity or the God-man personality of Christ or the meaning of 'This is my body'. Nor, similarly, will it allow a loyalty to something called 'Wales' that is embodied nowhere in particular (like Abercuawg) and yet is not simply an abstract idea.

This failure would not by itself have saved him from 'enduring like a tree', like Wordsworth, into a garrulous but poetically null old age. 'Country clergy' could have become representative of the poet's decline, as an unresolved struggle between empiricism and his religious beliefs froze the growing point of his mind.

To misquote R. S. Thomas's line, however, the stars themselves were too curious for the tree in him to endure as 'a winner of wars'. One of the striking things about science in our time is its total absurdity from an observer's point of view. To observe something has become a catastrophe. It changes the world to the extent that what is observed is quite a different situation to what is not. In physics, the Indeterminacy Principle, whereby if you measure the location of a particle you cannot, *in principle*, know its velocity; and if you measure its velocity, you cannot know where it is. In cosmology, the theory of Relativity. In biology, the growing realization that we are ourselves a part of the ecosystem and there is no outside laboratory from which to observe it. In psychology, the implications of 'transference' whereby, in order to diagnose a mentally sick person, you have to enter into a relationship with him or her which drastically changes the diagnosis.

Above all, the dominance of mathematics in our scientific culture has rendered an empirical stance in a poet simply a badge of suburbia. When I did pure mathematics in the sixth form, it gave me a wonderful feeling for the usefulness of the absurd. You could take a number that cannot possibly exist, like the square root of minus one, and use it as a tool to explore real problems like the relation of time and space. It is no accident that when a mathematician came to write a literary masterpiece, the result should be *Alice in Wonderland*.

So, at the end of *Song at the Year's Turning*, R. S. Thomas in 'No through road' confesses his failure as a Wordsworthian 'nature poet':

> All in vain. I will cease now
> My long absorption with the plough,
> With the tame and wild creatures
> And man united with the earth.
> I have failed after many seasons

To bring truth to birth,
And nature's simple equations
In the mind's precincts do not apply.

But where to turn? Earth endures
After the passing, necessary shame
Of winter, and the old lie
Of green places beckons me still
From the new world, ugly and evil,
That men pry for in truth's name.

(p. 68)

That's what it felt like in 1955. One must be careful not to exaggerate the extent of R. S. Thomas's interest in science. Up to *H'm* (1972), certainly, though scientific terminology gradually increases – 'virus', 'molecules', 'nucleus' and so on – it is little more than any reader of the *Guardian* might pick up at a cursory reading. The references are nearly always hostile – part of what Wynn Thomas describes as the poet's 'black-fly syndrome', quoting from *Y Llwybrau Gynt*:

> I bend over to sniff one of the flowers – but something nasty is waiting for me there! Quick as a flash it's up my nose, and I start to scream. My mother rushes over to me, scared out of her wits. After I have blown my nose like a dragon into her handkerchief, the enemy is revealed: a harmless little black fly! But I remember the experience to this day, and I still take great care when smelling a flower. (Translated by M. Wynn Thomas, *Internal Difference* (1992), 107)

Even in that fine poem, 'The moon in Lleyn' from *Laboratories of the Spirit*, I am not sure he understands the difference between the normal waxing and waning of the moon and a lunar eclipse. For most of the time he talks as though it was a question of the old moon giving place to darkness and then to the new moon again. Then he suddenly says,

> Even as this moon
> making its way through the earth's
> cumbersome shadow, prayer, too,
> has its phases –

where earth's shadow refers to an eclipse, but 'phases' can only refer to the normal cycle, which has nothing to do with earth's shadow but simply to the body of the moon itself hiding from us the sun's reflected light on its further surface. An eclipse always takes place when the moon is full.

197

One has to take the poet's scientific learning, therefore, with a pinch of salt. Even so, it is certainly present as an atmosphere, even as an ideal or a metaphor for positive things – as the title, *Laboratories of the Spirit* indicates. I think he probably realized both that science told us something about a God who delights in form and number, that science (as opposed to technology – 'the machine') was a useful tool for a poet, and that science, and particularly mathematics, was a kind of game. R. S. Thomas is full of tricksiness, and a good deal of his poetry occupies a *Through the Looking-Glass* world, with God playing a kind of zany chess with mankind.

One of the first symptoms of escape from the dead weight of empiricism in R. S. Thomas's poetry is a sudden proliferation of different perspectives and points of view – some of them quite remarkably far-fetched. When we remember Iago Prytherch's vacant gobbing into the fire, it is startling to find him asked out of the blue,

> You never heard of Kant, did you, Prytherch?
> A strange man!
>
> ('Green categories')

The element of dry wit, for which R.S. is famous in Wales, becomes a lever to shift poetry into dramatic confrontation:

> Who put that crease in your soul,
> Davies . . .
>
> ('Chapel deacon')

Frequently he talks about himself in the third person (as in *Neb*) with an effect of looking through mirrors reflecting backwards and forwards to infinity. Whereas the dominant literature of empiricism has always been the novel, now dramatic lyric is the order of the day. His poems talk to specific individuals, whether or not imaginary ones; and specific individuals talk back. For a poet who has never shown the slightest dramatic gift or inclination to write plays, this dominance of his poetry by dramatic speech is remarkable in itself. Drama is the art-form *par excellence* that empiricism is very bad at.

These transitional pieces are often stylistically unsatisfactory. The Davies poem, 'Chapel Deacon', after its vernacular opening goes into typical early R.S. top gear with lots of spondaic, usually adjective-plus-noun blocks:

Who put that crease in your soul,
Davies, ready this fine morning
For the staid chapel, where the Book's frown
Sobers the sunlight.

The vigour of confrontation is being wasted in the poet's determination to load every rift with ore. It is one thing to do this in a descriptive piece, quite another in dramatic speech. One understands his need to refashion his language in the direction of ordinary speech – the influence of William Carlos Williams was timely enough.

One cannot overestimate, I think, the release that dramatic confrontation – with other people, with himself and with a constantly elusive God – gave to his poetry. Coupled with the game-like model he derived from science, it made possible an œuvre where every poem is a new departure, every situation a different set of configurings. Instead of the heavy presence of the Wordsworthian suffering observer of the early work, you get an always changing, shimmering, 'tricksy' poetry, however grim in its import, that constantly yields new perspectives. Poems contradict one another – it is part of his greatness.

Brian Cox is quoted in the blurb as saying, 'His poetry uncompromisingly records the shifting moods of the believer, the moments of spiritual sterility as well as of epiphany.' The two words to which I would take exception here are 'records' and 'moods'. Does a Hamlet soliloquy 'record' a mood of Shakespeare's mind? The English empiricist fails to come to terms with genuine poetic creation, in all its drama and suddenness. It cannot see religion as anything other than a kind of 'experience' which is probably fallacious anyway. R. S. Thomas's poetry reminds us that real life is not just a sorting office where the ego delves into its sense data to build up a total pattern. Real life is made up of moments of confrontation, minute by minute changing, waiting for something to happen, absence as well as touch, nothingness as much as conscious understanding.

# 14

## *Roland Mathias:*
## *headmaster, critic and poet*

~

Roland Mathias was born in 1915 in Talybont-on-Usk, in what is now Powys, but he left Wales when he was four and did not live there again until he got a teaching post in Pembroke Dock in 1948. Both his parents were from Wales – his father Welsh-speaking from Carmarthenshire, his mother a monoglot English-speaker from Brecon. Though he admired his father, who was an Army chaplain, it was his mother's lead he followed in becoming a pacifist; and because he lived so much outside Wales he never learnt the Welsh language. But his nostalgia for things Welsh is palpable. He was the co-founder with Raymond Garlick of *Dock Leaves*, later *The Anglo-Welsh Review*, and when Garlick left to teach in the Netherlands he edited it for many years from Derbyshire and Birmingham where he was a headmaster, and then, after his retirement in 1969, from Brecon.

Roland Mathias is the only considerable Anglo-Welsh writer born before 1920 to have ventured into critical exposition on any scale, apart from Glyn Jones whose work must now be seen as introductory, emphasizing the possibility and existence of Anglo-Welsh literature rather than its moral and philosophical implications. Mathias belongs by birth to the generation of Dylan and R. S. Thomas, Alun Lewis and Emyr Humphreys; Caradoc Evans, Gwyn Jones, Rhys Davies, David Jones and Vernon Watkins were (or are) his older contemporaries. Although his significant criticism deals almost entirely with these two groups, it does not arise out of their work directly; rather its preoccupations are those of a subsequent generation, the Anglo-Welsh writers born in the twenties and thirties who mainly surfaced in the sixties and are associated with the first issues of *Poetry Wales*. Mathias as a critic is concerned with establishing a tradition. The writers he is interested in were those who, for whatever reason, had left Welsh Wales behind them but still carried the mark of the pariah, the W. N. of the Welsh not, as a badge of office into English-language culture. Hence his sometimes over-anxious apologies for his subjects' (and his own) lack of Welsh. Hence his later despair that Anglo-Welsh culture and his own poetic tradition were dying as the Anglicization of Wales moved into its final phase.

Apart from uncollected articles and reviews and a monograph on Cowper Powys's poetry, his major contribution to criticism is contained in two books, the Writers of Wales volume on Vernon Watkins (1974) and his selected essays, *A Ride through the Wood* (1985). The later *Anglo-Welsh Literature: An Illustrated History* (1987) is mainly of antiquarian interest, a catalogue that oscillates between the perfunctory and the quaint. He had not the gift of a good literary historian who can sum up the significance of a writer's work without foreclosing on its value. His very real critical intelligence requires a great deal of space before it starts to show returns.

Mathias brought to criticism experience and skills unusual in these days of academic specialization. He is the son of an army chaplain who nevertheless went to prison for his pacifist beliefs. He is profoundly Christian and Nonconformist. He is a historical scholar by training. Until 1969 he was a schoolteacher and headmaster. Each of these lives, Nonconformist, scholar and headmaster, contributes to *A Ride through the Wood* at every turn. This note from the essay on David Jones will illustrate the headteacher's insight:

> A surprisingly high proportion of secondary schoolboys seen voluntarily square-bashing in the CCF after school hours used to belong (if they do so no longer) to the category of those who, as a result of serious 'spoiling' at home, were incapable of hard or consistent work at their academic studies.

To connect that 'surprise' with David Jones, incapable of prescribed academic work yet yearning for order, discipline, *imperium* and Rome, is surely proof of critical intelligence; but the sensibility to children's problems has been acquired the hard way, in the classroom and the community. Mathias usually looks closely at a writer's upbringing. Most critics do it perfunctorily, but with Mathias it leads directly into his most profound insights.

Perhaps the triumph of this approach is the masterly essay on David Jones, who must surely represent a Blakean 'contrary' to him. Jones was an artist incapable of any other career, Mathias a successful headmaster who even in his retirement was until recently a man of affairs, a member of committees. Jones lived as a hermit, who actually feared working-class Welsh people, while Mathias is a sociable man, remembering his childhood holidays in the Rhondda with affection. Jones was a soldier in the trenches; Mathias went to prison for his pacifist beliefs. Jones was a convert to Catholicism, attracted by its ritual and metaphysics; Mathias a lifelong Protestant, heir of the puritans. Jones was tempted by Fascism, looking for authority, while Mathias is a democrat to the bone. For David Jones Wales almost stopped in 1282; for Roland Mathias it only started in 1536.

These differences do not preclude affection or respect. They give the critic purchase in a difficult terrain. When people are faced with the cunning mixture of army roughness, artistic integrity and saintlike innocence that was David Jones, they tend to reach for their absolutes. The result is not criticism but hagiography. But it is a virtue in headmasters not to be taken for a ride. Mathias knows a spoilt child when he sees one. Nor is he prepared to pass over an addiction to empires, Papism or Mussolini as if they were not features of the real world, features that he basically dislikes, but somehow part of the sanctity, miraculously translated in David Jones like the Virgin Mary into heaven.

Mathias's insight goes far beyond that of a headmaster, but his teaching experience stands him in good stead, for it helps him, with his scholarship and his Nonconformity, to identify the spiritual morass that threatened to engulf David Jones. For what the essay triumphantly shows is that David Jones was not engulfed. Roland Mathias puts it like this: '. . . my thesis, in this paper, is that Wales, after many vicissitudes, won a great battle for him. It became, so to speak, the shibboleth with which he could put aside fear.' Step by step, and with scrupulous care, he uncovers what David Jones had of Welshness, and what his imagination made of it. How it became a last-ditch defence of the 'holy diversities' against the Ram, the 'necessity' of Empire, the preservation of once-paramount values by force:

> The *imperium* had been the emblem of his own need for strength and reassurance: Wales spoke to him constantly of freedom and a separate tradition. In the later years of his better health Wales came, of the two, to seem the more desirable and he moved towards it as far as he was able.

Wales as a moral force, a champion striving for the allegiance and spiritual health of her people, is one of Mathias's main themes. It is almost a new criterion of Anglo-Welshness, going far beyond the simple meaning, 'coming from Wales but in the English language'. In the simple sense, David Jones is hardly Anglo-Welsh at all. Under this moral criterion he becomes one of our most prized authors. Writers like Dannie Abse, who are from Wales but whose pith and direction turn towards London, are more of a problem. Of course, the situation is complex: Wales is a nation in eclipse, and exerts moral pressure in a quite different way to England or the United States.

On Dylan Thomas, Mathias tries to put the English apprehension of him as quintessentially Welsh into some kind of perspective. His social milieu was un-Welsh, he gravitated to London, his view of the poetic life was based on Keats. Even his precocity and his foreboding of early death were derived from the English Romantics. But he derived from his Welsh background a biblical, preaching tone and a habit of affirmation: the trappings of Nonconformity without the faith. He shared with many Welsh poets an interest in complex forms, though whether this was due to lingering and obscure influence is not clear. Myself, as I have noted in connection with Idris Davies,[1] I think that English people see Dylan as Welsh because he is palpably not English. The words he uses seem so unaware of their own history. The English culture of the Thomas family was 'all in the head', as Lawrence would say. It hadn't had time to be natural. Dylan's Welshness is a lack of Englishness as much as anything homespun from Wales.

It is when Mathias leaves discussion of Dylan Thomas's Welshness and descends to the poetry that my doubts start. For one thing, he sounds very concerned to avoid such assessment. Here, for example, in a sentence that disclaims any such thing, he coils around it until 'murder will out' and he abuses it with considerable animus:

> It is not my purpose to examine this subject-matter closely: it must be sufficient to say that whether, using John Donne and others, he attempted a metaphysic of the bodily functions, whether his work was a genuine reflection of a loss of identity in the womb (as David Holbrook would seem to be suggesting in *The Code of Night*) or whether, as Raymond L. Hogler has recently indicated (in *The Anglo-Welsh Review* Nos. 47 and 48) he deliberately played the poetry market until he found a subject-matter and a mode that would make his mark for him in the shortest possible time, one thing is obvious enough: his poetry was inchoate, suffocatingly romantic and obscure, reflecting very little of what might be called objective life and background experience in the community to which he nominally belonged.

---

[1] See above chapter 4, p. 52.

It would be hard to fault that as an example of the convoluted rhetoric of dismissal. The huge differences between the threefold 'whethers' are reduced to inconsequence, for example, but their clauses subtly arranged so that the most disreputable interpretation is climactic. The iconoclasm attributed to Raymond L. Hogler made me look his articles up. I was disturbed to find that I could not for the life of me see where he advances the view Mathias quotes from him. He makes the point that Dylan Thomas's poetic method is more relevant to the appreciation of his poetry than any worrying after a paraphrasable meaning; and that once Dylan found that method he kept to it. He also insists that the poet knew what he was about. 'I can only assert', he says, 'that Thomas's method of poetic creation is basically the method of all poetic creation.' But as for playing the poetry market, two or three readings of his articles have failed to bring Mathias's interpretations to light.

More seriously, Roland Mathias's description does not answer my own experience of *18 Poems*. Far from being inchoate, the best of them strike me as wonderfully ordered, formal pieces of work, intricate as a passacaglia or fugue. The fact that one cannot be sure of their paraphrasable meaning (though to judge from the poet's note to the later and even more difficult 'I make this in a warring absence' it is likely he considered they had one) does not make them inchoate. Some of them, such as 'Especially when the October wind' or 'Light breaks where no sun shines', have a texture which seems to me beautiful and limpid. The poetry of *18 Poems* was a rare achievement but a precarious one. Even before the collection was finished, poetic cramp was making inspiration difficult. Leaving Swansea may have made the break irreparable; but it is likely that the poise and formal perfection of *18 Poems* was not repeatable. The turgid muscle-bound poems that followed from time to time in Dylan's 'capital punishment' are quite different from these extraordinary pieces. It is only with the poetry of metamorphosis that begin with 'Ballad of the long-legged bait', 'The hunchback in the park' and 'Poem in October' that any new vigour or clarity entered his verse.

Roland Mathias is not very helpful with the later poems either:

> The issue, for me, is not whether 'Over Sir John's Hill' is the finest poem in English of its decade – there is no dispute over the continuance, even the perfection, of Dylan Thomas's technical gifts – but whether this poem, together with 'Fern Hill', 'Holy Spring', 'In Country Sleep', 'A Winter's Tale', and 'Poem on his Birthday', do not demonstrate such a narrowing and closing of poetic interest that the end is clearly foreshadowed.

Mathias does not demonstrate this thesis in terms of the poetry: he only quotes one poem in passing ('In country sleep'). Anyway, is the main issue of poems like these to demonstrate biographical theories? And what sort of poetic fineness depends on the 'continuance' of 'technical gifts'?

Reluctance to face this poetry is evident, and a dislike of it so bitter that it twists his rhetoric and even makes him misconstrue its critics. Some personal animus may be present – Mathias has been the slowest to develop of the poets of Dylan's generation, and his dislike of precocity is obvious. But more than that, the headmaster is disturbed by the spoilt brilliance of the pupil. The conservative dislikes the posturings of the avant-garde (see his treatment of Keidrych Rhys's editorship of *Wales – A Ride through the Wood*, 298-300). Mathias often echoes Victorian habits of criticism – in Susan Butler's *Common Ground* he acknowledges Hopkins, Browning, Tennyson and Housman as influences. His emphasis on the 'thought' of Vernon Watkins or R. S. Thomas reminds us of Victorian explications of Browning's 'philosophy'. As a puritan also, he is perhaps uneasy about a beauty that is divorced not simply from morality but from truth. Certainly his historian's instinct is to want the subject matter of a poem rooted in a particular place and time. I cannot imagine him using anachronism as a deliberate technique. Indeed, his lack of interest in poetic form and his massively unschizoid view of the world both contribute to a rejection of modernism, at least in the form we find it in *18 Poems*. This is confirmed by the selection from Thomas in his and Garlick's definitive anthology, *Anglo-Welsh Poetry 1480-1980*, where all the guts are tidied away and you would never guess that Dylan Thomas was an *enfant terrible* of European modernism, admired by Stravinsky to the point of suggesting collaboration. It is a sad declension, Thomas's diminishing into the sacrificial victim facing death 'certain only of the equipment of a child', as Mathias puts it, in the 'sacramental covert' of Laugharne.

Each essay in *A Ride through the Wood* holds great interest. Like all original critics, Mathias invites thought, sometimes to develop what he says, sometimes to qualify it. With the rest, we must be brief. 'Grief and the circus horse', when it was first published in 1971, was a great bringer of light into the jungle of Vernon Watkins's early poetry. It is still essential reading on the poet, hinging on the role of 'grief' in making Watkins question the regenerative power of Platonic myth and move towards a belief in Christianity. Mathias says: 'Whether this was a specific grief it is impossible at this stage to say . . . It seems possible, even likely, that the early death of schoolfellows – and I couple with this the death of 'The

Collier' and other like unfortunates – compelled Vernon Watkins . . .'
But (is it quibbling to protest?) in his own monograph on Watkins in the
Writers of Wales series, published three years later, Mathias makes it
clear that this grief was nothing of the kind. It represented the poet's
failure to grow up, connected with a golden age he could neither recover
nor forget that he experienced in his last year at public school. And yet
the earlier essay is reprinted without change or footnote. It seems very like
not letting your left hand know what your right is doing.

With Alun Lewis and Emyr Humphreys, Mathias obviously feels at
home. With them the book as a whole can be seen to centre on the
struggle of Welsh idealism, grounded as it was in puritan Nonconformity,
to survive in an alien world. Roland Mathias proposes a view of Anglo-
Welsh literature as a kind of Paradise Lost, in which Eden is represented
by the Welsh-speaking Nonconformist and rural communities of
nineteenth-century Wales. The Anglo-Welsh struggle on as best they may,
with this or that legacy of Eden, attempting to navigate the wasteland
around them. This is his 'main ride', the generations from that of David
Jones (born in 1895) to that of Emyr Humphreys (born in 1919), which
have exercised such hegemony on Anglo-Welsh life ever since the thirties.

*A Ride through the Wood*, then, is clearly the most comprehensive
book on these authors that has yet appeared. Whether or not the author
intended it, it proposes a canon of great Anglo-Welsh writers, and it
posits a centrality of moral and idealist concern. As for the canon, David
Jones, Dylan Thomas, Vernon Watkins, Alun Lewis, R. S. Thomas and
Emyr Humphreys are all of them sons of middle-class families that had
seen fit deliberately to stop speaking Welsh. But one of the features of
Anglo-Welsh verse and prose is that its writers belong to a much wider
class-spectrum than we find in England. I think that most Anglo-Welsh
critics who are younger than Roland Mathias would find Idris Davies, for
example, at least as important as Vernon Watkins. But of course Idris
Davies (or Lewis Jones or Jack Jones or Gwyn Thomas) would extend
not merely the canon but also the field of moral and idealist concern.

Roland Mathias's inquiry into the often very difficult authors that he
treats goes very deep. It is perhaps typical of the situation in Wales that
our major critic waited till he was nearly seventy before a collection
appeared. However one disagrees with him (and I do), his penetration
and originality give one more purchase on the subject than any
comparable body of work I can think of.

Mathias's poems may be roughly divided into two kinds: first, his Browningesque dramatic monologues and historical pieces ('A letter', 'For Jenkin Jones, prisoner at Carmarthen, these') which often – not always, as the first example shows – refer back to sixteenth- and seventeenth-century Wales, the Catholic recusants, the partly Anglicized squirearchy and the puritans. Mathias has explained how in his diffident attempt to find roots he researched the Recusancy of the Border counties of Wales, thinking that that was probably as far in as he could get into Welshness without presumption. As he says, 'The history we choose speaks largely of ourselves' ('Memling'). His historical myth, therefore, is neither that of the medieval Catholic Wales, independent or hankering for independence, that appeals to Saunders Lewis or R. S. Thomas; nor is it that of the Methodists, the *buchedd* or 'Welsh way of life', a democratic people loyal to Britain rather than a nation in itself. As a group, the gentry of Tudor and Stuart Wales seem torn in two. On the one hand, in terms of worldly success, as a group they were adventurers only too willing to cash the blank cheques that the Act of Union gave them on English prosperity. On the other hand, they seem worried, tentative, afraid they're throwing the baby out with the bathwater, conservative in politics, clinging to the skirts of a monarchy even when it no longer offered them opportunity or riches. They seem vulnerable spiritually, like undercapitalized enterprises in a recession. The Recusants and the puritans pointed backward and forward to their various utopias; but Wales went with neither, in the doldrums 'in the turn of a civilization' when, as David Jones says of God, 'it is easy to miss Him'.

But secondly, there are the lyrical pieces in which Mathias speaks in his own person, and which surely form his important work as a poet. The typical Mathias poem starts off as an almost private meditation, full of eccentric and obscure vocabulary verging on verbiage as he strives to bring the objects of his contemplation into emotional focus:

> They have not survived,
> That swarthy *cenedl*, struggling out
> Of the candled tallut, cousins to
> Generations of sour hay, evil-looking
> Apples and oatmeal porringers.

One is reminded of Hamlet in the graveyard scene exercising his melancholy wit on the skull of poor Yorrick. A 'cenedl' is both a nation and a generation – Mathias says in his notes in *Common Ground* that it means a 'tribe'. 'Tallut' is more impenetrable but he does not notate it in his collections: it is only the notes to the last-named anthology that tell us that it is a Gower version of the Welsh 'taflawd', a hayloft.[2] A 'porringer' is standard but archaic English, and means a small basin from which children eat soup etc. Or, in other words, a bowl of porridge.

Let me paraphrase therefore what this mass of words is saying: the tribe of swarthy people (we learn later they were his collier cousins in the Rhondda) who came ('struggled') from the haylofts of Gower where they were agricultural labourers, lit by a candle, sleeping on hay and eating poor-quality apples and oatmeal gruel – háve not survived. Even to expand it like this into a prose sentence makes it seem unnaturally congested. To make it easily accessible public discourse a whole paragraph of several descriptive sentences would be required.

What this use of language acts out is a kind of mimesis: the poet is rummaging round in the glory-hole of his memories and half-acknowledged insights, like a man in a dump looking for treasure. Each glinted clue is prized open for its significance. The rhetoric only pretends to be descriptive: actually it is the savouring of the activity that counts, the disturbance and the echoes that it generates. It hardly matters how many of his readers are acquainted with Gower haylofts or know exactly what a porringer might be. We respond to the process as a private one, a man rooting round half in a junk yard and half in his own mind. Most description is an extrovert identification of things 'out there': Mathias's clotted notation is profoundly introvert. Sensations are not objective guides to the world, to be clarified and ranked in order: but neither are they mere illusions. What they do is place the experiencing mind in the context of what to experience. Consider the phrase 'struggling out of the candled tallut'. Mathias is feeling the sensations of a man getting up in a Gower hayloft, struggling down the ladder from the sour hay of his bed and sniffing the dead tallow of the candles. And what about 'generations'? Is the word really innocent of the Welsh word 'cenedl'? Does 'cenedl' mean just 'tribe' to Roland Mathias? Or are we thinking of the 'generations' of procreation, struggling out of the act of sex on this same 'sour hay' in the 'candled tallut'.

---

[2] Susan Butler (ed.), *Common Ground: Poets in a Welsh Landscape* (Bridgend: Poetry Wales Press, 1985). Mathias seems to have found the word in 'Some features of Gower dialects' by David Parry, which as editor he published in *The Anglo-Welsh Review* (Winter 1967). 'Tallut' is found all over south-east Wales, not just in Gower.

A common objection to Roland Mathias's poetry is that it is needlessly obscure and convoluted, and that he uses hard words and unfamiliar allusions without bothering to explain them. There is something of a magpie about Roland Mathias, rummaging for Anglo-Welshness to decorate his nest. But if you don't know what the exact flavour is of struggling out of a candled tallut in nineteenth-century Gower, neither I suspect does the poet. Yet to say it means 'hayloft' is misleading. It means a hayloft *in Gower* where Welsh words have been a kind of worn-down fossil for centuries. The phrase also suggests by its sound a 'tally', candled by accounting generations. And of course the *cynghanedd* of 'cenedl' and 'candle' gives the latter a sexual, phallic overtone that Mathias makes overt in the next sentence:

> A quick incontinence of seed
> Cried in the barn, a mind to spit
> And squat harried the gorse
> Into burning, and the melancholy
> *Rhos* burst into plots, as circumscribed
> Only as the lean muscle yearning
> Carefully for love could lay
> Around each house.

Notice the distaste, 'a quick incontinence of seed', an anti-lyrical view of sex which reminds one of some moods in R. S. Thomas. Presumably it has something to do with Welsh puritanism – it certainly is one element in Mathias's dislike of Dylan Thomas's early poetry, which revels in sexuality as a process.

A *rhos* is a moorland but it is quite difficult to be sure where all this is happening – in Gower (or wherever the family came from) or in the bleak upland valleys of the Rhondda. I take it we are still in the country before the 'new swarming' which is to the coalfield. The plots are 'circumscribed' by lean muscles 'yearning carefully for love'. Does 'carefully' mean just 'painstakingly' here, or is there more than a hint of its older meaning, 'caringly'? The word is not used about the plots being circumscribed; it is the muscles that carefully yearn. Again, the complex of empathies is almost too much for language to cope with. Yearning is being felt as dangerous, as something you have to take care with or you get nowhere.

> But of that
> Merely a life or two, enough to multiply
> Cousins like bloodspots in the wasted
> Grass.

The terrible toll of rural poverty and overpopulation is sketched in that image. It is the second time we've had the word *cousins* – it comes again in the last four lines of the poem. Each time it does so it becomes more particularized. In the third line, the swarthy *cenedl* is said to be 'cousins to generations of sour hay' where it seems largely a metaphor. Here, in the middle of the poem, the cousins multiply 'like bloodspots' – *cousins* means no more than members of the family, the tribe. It is a nightmare image, where bloodspots in the wasted grass multiply like some fungus or bacteria. But in the last four lines the poet says: 'For this dark cousinhood only I / Can speak.' They have become his own cousins by then, whom we know from his reminiscences of the Rhondda. 'Cousins' is in fact a paradigm of the way Roland Mathias's poems often spiral down through a maze of generalized empathies to a particular situation and finally to the poet himself as both part of the situation, the 'cousinhood', but also distinct from it – only he can speak.

The actual move to the coalfield is described in characteristically difficult mixed metaphors:

> Then a new swarming, under
> An aged queen, before they walked
> Their milgis over the ragged hill
> They ghosted every shift, farming
> A memory of that last-seen
> Country that was never theirs.

They are first compared to a swarming of bees; but it is difficult to be sure who or what the 'aged queen' is – an actual family matriarch? a personification of coal? or Wales? One reader suggests we should take 'aged queen' literally, as referring to Queen Victoria; but the idea of Victoria as a queen bee leading a swarm, metaphorically a mass migration to the coalfield, is hard to swallow. (It is worth noting that, with honey-bees, the old queen swarms first, before the new queens are properly hatched: to describe it as a 'new swarming' is therefore misleading.) The 'swarm' are then described as walking their *milgis* (greyhounds) over the 'ragged' hill that they 'ghosted' every shift, and in the process 'farming a memory'. There are at least three or four incompatible metaphors here, besides the difficult syntax and the puzzle of what a 'last-seen country that was never theirs' might be.

The puzzles mostly are soluble, it is true. One gets the general drift, and the obscurities do reverberate, with the peculiar cluttering echoes that Mathias's poetry rings with. But for all the suggestions of visual exactness – 'swarming', 'ragged', 'ghosted' – I don't in fact *see* anything, though I certainly feel what it's like to see these things. The effect I think is more like a person putting on ritual garments, as a priest or a Freemason might do, solemnly feeling what each one means without necessarily *looking* at any of them.

My real difficulties start with the next four lines:

> It was not will was lacking then
> So much as instinct, a gift
> Of seed for their backyard culture,
> A grip on the girl who bears.

Will to do what? In the last sentence they have swarmed, walked their *milgis*, ghosted every shift and farmed a memory. Does Mathias mean that they could only farm a memory, not the real thing, because instinct was lacking? What instinct? He talks as if it was sexual – almost as if they were impotent, lacking a grip on the girl who bears, lacking a gift of seed. Perhaps he means simply that, deprived of the country, they lacked the instinct to marry and have children, even though they wanted to, i.e., even though they had the will to do so.

If he does mean that, it would certainly explain why 'they have not survived' and why the tribe, the *cenedl*, died out. The poet describes how they suffered and died:

> Coughing in terraces above
> The coal, their doorsteps whitened
> And the suds of pride draining
> Away down the numbered
> Steps to the dole, they denied
> Both past and future, willing
> No further movement than the rattle
> Of phlegm, a last composure
> Of will and attitude.

There is a kind of pun on 'steps'. The actual soapsuds are called 'suds of pride' because it was the pride of every household to keep its front step clean and white – not to do so was to invite contempt as a slut. The suds are imagined draining away down the steps to the Labour Exchange – the 'dole'. But the whole process is a metaphor. The pride of these people drains away like soapsuds, down 'the numbered steps', each stage numbered and counted out, to the humiliation of the dole.

So far, so good. They have denied 'both past and future', the past because they have left farm labouring and the future presumably because they have had no children. They have willed 'a last composure of will and attitude'; and once again I find myself flummoxed. It is a striking thing to do, to 'will a last composure of will', the poet ought certainly to have told us more about it. How do you perform it? Is it a form of yoga? Does the poet approve or disapprove?

I used to dislike Roland Mathias's poetry: it made me feel claustrophobic and even physically angry. But now I feel that the congestion, the ever-present threat of obscurity, the frequent lack of clear images, are probably endemic to the sort of thing that it does and the sort of greatness that it has. For despite my reservations, 'They have not survived' is a great poem. By the time you've read it, penetrated its complexities, suffered its empathies, donned its humanity like a ritual, you find you have a context for some of the most moving and direct lines in our poetry, lines whose honesty and sorrow are breathtaking:

> For this dark cousinhood only I
> Can speak. Why am I unlike
> Them, alive and jack in office,
> Shrewd among the plunderers?

It is lines like these that critics who talk of Mathias as a great poet are surely remembering. There is the sense of a man betraying himself almost by what he is, or by the fact that he exists at all:

> It is enough to unpile and shift
> The endless loops of this waste, hearing the crackle behind
> And knowing the smell of a life ill lived as it passes down wind.
>
> ('Burning brambles')

There is a constant sense of a refugee from Time, someone I imagine a bit like Snipe in 'Snipe's Castle',

> quiet
> And speckled, grubbing a while longer in the dull
> Dark rain,

wandering around looking for old significances and certainties that once were valid for a whole society but now

> Each on his own must stand and conjure
> The strong remembered words, the unanswerable
> Texts against chaos.
>
> ('Brechfa Chapel')

212

More than any other Anglo-Welsh poet – even R. S. Thomas – Mathias has this sense of *lacrimae rerum*, the tears in things, the still sad music of humanity. To read him is to feel lost and yet still human, cut off yet still in the bloodstream. He is so much a poet of history, and yet his best work is almost not historical at all: a moment of sorrow or realization when time stands still and the past reasserts its grip on the eternal.

He is the least dramatic of poets, and yet his style is often touched with the histrionic: thus he adjures the river in 'The flooded valley':

> You did not despise me once, Senni, or run so fast
> From your lovers. And O I jumped over your waist
> Before sunrise or the flower was warm on the gorse.
> You would do well to listen, Senni. There is money in my purse.

The speaker here is a farmer who has sold his land to make a reservoir. The sudden bizarre echo of Iago talking to his gull Rodrigo ('Put money in thy purse') underlines the farmer's sense that he has betrayed both his land and his birthright. It is worth remarking how much better centred and 'felt through' this poem is than Leslie Norris's 'A small war', also on the flooding of the Senni Valley:

> When I open the taps in my English bathroom
> I am surprised they do not run with Breconshire blood –

or even than R. S. Thomas's very different 'Reservoirs' with its magisterial distaste – 'There are places in Wales I don't go.' Roland Mathias – and it is surely one of his strengths – could never say a thing like that. 'The flooded valley' ends with the farmer's naming the names in the Senni churchyard:

> So you are quiet, all of you [the rivers], and your current set away
> Cautiously from the chapel ground in which my people lie . . .
> Am I not Kedward, Prosser, Morgan, whose long stones
> Name me despairingly and set me chains?
> If I must quarrel and scuff in the weeds of another shire
> When my pounds are gone, swear to me now in my weakness, swear
> To me poor you will plant a stone more in this tightening field
> And name there your latest dead, alas your unweaned feeblest child.

Consider the phrase 'quarrel and scuff' – children scuff their shoes by dragging their feet and kicking at stones. It seems to me a marvellous transformation of a headmaster's kind of language and apprehension of his charges into high lament: a farmer stripped of his birthright by his own fault has nothing to do in his exile except behave like a recalcitrant schoolboy; and this prepares us for the metaphor in the last line where he imagines himself as an 'unweaned' baby, but still nevertheless part of the 'tightening field', the graveyard's 'field full of folk' who wait for the resurrection of the dead. 'Tightening' because it is filling up with corpses; but also connotating the tightening of the throat under emotion, the tightening of a purse full of the money that has betrayed him, and perhaps the tightening conditions of salvation – strait is the way – where many are called but few are chosen. Certainly 'unweaned' carries with it echoes of one of the great controversies of Christianity: can a baby be saved who has not reached the age when it is possible to believe in Christ – saved by virtue of belonging to a Christian household or a Christian community? Or, in other words, is the baptism of babies efficacious? The farmer is asking for the status of an 'unweaned' baby and also – for he uses the word 'feeblest' – the status of a sinner who can be forgiven his treachery and received back into the 'holy people' of God's acre. This 'eating your cake and having it' is typical of the paradox of Christian salvation; for we are bidden to 'repent for the Kingdom is at hand' – i.e. behave as adults who have sinned – and yet we are told, 'except you become as little children you shall not enter the Kingdom'.

Though 'The flooded valley' is a 'dramatic monologue' the form is used entirely for lyric purposes. Even in the historical pieces, there is no emotional space left for the give and take of genuine dialogue. Take for example 'The remonstrance of John Poyer' from 'Tide-reach: A sequence of Pembrokeshire poems written for music'. John Poyer is grumbling about his enemies who have indicted him, and quotes phrases from their accusations. But there it stops. The enemies ('Goody Elyot' and the rest) have no imaginative existence for us except as refracted through Poyer's mind. (Incidentally, the fact that it was written for music doesn't seem materially to alter Mathias's usual procedure in this regard.) Compare a genuine dramatic lyric, such as Emyr Humphreys's 'A Roman dream': a bored Roman emperor decides he wants a scholar first to kill a prisoner, then to die for him. It is a three-dimensional vision of monstrous tyranny, with the emperor and the scholar both occupying their own space, still affecting each other, however one-sided and extreme the outcome.

Mathias, in the interview with him in *Common Ground*, has said he has 'very little use for confessional poetry, written in the tiresome belief that the poet's experiences are in some way unique'. He has described his struggle against sentimentality, and the way he had to wait for years before he could master his emotions sufficiently to write a poem – in fact the very poem we have been struggling with, 'They have not survived'. And yet it seems to me that his greatest poetry is almost all of it about himself, and if not confessional is at least about a unique consciousness. His finest poetry is also (most of it) very late. His struggle against emotion, his fear of sentimentality, as well as his Christian guilt and the insecurity of his Welshness – these things seem to have led him a fine dance before he could find himself as poet. And when he did, as often as not, it is his feelings as a boy that he reaches home with, a kind of belated acknowledgement that what he felt then was valid after all. The next poem to 'They have not survived' is called 'Testament' and seems to me one of the most perfectly achieved he ever wrote. At every turn it risks sentimentality; and if this is not a confessional poem about a unique experience I don't know what the words mean! At the same time it places that experience in the context of a whole generation and a whole Christian tradition, and gives back to the 'little trembling fellow' a moral weight that only age can endorse:

> I cannot be sure what
> I remember, but it was
> Not a heroic escape, a grave
> Hypocrisy strangled, the cortège
> Of deacons stunned by one
> Honest stroke. I was the child
> Of belief, aching pitifully
> In the unready hours
> At the wounds I must suffer
> When I walked out weaponless
> And grown.
>
> They were all heroes then,
> All bullyboys kicking the pews
> In, stirring their history up
> In a pint-pot, jeering
> The shabby unmuscled parades
> Of the old Model Army.
> But I was a little trembling
> Fellow who had known love
> And saw only greed
> And false heart in such great
> Drunken tales.

# PART V

## 15

### *Exile and elegy in the poetry*
### *of T. Harri Jones*

~

After the 1939–45 war, the *buchedd* was in tatters, but *buchedd*-values were still powerful. The ruins of *buchedd* Wales were everywhere, in depopulated villages, run-down industry, still-powerful chapels. In fact the war had breathed new life into some *buchedd* institutions: the coal industry had revived from the years of Depression, and the Labour government had at last nationalized the mines. Aneurin Bevan's National Health Service was based on the model of the colliers' own medical scheme and aimed to be genuinely classless, with free medicine for all. The same was broadly true for secondary education. The paradox of all this socialist effort was that it would require a much larger middle class than ever before to service it. Doctors, teachers, administrators, social workers and so on had to be trained. There was a period of ill-adjusted growth, when a new middle class was in being, students were coming out of college looking for jobs, but Wales was not yet affluent enough to absorb them. Traditionally Welsh students had gone into preaching and teaching and those occupations were already over-subscribed. As yet the universities had hardly expanded at all, and it was very hard indeed to get an academic job, particularly if you'd not been to Oxford or Cambridge.

Exile is what divides the post-war Anglo-Welsh generations. The poets who were looking for jobs in the late sixties and seventies were not automatically shunted out of Wales. It means they don't always see what the fuss was about. They take Welshness calmly. If it shows, well, you've got to come from somewhere, haven't you? But for their elders, starting a career in the forties and fifties, the need to emigrate was evident. Harri Jones ended up in Australia, Dannie Abse in Golders Green. But even poets who were to return to Wales, John Ormond, John Tripp (1927–86), Gillian Clarke, Sally Roberts Jones (1935– ) and myself, had long or

217

short spells working in or near London. It hardly occurred to any of us that we could or should try to get professional jobs in Wales itself – the job-market, though slightly better than before the war, was still depressed, the general mood of bewilderment and lack of centre survived from the thirties. What was left in Wales was narrow, petty-bourgeois and hypocritical puritanism. The trauma of exile, therefore – together with the deaths of Alun Lewis, Idris Davies and Dylan Thomas – was a major factor in the post-war blackout of Anglo-Welsh poetry.

Then, like everywhere else, Wales started to be affluent. There was a possibility of coming back. Even for poets who did not return, the changed conditions of the mid-sixties led to a profound nostalgia for Wales, a centripetal and lyrical reaffirmation of Welsh distinctiveness. This is what Meic Stephens called the 'Second Flowering'. T. Harri Jones (who died before it was properly under way), Leslie Norris, John Ormond, John Tripp, Bryn Griffiths (1933– ), Sally Roberts Jones and Meic Stephens (1938– ) himself are some of its more distinguished practitioners.

## T. Harri Jones

T. H. Jones was a country boy from Breconshire who interrupted his degree at Aberystwyth to serve in the Navy during the war. He returned as a married man, took a good first in 1947 and did research on the Metaphysicals; but he failed to find an academic post. He resigned himself to schoolteaching in Portsmouth Dockyard, teaching apprentices English. Hart-Davis published the first of his four books of poetry in 1957. In 1959 he emigrated and became a lecturer at the University of New South Wales. His third and best book of verse, *The Beast at the Door*, appeared in 1963. He also published a study of Dylan Thomas in the Oliver and Boyd 'Writers and Critics' series. He was found drowned at the foot of a cliff near his home in New South Wales in January 1963.

Harri Jones is a very uneven poet, and little of his first two volumes offers anything new. Much of it is indifferent pastiche of Dylan Thomas, Auden and Robert Graves. He is one of the first Anglo-Welsh poets to surface as a camp follower of English poetic fashions. His love-poetry has been praised, but I find it (almost always) slick, taking easy ways out and too often relying on charm to hide the fact that he is saying very little. He is usually much better writing about his family than about his girl-friends:

> My daughter of the Mabinogion name
> Tells me Ayer's Rock is ten times higher than
> A house, and she, being seven today,
> Would like to see it, especially
> To ride there on a camel from Alice Springs.
> She also says she wants to be a poet –

Will this rock in the middle of Australia, he asks, haunt her mind and dreams as Allt-y-clych haunts his:

> bedraggled with wet fern
> And stained with sheep, and holding like a threat
> The wild religion and the ancient tongue,
> All the defeated centuries of Wales?

> ('Rhiannon')

It sounds more like druids and Ancient Britons than respectable chapel-goers of twentieth-century Breconshire! These three aspects of Wales, its wildness, its defeat and its threatening quality, dominate his thinking about his homeland; but there is another thing too which he recognizes – the sense of belonging that was there. For all his lack of the language and his coming from near the English border, Harri Jones was an insider in Wales in a way that neither Dylan nor R. S. Thomas ever was:

> When the cataracts came down, creeping
> Curtains over his shepherd eyes,
> He talked to me.

> The old names still resound
> For me of farms, men, ponies, dogs,
> The old names that are all that I possess
> Of my own language, proud then
> And prouder now to call myself only
> Young Crogau, old Crogau's grandson.

> I remember when the cataracts came down.

> ('My Grandfather going blind')

It took him half a lifetime to articulate the insiderness he had. In perhaps a dozen poems he wrote of Wales with complete authority, with sardonic passion and deadpan pity, without any of the charm or evasiveness that marred so much of his work and owing little to the fashionable voices of his time, R. S. Thomas included. Look at his grotesque yet strangely moving evocation of the chapel ('Pisgah' may be the chapel's name; it was the mountain from which Moses looked down on a Palestine he was never to enter):

> And the capel, God in a little bwthin
> Once whitewashed – but God in the voices
> Of the mean, the crippled, the green bacon eaters,
> The lead me beside still waters buggers, the wild boys,
> The sin-eaters, and the godly daughters,
> All of them suddenly in unison
> In the ugliest building I have ever seen
> – Pisgah I shall never see again –
> All suddenly bursting – not bursting,
> All suddenly startled into song, to praise
> The god of fornication and the world we lived in.

The energy of sardonic contempt is beautifully controlled; but the effect is not wholly reductive. Despite the irony and the ugliness it is a genuine religious and anarchic experience he is remembering, and one which totally belongs to him, flesh of his flesh, bone of his bone. The final summing up, with its ironic dialect and dry officialese, is dramatic and achieved:

> Boyo, if you come from a country like that
> You can talk to me of sin and related matters.

Other poems are neither nostalgic nor satirical. 'My grandmother died in the early hours of the morning' is a poem of visionary loss:

> It was cold in that room, after the cold hours
> Of keeping company with the big, shrunk man
> Who had been her husband, my father's father.
> Her sallow face seemed peaceful as ever,
> Her straggle of hair blanched into the pillow
> – You would not have guessed at a body under the bedclothes.
> Past tiredness, I was a boy, incurious.
> A little woman was dead, a little old woman
> Who had long confused me with her youngest son.
> I did not even think, How small she looks.
> And certainly had no thoughts for her life of labour,

> Nor wondered how she who had always been old to me
> Had once been whatever beauty the world has
> To the old man I now led out of the room,
> Out of the house, up the narrow road,
> In the dawn he could not see for tears, taking
> My hand in his as he'd done when I was small,
> Both of us wordless against the dawn and death.

'It was cold in that room, after the cold hours' – it is a few minutes after she's died, yet already the pluperfect ('who had been her husband') is the appropriate tense. The hours of waiting have been cold for the boy that 'kept company' (almost like an old-fashioned lover) with his grandfather, but now 'it was cold in that room'. In this context, cold on cold, the oxymoron, 'big, shrunk man' seems natural and effective: 'who had been her husband, my father's father' – big, protecting, masculine words, now shrunk by the cold to a pluperfect that prepares us for the later reversal of roles as the tired boy takes care of his grandfather at the end, 'both of us wordless against the dawn and death'.

Perhaps central to Harri Jones's sensibility is the headlong flight from the super-ego, God or his parents or whatever, that imposes punishment and guilt. This can surface anywhere, for instance in a poem that starts as a description of a dying deer:

> There were no hounds after her; only winter,
> Remorseless as God or parents.
>
> ('One Memory')

The same combination of terrors, 'God or parents' is what gives 'A storm in childhood', from his last, posthumous volume, *The Colour of Cockcrowing*, its compelling force. A group of schoolchildren walking home from school take a long way home in order to stay together longer, even if they get home later. They are surprised by a thunderstorm through the wooded hills, and panic:

> We ran, between the trees and the trees,
> Five children hand-in-hand, afraid of God,
> Afraid of being among the lightning-fetching
> Trees, soaked, soaked with rain, with sweat, with tears,
> Frightened, if that's the adequate word, frightened
> By the loud voice and the lambent threat,
> Frightened certainly of whippings for being late,
> Five children, ages six to eleven, stumbling
> After a bit of running through trees from God.

They eventually reach home:

> The lightning struck no trees, nor any of us.
> I think we all got beaten; some of us got colds.

The ironic eye of the adult academic is only just in control: 'after a bit of running through trees from God' and 'some of us got colds' as though they'd just been jogging in the rain. The tension between primeval terror and guilt and the sophisticated balance of maturity is a difficult one to accommodate and probably undermines his poetry more than it helps it. The poet often seems to trifle with his feelings precisely because they threaten to overwhelm him. In this poem, though, the throw-away succeeds. If anything, it increases our sense of his childish terror.

This bedrock of fear and guilt was certainly reinforced by his experience in the navy of wartime convoys through the Mediterranean, with all hell let loose around him, and his friends and messmates killed. 'Lucky Jonah', which is subtitled 'In Memoriam – friends killed on active service', tries to deal with this experience directly, but the memories are too much with him and he fails to shape the poem incisively enough (it is a problem we also find in the sea-poems of Bryn Griffiths):

> Voices: '*Remember me, mate? Had a run ashore*
> *With you in Alex once. We found a girl*
> *And christened her the Nut-Brown Maid.*'
> '*Remember me? I hit a gharri-driver once*
> *Because he wouldn't let me have his whip.*'
> '*Remember me? I fell out of the motor-boat.*'
> 'Remember – ' all the frantic runs ashore
> With Jacks who are not jolly any more.
> Alex, Benghazi, Tripoli, Algiers,
> Beirut, Valetta, Famagusta, –
> O ports and harbours of my sunken years.

The next paragraph partly recovers itself:

> And all of life a long survivor's leave
> For lucky Jonah, spewed up from the maw
> To wait and wait and wait for death.
> The sea's a populous city – half my world
> Is walking there, up home with mermaids,
> Cold, picked clean to the white bones,
> And braggarting to fish, 'The Navy's here.'

We are left with a sense of 'five long years of waiting to be drowned'.

It is probable that this undercurrent of fear and guilt, and the ego's attempt to keep its balance in spite of hysteria, also led Harri Jones to write his other long poem, about the seventeenth-century witch trials, 'Cotton Mathers remembers the trial of Elizabeth How: Salem, Massachusetts, 30 June 1692':

> The horns that sounded across Essex county
> At midnight, the unaccountable mazes
> In which men and women and beasts were wildered,
> All the afflictions and torments, the agony
> Of those who judged those who were only tried,
> God's guidance for which I so strongly cried –
> Were these things here in Salem? Did help come?
> Is God's good wilderness now purified?
> Or must we fear and go in constant sorrow
> That we are still afflicted, that tomorrow
> May bring back to Salem that delirium?

It is a more disciplined performance than 'Lucky Jonah' but perhaps too dependent on Mathers's own words to be more than a historical exercise.

There are one or two love-poems which escape the general fatuity (as I feel it); the often anthologized 'Girl reading John Donne' is one, about an academic dodging or postponing the pitfalls of sex:

> Her arms bare, and her eyes naked,
> She tells her borrowed book, *I am in love*,
> And the fierce poem jumps about under her skin.
>
> Mr, the almost anonymous lecturer
> Who prescribed this text for her undoing
> When he said *Goodmorrow* to his shaving self,
> Remembered how she crossed her legs in class,
> Thought vaguely of writing a poem, a declaration,
> But after breakfast went on marking assignments.

Even this is a bit two-dimensional. The best of his love-poems, to which I've already referred, is almost not a love-poem at all – 'One memory', about a dying deer:

> There were no hounds after her; only winter
> Remorseless as God or parents; and I was sick
> For her boned beauty only for a little while,
> And still do not dare to think of how she died.

But I know she died: the quick mouths of hounds
Would have been more merciful, some grace
Among that slaver and baying she could not find
In the slow sleep in the last drift she stumbled into.

And there, where houndtooth could not reach
Nor cabbagetop entice, there the bone of her beauty
Still whitens against the offwhite of bogcotton, as you
Still intrude with a bony gleam into my life.

It is a haunting and mysterious poem, and full of pain, that yet says a lot more about love between the sexes than all his compliments and evocations of lust.

It is at least possible that Harri Jones would have developed into an Australian poet: 'Sawmill incident' seems a promising pointer in that direction; but as it is, his best work is about Wales. 'Spoiled preacher' is a nightmare about what would have happened had he succumbed to the claustrophobic pressures of his parents' desire for him, and become a minister:

Suppose
You think, you had gone through with it,
Suppose a war hadn't come conveniently,
Suppose – this is the moment when your scream
Awakes you to your own sweat and dirt – suppose
You had let yourself be dipped in the Chwefru
(Below where the trout were, and where they washed the sheep),
Suppose you had learnt from the ghosts of Christmas Evans
And Evan Jones 'the man from Eglwyswrw'.
And you lived now in a meagre manse –
How beautifully you would have been able to thunder
Against sin (meaning only one thing, that thing)
To your thin and sinning congregation . . .

Pastor you would have been – and what a hypocrite
You would have been in the glory of the pulpit –
Hair flowing all over the place, and hellfire texts
All endlessly against fornication
To a few thin and avaricious buggers
Of both sexes heedfully laying up their treasure
In the bank and whatever they thought was heaven.

The poem marks a crisis in the *buchedd*, the Welsh way of life as a whole, not simply a nightmare of Harri Jones. Its representative institution, the chapel, was ceasing to inspire idealism. Poor parents scraped their pennies together to give their sons the education that would make them ministers, leaders of the *buchedd*; but the chapel was failing them, the children ended as hypocrites or exiles. The collapse since the Second World War has been rapid and seemingly irreversible. The respectable have stopped seeing the chapel as a desirable career for the young, and therefore respectability in Wales has no centre to it, no institution (except the language for those who speak it) any different from respectabilities elsewhere. Once, the desire to be a minister focused a boy's ambition; but increasingly it was becoming the negation of all that was modern, a claustrophobic nightmare of hypocrisy and provincialism.

In 'Spoiled preacher' we are witnessing the birthpangs of the post-war middle class out of the Welsh way of life, the *buchedd*. The new Welsh professional looks back in horror at the trap he has escaped; but the cost of his escape is exile and guilt. But by the middle sixties the economic necessity for exile and the psychological pressure towards guilt were both beginning to diminish. Not long before he died, Harri Jones's wife suggested that 'one way out of his personal impasse would be to go back to Wales'.[1] The result was 'Back', dedicated to R. S. Thomas:

> Of course I'd go back if somebody'd pay me
> To live in my own country
> Like a bloody Englishman.

With that stanza – and it had to be in English, it had to be published in London – the new Welsh middle class is at the door, claiming its inheritance.

---

[1] Julian Croft, *T. H. Jones*, Writers of Wales (Cardiff: University of Wales Press, 1976).

# 16

## *Telling the dead go home:*
## *the poetry of Leslie Norris*

~

T. H. Jones represents the new 'red-brick' academic middle class failing
to live with its guilt and at the same time failing to claim its inheritance
by getting a job in Wales. Leslie Norris from Merthyr suffered a similar
guilt – particularly about surviving the war when so many did not, but
also more generally about detaching himself from the poverty-stricken
*buchedd* folk he grew up with, to become expatriate and successful.
Norris came to terms with it, largely (as far as one can see) by
externalizing it in poetry and, as he says, 'telling the dead go home'.

Born in Merthyr Tydfil in 1921, the son of a milkman, Leslie Norris
was invalided out of the RAF in 1941. He published two volumes of
verse in 1943 and 1946, and in 1948 entered the Teacher Training College
at Coventry and subsequently taught at various schools and colleges in
the south of England; and latterly in America. After 1948 he has never
worked or been domiciled for more than holidays in Wales.

For twenty years Norris had published almost nothing; then, in the
mid-sixties, he began writing poems again – complex and sensitive
confrontations with his own past, meditations on the poetic life,
dramatic lyrics, pieces about the Merthyr of his youth. Ten were printed
in a Triskel pamphlet of 1967, *The Loud Winter*, and of these, seven
subsequently appeared in *Finding Gold*, his first major collection (also
1967). Perhaps this group constitutes Norris's most secure achievement.
'The ballad of Billy Rose' has deservedly been popular, a fine expression
of compassion and a sure-footed evocation of south Walian boxing. It is
one of the rare successful matches between poetry and sport. Equally fine,
however, and more typical, are poems like 'An old house' and 'Early frost'.

These are among the finest achievements of Anglo-Welsh poetry since
the death of Dylan Thomas. Memories and experiences overlay and
change one another. Here is no static imagism but the stuff of real

human experience, the bitter learning process that we can oppose to innocence. In 'An old house', for example, the house is explored very convincingly in the present by Norris and his dog; it was played in when he and his friends were children; and before that it was the scene of a girl's murder. The three times react on one another, in the context of a whole life. The children have some kind of horrid experience in the house while Norris is left sceptical and angry:

> What they had seen I could not make them say.
> In the harsh sun I found my freckled courage,
> Jeered, was angry, went home a different way.
>
> And walk a different way for a whole life.
> Five simple years soon took them to the war
> That burned their vision on all Europe's houses.
> In the old house it was their death they saw.

How alive the language is – 'freckled courage' which gives both the effect of the sun on the boy's face (it brings out his freckles) and the precariousness of his bravery – freckled, dappled as it were, by insecurity. And the 'five simple years' – what a marvellous word *simple* is there! Or if you want verbal fireworks in the Dylan tradition (but so controlled!) how about:

> For these are ghosts, the boys who from this house
>
> Burst with hysteria in their spitting feet,
> The whimpering ends of laughter in their mouths.

The relation of such poems to Dylan Thomas's work requires careful analysis. It is not just a simple matter of tricks of style but a re-enactment of some of the strengths of Dylan's later poetry in terms of Norris's very different sensibility. Dylan Thomas had perfected a technique in which, under strong lyrical feeling, memories acted rather like metaphors in Romantic poetry, with a kind of chemical or imaginative change, so that two experiences, two kinds of experience even, irreversibly become one. To take a simple example, in 'Poem in October' the 'rainy autumn' of the present, his thirtieth birthday, conjures up 'over the border' his childhood world, the sun of October 'summery on the hill's shoulder'. Against the still life of imagism, Dylan posits a world where 'time past' is really 'contained in time present' and both look forward and outward into 'time future'. Dylan Thomas's later poems are equipped to take advantage of the poetic insights of *Four Quartets*. In terms of their very different sensibility they too re-enact the 'moment of the rose-garden' and the 'moment of the yew' and show the two fused in the weft and warp of continuing consciousness, as a metamorphosis and forgiveness of separation.

In Dylan's poetry, the metamorphosis is celebratory and ecstatic – but is also part of a wider formal concern with the synthesizing of images, a dialectic where each image continually generates its contrary to make 'the peace that is a poem'. Leslie Norris, in these first poems of his maturity, inherits this synthesizing art of Dylan Thomas, again transposed into a very different sensibility, one that (here at least) reminds us at least as much of Edward Thomas, both in its evocation of terror and its particularity of sensation, as it does Dylan.

Finally, however, Norris cannot or will not take responsibility for the past he has conjured up. The poem ends:

> After such roads I stand in the rind of the day
> With my poor ghosts. Headlights stain the snow.
> Light leaves the monotonous sky. Heavy with night,
> Down the steep hill the wary motorists go,
>
> Stiff on the packed ice. I whistle to my dog.
> His eyes rejoice. The fall I call him from.
> Now winter bellows through the travellers' air
> And with a sigh I tell the dead go home.

It is a leave-taking he re-enacts many times, and at the end explicitly about Wales, the 'green bridge to death' as he calls it. In the strange, much later poem about the drowning of the Senni Valley in Breconshire, he half offers to take responsibility – but only on his own terms:

> I would not fight for Wales, the great battle-cries
> Do not arouse me. I keep short boundaries holy,
> Those my eyes have recognised and my heart has known
> As welcome. Nor would I fight for her language. I spend
> My few pence of Welsh to amuse my friends, to comment
> On the weather. They carry no thought that could be mine.
>
> It's the small wars I understand . . . I'd fight for them.

(It seems worth remarking, concerning these 'few pence of Welsh', that in his *Selected Poems* there are translations of seven poems by Dafydd ap Gwilym, two from the Welsh of Gwenallt, and one adapted from the Welsh of Llywarch Hen: about an eighth of the book!)

One does not wish to undervalue small-scale struggle. As Homer remarks in Patrick Kavanagh's 'Epic', 'I made the Iliad from such a local row.' But it seems to me that Norris would be a disaster to have on your side. His mind has already acceded to the 'arguments' – the great towns' need of water, and so on. He has nothing to put against them except his heart, the stubborn loyalty of the Welshman to his *bro* or district. To mention Kavanagh is to show Norris's offer for what it is, because Kavanagh did take responsibility for his past, as far as lay in him as a poet. 'The great hunger' alters the way we look at people now, not simply laments what has passed. But when Norris finishes his poem on the Senni ('A small war' it is called),

> When I open the taps in my English bathroom
> I am surprised they do not run with Breconshire blood –

then I, for one, want to cry out, 'Come off it, who do you think you're kidding?' It is on a par with his desire to conserve wild life: his sorrow over pheasants wiped out by motor cars does not stop him driving. Like any middlebrow Englishman, emotionally he eats his cake and has it too. It is a condition that is usually called 'soft-centred', like chocolate creams.

After the tragic knowledge of 'An old house' and 'The ballad of Billy Rose', what forgiveness? Norris had his main subject matter in his Merthyr past; and yet with a sigh he tells his dead go home. What to do next? My impression is that he spent a good deal of energy projecting his *persona* – a process he actually mocks in himself:

> Well, let us admit it, I make
> A pleasant picture here. A check
> Overcoat, fresh from the cleaners,
> Discreet suede shoes (I use a wire brush) . . .
> Even my dog, unfashionable but
> Successful, adds to my satisfaction.
>
> ('An evening by the lake')

More and more the poetry, when it is not simply 'genre' painting like his pieces on Merthyr characters or the extraordinary and beautiful portrait of a prize bull, seems to concentrate on Norris's consciousness of his own emotions, his sensibility and his projection of himself. He tells Edward Thomas:

> I have my small despair
> And would not want your sadness; your truth,
> Your tragic honesty, are what I know you for.
>
> ('Ransoms')

The 'I' there is quite different to the 'I' of 'An old house' – 'I found my freckled courage', for example. It is much more self-regarding, almost asking to be admired for its modesty. These poems project an image of himself as a charming, rather natty, cultured man, a motorist full of regrets, a professional poet who suffers from insomnia and bad dreams. He is nowhere at home now.

I think there is no doubt that the poetry is a lesser thing. Even on a verbal level, it loses that kind of tingling richness of response that we noted in 'An old house'. There are compensations, however. Norris's *Selected Poems* is an enjoyable and varied collection, often memorable, never irritating by bad craftsmanship or needless obscurity. Norris's insistence on being an uncommitted *persona* does sometimes depress me, for example, in his translation of Gwenallt's great elegy for the Valleys ruined by the Depression. Gwenallt was of course an intensely committed man, who went to prison for his socialist beliefs in the First World War and then became an Anglo-Catholic. 'Y meirwon' is an elegy for a whole way of life. It begins,

> Bydd dyn wedi troi'r hanner-cant yn gweld yn lled glir
>     Y bobl a'r cynefin a foldiodd ei fywyd e',
> A'r rhaffau dur a'm deil dynnaf wrthynt hwy
>     Yw'r beddau mewn dwy fynwent yn un o bentrefi'r De.
>
> (When he's turned fifty, a man sees with fair clarity
>     The people and places that moulded his life,
> And the steel ropes that tether me strongest to them
>     In one village of the South, are the graves in two cemeteries.)

Norris begins his adaptation conversationally:

> Reaching fifty, a man has time to recognise
> His ordinary humanity, the common echoes
> In his own voice. And I think with compassion
> Of the graves of friends who died.

The effect of the Welsh is to identify the poet with the community that moulded him. (It is worth mentioning that the verb *moldiodd* is peculiarly relevant to a village that made steel and to a poet whose father was killed in the steelworks.) What Norris does is to distance the speaker from what he is talking about: Gwenallt 'sees', Norris 'has time to recognise'. Gwenallt is tethered by steel ropes to a particular village, Norris recognizes his own 'ordinary humanity' and 'thinks with compassion' of his dead friends.

> Sleifiem i'r parlyrau Beiblaidd i sbio yn syn
>> Ar olosg o gnawd yn yr arch, ac ar ludw o lais;
> Yno y dysgasom uwch cloriau wedi sgriwio cyn eu pryd
>> Golectau gwrthryfel a litanïau trais.
>
> Nid yr angau a gerdd yn naturiol fel ceidwad cell
>> Â rhybudd yn swn cloncian ei allweddi llaith,
> Ond y llewpart diwydiannol a naid yn sydyn slei,
>> O ganol dwr a thân, a wŷr wrth eu gwaith.
>
> (We slunk into Bibled parlours and looked amazed
>> At cinders of flesh in the coffin, at ash of a voice;
> That's where, over lids screwed down beforetime, we learnt
>> Red revolution's collects, and litanies of rape.
>
> It was not Death on his natural rounds, like a gaol warder
>> With a warning in the clink of his damp keys,
> It was industry's leopard leaping, sudden and sly,
>> From the midst of water and fire, on men at their work.)

Norris again distances the speaker:

> It was all
>
>> Done at last, and I crept in to look
>> Over the coffin's edge and the black
>> Rim of the Bible, at the dry flesh free
>> Of breath, too young for the cemetery.
>
>> And I protest at such death without dignity,
>> Death brutally invoked, death from a factory,
>> Immature death, blind death, death which mourning
>> Does not comfort, without tears.

Where are the collects of red revolution, the litanies of rape? Instead of social anger and a community's grief, Norris gives us personal sadness and protest that seems as much directed at the human condition as at deplorable economic exploitation. So to the final débâcle:

Gosodwn Ddydd Sul y Blodau ar eu beddau bwys
    O rosynnau silicotig a lili mor welw â'r nwy,
A chasglu rhwng y cerrig annhymig a rhwng yr anaeddfed gwrb
    Yr hen regfeydd a'r cableddau yn eu hangleddau hwy.

Diflannodd yr Wtopia oddi ar gopa Gellionnen,
    Y ddynoliaeth haniaethol, y byd diddosbarth a di-ffin;
Ac nid oes a erys heddiw ar waelod y cof
    Ond teulu a chymdogaeth, aberth a dioddefaint dyn.

(This Sunday of Flowers we place on their graves a bunch
    Of silicotic roses and lilies pale as gas,
Between premature stones and the curb never ripened
    Gather from their funerals old blasphemy and curse.

Utopia vanished from the peak of Gellionnen,
    Abstract humanity, without frontier or class:
Today nothing's left at the bottom of memory
    Save family and neighbourhood, man's sacrifice and pain.)

Norris translates this as:

### Terrible

Are the blasphemous wars and savageries I
Have lived through, animal cruelty
Loose like a flame through the whole world;
Yet here on Flower Sunday, in a soiled

Acre of graves, I lay down my gasping roses
And lilies pale as ice as one who knows
Nothing certain, nothing; unless it is
My own small place and people, agony and sacrifice.

It is an extraordinary emasculation of a poem, and one is entitled to ask why Norris chose to 'imitate' (to use Lowell's word) Gwenallt's elegy in this destructively namby-pamby way. That it is deliberate is certain: no one mistranslates 'lilies pale as gas' as 'lilies pale as ice' without knowing what they're doing. The change from 'silicotic roses' to 'gasping roses' is instructive: 'gasping' may certainly be one connotation of silicotic, but it lays all the stress on the physical sufferings of the roses themselves. 'Silicotic' – which I take as basically a synonym for blood-red referring back to the red mess in the bucket earlier in the poem – is not primarily descriptive of the roses but of the sufferings to which they pay tribute.

Norris was from Merthyr, the largest mining community in Wales; but he was not altogether of it. His father, who came of a farming family, had been a miner, it is true, but during Leslie's childhood he earned his living as a milkman. Leslie was once the only boy in his class to have shoes. There is a sense, I believe, that even as a child Leslie had a touch of the outsider about him, looking at the mining community with interest – it was a very lively one – even sharing in it to a degree, but identifying as well, and possibly even more, with the rural world of his relatives. His family was upwardly mobile and education was seen as the key to a wider world.

Gwenallt – steelworker's son, socialist, Welsh-speaker and poet, a thorough insider, committed to his community and his nation – must have presented Leslie Norris with a challenge. Gwenallt's poems about the Depression  powerfully echoed  his own experience, and yet the interpretation, the use that Gwenallt made of it, differed radically from his own. To translate Gwenallt was more than a poetic exercise: it was like a hand-to-hand struggle with his own shadow. Or was he the shadow, Gwenallt the flesh and blood?

At any rate, Norris made a full-blooded attempt to translate 'Y meirwon' into his own idiom and mode, even at the cost of scrapping much of the imagery and particularity of the original. We can see what he has to leave out of the reckoning, and that the 'remainder' is almost a paradigm of what his poetry in general has to ignore in order to exist; that is, it tabulates the cost of fashioning for himself an uncommitted 'voice' in the English manner. The detachment of exile or 'Britishness' is one option for an Anglo-Welsh writer; but, just as much as any other option in Wales, to choose it means a self-wounding limitation on the power to see life clearly and to see it whole.

# 17

## *Funland and the work of Dannie Abse*

~

Tony Curtis (1946– ) opens his Writers of Wales booklet on Dannie Abse, 'Dannie Abse is one of the two most widely read and respected living poets of Wales . . .' and goes on to contrast him with the other one, R. S. Thomas. It made me pause. I cannot vouch for other poets of the so-called Second Flowering (the Anglo-Welsh poets who became prominent in the late sixties) but, to speak personally, it would hardly have occurred to me to compare the two, or even to say that Dannie Abse was a widely read and respected poet *of Wales*. He was of course widely read, and he certainly came from Cardiff. Nor did we lack respect for his very considerable art. But his concerns seemed so remote from the Wales we wrote about – the Wales of Leslie Norris or John Ormond as much as that of R. S. Thomas or Harri Webb or John Tripp – that it would have been problematic for me, in those pre-Referendum days, to call him a poet of Wales at all. He was writing 90 per cent in an English context – even his defence of Dylan Thomas did not seem particularly relevant to what we were doing. Most of us were trying to forget about Dylan anyway, or at least to 'place' him as a historical feature, his style no longer a booby-trap to young poets looking for Welshness.

But to Tony Curtis's generation, the poets of the late seventies and eighties, Dannie Abse is clearly very important. He acted as a kind of foster-father to their publishing house, the Poetry Wales Press, lending it his holiday cottage to work from. Curtis himself shows in his poetry many signs that he has learnt from Dannie Abse; but not many that he has been influenced by R.S. The whole concept of the lyric as a short-story form – not that Abse invented that, of course, but he certainly developed it and made it available as a model for young poets from Wales – has been immensely liberating for Tony Curtis. One should not ignore the work of Leslie Norris, of course, perhaps particularly as a formative influence on John Davies. But Norris inclined too much to the past. What was exciting in Abse was his sophistication, his up-to-dateness, and the fact that he was up there in Golders Green, more than holding his own among the poets of Oxbridge and London.

There were deeper things involved than modishness. Dannie Abse has a sense of human tragedy, a lively interest in people and their heroism, that is rare in English lyric and which was moving into focus in Anglo-Wales in the seventies and eighties as a master-insight of the time – certainly in the tragic lyric of Curtis himself. The Second Flowering had found its main centre in elegy. It mourned an order of things, a Welsh way of life dead or dying, fatally wounded by economic Depression and Anglicization. It was also a way of implying that the elegists, and the Anglo-Welsh professional middle class to which they belonged, were the heirs of this way of life and the natural leaders of the new Wales that was to be. Abse, though he is not without reminiscences, as a poet is more interested in ways of death than ways of life – that is, in tragic lyric rather than elegy:

> Never,
> not for one single death,
> can I forget we die with the dead,
> and the world dies with us . . .
>
> ('A smile was')

Abse's victim-status is almost embarrassingly well authenticated: he is a Jew who has inherited the memories but not the faith of his race; he is a doctor continually reminded that his patients are not just cases but people with feelings of their own, and therefore frustrated because his profession so often treats them as just cases; he is a London Welshman; he is a middle-class radical, praising the impotent ardour of anti-Vietnam demonstrations, at least as much for their impotence (one gathers) as for their ardour. The great virtue of all this has been that Abse's poetry could swim the tides of fashionable feelings. He would have all the right things to say about the thalidomide babies, for example, supposing he wrote about that particular drug-tragedy. And he is a very accomplished poet. He can compete with the Colour Supplements almost on their own terms. He has Auden's command over the journalistic phrase together with the necessary irony:

> Perhaps some girls entered for a giggle,
> but all walk slave-like in this ritual fuss . . .
>
> ('Miss Book World')

> Once his voice had been so thrilling,
> the twelve women all agreed. Off and on TV
> he was charming, he was charismatic
> yet without side. He was their pin-up.
>
> ('The bereaved')

Having the correctness of his feelings given to him on a plate, as it were, has meant that he was free to perfect that very desirable feature of the middlebrow poet, the personal tone of voice. One of his blurbs quotes a review by Alan Brownjohn in the *New Statesman*: 'Abse is talking quietly and persuasively to people who will understand, listen and agree . . . At his very best he uses this warmth and approachableness to lead the reader on to accept some disquieting, original and memorable effects.'

It was not just that his early poems seemed often excuses to rehearse fairly stock liberal attitudes that one registered dissatisfaction with them. There was a characteristic failure, in many of them, to follow a poem's logic through, except to cliché and indecisiveness. The scientific name-dropping in the famous 'Letter to Alex Comfort', for example, led to nothing more impressive than romantic gestures:

> But nothing rises. Neither spectres, nor oil, nor love.
> And the old professor must think you mad, Alex, as you rehearse
> poems in the laboratory like vows, and curse those clever scientists
> who dissect away the wings and haggard heart from the dove.

Quite often one found an arbitrary use of myth to smuggle self-pity through the censorship of a stiff upper lip – see, for example, 'The victim of Aulis', 'The second coming', and 'The trial'. The pathos was being relished too much; and the gestures of revolt too often remained just gestures, part of the customary apparatus of the suburbs:

> Still I'd shout out, 'No',
> like a Daniel condemned
> to prove timeless honesties.
> Let spellbound lions know
> an angel in the den
> lest they bite to please
> the vast majorities.
>
> ('New Babylons')

What exactly does he mean by saying that the lions will be 'spellbound' this time? And the end of the poem denies the untested defiance with which it opened:

So hearing in the Square
another maverick's despair,
as crowds draw near and shout
dark curses in the air,
where is the Daniel who
will not kneel in doubt
and will not turn about?

This, the Image of the Age:
police bring truncheons down
and each blow is our own.
When Nebuchadnezzars rage
no maverick is immune
for it's we, ourselves, who cry
'Conform, conform and die.'

The 'maverick' – the individual rebel against conformity, the one who evades the guards like the lovers in 'The frontier' and strikes out into 'the possibility of being: Utopia and grace'[1] – the hope of the maverick is always undercut by doubt. The searchlight finds the lovers 'kneeling in prayer below the Gate' but even worse the poem finally asks whether that possibility is 'a land or a mirage?'

These poems remind us how much Abse was a poet of the fifties, how much he has in common with the right-wing 'Movement' that his *Mavericks* anthology officially opposed. The fifties poets remind me of the bodies of the girls, freed in theory from constraints of corset or chaperon, but still waddling in roll-ons and playing anxious games with the telephone – 'he loves me, he loves me not'. What Abse was later to characterize and eschew as 'allegorical or symbolical structures' were the orthodoxy of the time, inherited from Edwin Muir and Auden: every other poem you read in those days seemed to involve the Garden of Eden – as indeed does 'The frontier' if in a somewhat unauthorized version.

What the fifties poets all wanted was clarity, after the apocalypse and obscurity that passed for poetry in the previous decade. But, as these poems show, the clearer you got, the more you exposed the fundamental precariousness of middle-class sanity in the Age of Affluence and the Bomb. There was a schizophrenic feeling in all this poetry, Movement or Maverick alike, a zany kind of precision guarding the self from panic.

---

[1] For my own purposes I have slightly re-punctuated this line, which reads in the original: 'the possibility of being. Utopia and grace'.

Defensive irony became the new civilization of suburbia. Many poets took refuge in Academia, some hid in minimalism, others in 'commitment'.

Abse certainly recognized a schizoid tendency in himself. His first important book, *Tenants of the House* (1957) starts with a section called 'Metaphysical ironies', beginning with a poem called 'Master':

> I know the gorgeous content guides the form.
> You wind my clockwork up and I perform
> with this unearthly voice that is not mine,
> I want 'yes', You say 'no', thus I decline.
>
> You strike my shuddering keys so I must dance
> mocked by the public, casual audience.
> You jerk on wires and I fall or leap,
> I have no tears of my own to weep.

Another poem ('Duality') begins in sub-Dylan style:

> Twice upon a time
> there was a man who had two faces,
> two faces but one profile . . .
>
> They dream their separate dreams
> hanging on the wall above the bed.
> The first voice cries: 'He's not what he seems',
> but the second one sighs, 'He is what he is'.

It ends in total confusion:

> I am that man twice upon this time:
> my two voices sing to make one rhyme.
> Death I love and Death I hate,
> (I'll be with you soon and late).
> Love I love and Love I loathe,
> God I mock and God I prove,
> yes, myself I kill, myself I save.
>
> Now, now, I hang these masks on the wall.
> Oh Christ, take one and leave me all
> lest four tears from two eyes fall.

Yet another 'The trial' is a long and indecisive ballad about the trial of a man who

> wanted to be myself, no more,
> so I screwed off the face that I always wore.

We should not be too surprised that Abse's masterpiece should take place in a mental hospital: the seeds of it had been in his poetry from the beginning.

After the large-scale gestures and commitment of *Tenants in the House*, his next collection, *Poems, Golders Green* (1962), seems much more circumscribed, as though Abse were settling down into suburban life – which may account for the title. He pictures himself as a water-diviner going through a bad patch:

> Late, I have come to a parched land
> doubting my gift, if gift I have,
> the inspiration of water
> spilt, swallowed in the sand.

> ('The water diviner')

He writes poems about public libraries, visiting English villages on Sunday, returning to Cardiff, memories of school. These footnotes to life are the stock-in-trade of English poetry since the war, where waiting for the next poem is equated with looking for a new subject matter, as in academic research.

One new feature of *Poems, Golders Green* is the sudden emphasis on Abse's Jewishness in the poetry. 'After the release of Ezra Pound' is a complicated and not altogether achieved poem – I am not quite sure who is laughing and who is not, or why: except that the circumcised do not laugh, because they remember the Holocaust. The attempt to fit Ezra Pound into the multifarious 'public neurosis' of Soho leads to incoherence, and I am not sure that the poem would not be improved by retaining only the last three paragraphs. But it is certainly a memorable rebuke to the glib liberalism of the intelligentsia – the 'gentle Gentile', Paul Potts, who asked the question:

> *In Jerusalem I asked*
> *the ancient Hebrew poets to forgive you,*
> *and what would Walt Whitman have said*
> *and Thomas Jefferson?*

> Because of the structures of a beautiful poet
> you ask the man who is less than beautiful,
> and wait in the public neurosis of Soho,
> in the liberty of loneliness for an answer.
>
> In the beer and espresso bars they talked
> of Ezra Pound, excusing the silences of an old man,
> : saying there is so little time between
> the parquet floors of an institution
> and the boredom of the final box.
>
> Why, Paul, if that ticking distance between ´
> was merely a journey long enough
> to walk the circumference of a Belsen,
> Walt Whitman would have been eloquent,
> and Thomas Jefferson would have cursed.

'The liberty of loneliness' is a great phrase, contrasted as it is with the horrifying claustrophobia of the 'ticking distance' round the circumference of Belsen. Perhaps it was this crisis of conscience that made Jewishness available to his poetry, and in fact, latterly, allowed his work to profit from Jewish wisdom and tradition.

The death of his father in more ways than one marked a watershed in his work. The event itself seems to dominate his next book, *A Small Desperation* (1968), if only because 'In Llandough Hospital' is the most moving poem in it:

> 'To hasten night would be humane',
> I, a doctor, beg a doctor,
> for still the darkness will not come –
> his sunset slow, his first star pain.
>
> I plead: 'We know another law.
> For one maimed bird we'd do as much,
> and if a creature need not suffer
> must he, for etiquette, endure?'

Linguistically, this is mixing registers quite a lot. The basic rhythm suggests a romantic lyric or even a broadside – though without rhyme to pull it together. Abse *may* have said to his fellow doctor 'To hasten night would be humane' – many things are said in conversation under pressure – but the poet does not make it believable as authentic speech: it is conventional literary metaphor, a register signalled to us also by the parallelism of the gloss upon it: 'his sunset slow, his first star pain'. But then an eighteenth-century note, with Doctor Johnson's 'On the death of Mr Robert Levet' somewhere in the background, rounds out the moral point: 'must he, for etiquette, endure?' And yet the poetry comes across as powerful lyric utterance, its awkward poeticism amply justified both by the awkwardness of the emotion itself and by what it leads to. It is spanning a linguistic chasm, between the agonizing prose of the doctor's consulting room and the poetry of the pathos of his father's dying. If Abse had followed our dogmas about speech rhythm, about preserving register and all that, this poem would not have been written.

As it is, the poem can develop in two different directions at once, both very important for Abse's future: first, it talks of the father as a patient and yet as a human being. And secondly it makes completely available to Abse the poet Abse's professional, human experience as a doctor:

> Earlier, 'Go now, son', my father said,
> for my sake commanding me.
> Now, since death makes victims of us all,
> he's thin as Auschwitz in that bed.
>
> Still his courage startles me. The fears
> I'd have, he has none. Who'd save
> Socrates from the hemlock,
> or Winkelreid from the spears?
>
> We quote or misquote in defeat,
> in life, and at the camps of death.
> Here comes the night with all its stars,
> bright butchers' hooks for man and meat.

The sudden violence of the last line sharpens terrifyingly the idea of the first stanza, 'his first star pain', as 'at the camps of death' generalizes from the phrase 'thin as Auschwitz' – in itself bold because risking a too facile use of the Holocaust, but I think completely justified by fellow feeling in the face of grief. But then Dannie Abse feels himself becoming a child before his father's courage and suffering:

> so like a child I question why
> night with stars, then night without end.

The opening plea is in fact reversed by the end: he does not plead to be humane, to 'hasten night'. Rather he questions the human condition itself, 'night with stars' – the stars of pain, certainly, but surely other stars as well – then 'night without end'.

A more scrupulous poet would not have got to this point. He would have been afraid of the poeticisms and the awkwardness. There is a certain coarse-grained quality in Abse as a poet which allows him to take this kind of risk. It is one of his strengths, even though sometimes it spoils a poem, often through over-emphasis or, as Barbara Hardy says, through not trusting the poetry to do its own job.[2] But this poem is a breakthrough: formally it leads to other poems about individuals, particularly patients; and spiritually it clarifies Abse's tragic subject matter, the 'ways of death'. It sounds inhuman to praise the poem like that, for it obviously moves one with sympathy for his personal grief; but we go where there's heart, and make our bright achievements from suffering.

*A Small Desperation*, the book which contains 'In Llandough Hospital', is at the centre of Abse's work: here he perfects the 'short-story' poem, the short narrative, often about other people but sometimes ('A night out', 'Not Adlestrop') about himself. The format has many advantages: it makes suburban life available to poetry, both its strengths – involvement in people, sense of a job to be done, passions and basic civilization; and its weaknesses – polymorphic guilt and loneliness, a final irresponsibility, domestication of the human condition. But it does so at a certain cost. Like the anecdotal snippets in *Reader's Digest*, it implies a middlebrow approach to experience as something that can be framed and enjoyed in isolation, like a holiday snap. It tends to imply that people and worlds are knowable.

The paradox is that Dannie Abse does not believe in such knowledge. He is a poet of our ways of death – death being the most unknowable thing of all. Rilke as well as Dylan Thomas was a formative influence on him, but it is not only death that is finally unknowable:

> Every thing is alien, everyone strange.
> Regard an object closely, our own foot
> named, how queer it appears as its toes flex.
> Peer at it with greenhorn observation;
> thus magnified, what incongruous toenails!

---

[2] 'Aspects of Narrative', in Joseph Cohen (ed.), *The Poetry of Dannie Abse: Critical Essays and Reminiscences* (London: Robson Books, 1983).

> Or the tree outside, we pass every day,
> stand below it, stare at it flagrantly
> till it becomes uncomfortable, till
> its slender boughs, shyly naked beneath
> those veined, pellucid leaves, stir a little.
> Scrutinized, it grows unrecognizable.
>
> ('Surprise! Surprise!')

For Abse (as for Williams Parry) surprise is an existential emotion: 'What surprises is that sometimes we are / not surprised . . .' Abse's later poetry is very largely based on this paradox. His use of the short-story poem, which seems to imply a middlebrow, domesticated universe, is often turned in on itself to buckle and reveal a surprising wildness at its core. The anecdote, in fact, becomes a Zen Buddhist koan.

*Funland and Other Poems*, his fifth collection (1973), begins with the poet trying to face himself growing old. The persuasive air of collusion with the reader is starting to show unexpected cracks:

> Long ago my kinsmen slain in battle,
> swart flies on all their swart masks feeding.
>
> I had a cause then. Surely I had a cause?
> I was for them and they were for me.
>
> Now, when I recall why, what, who,
> I think the thought that is as blank as stone.

Indeed, this poem, 'An old commitment', seems to me one of the finest Dannie Abse has ever written. He journeys back into the blankness, tries to find the black behind the light:

> Travelling this evening, I focus on the back
> of brightness, on the red spot wavering.
>
> Behind it, what have I forgotten? It goes
> where the red spot goes, rising, descending.

Is he talking of some underground journey of the sun-god of Egypt, or else of some mystical experience of unknowing?

> I only describe a sunset, a car travelling
> on a swerving mountain road, that's all.

That's all. Who taught Abse to make Zen puns?

> Arriving too late, I approach the unlit dark.
> Those who loiter outside exits and entrances
>
> so sadly, so patiently, even they have departed.
> And I am no ghost and this place is in ruins.
>
> 'Black', I call softly to one dead but beloved,
> 'black, black' wanting the night to reply . . .

('Black')

Gone is the familiar victim-stance. Gone too is Abse 'talking quietly and persuasively to people who will understand, listen and agree'. The characters who inhabit his later work, 'those who loiter outside exits and entrances', are beginning to be important if only for their absence. He is no ghost and the place at the back of brightness is in ruins. He calls out to one dead but beloved, one of those presumably that he recalls with a thought that is as blank as stone. Mysteriously he calls the dead one 'black' – the forgotten thing at the back of brightness that he seeks. His wanting the night to reply 'black' is tempting but absurd, almost irrelevant. 'I only describe a sunset . . . that's all.'

Unfortunately few of the other short poems in the book show this authority and freedom from the *New Statesman* consensus. The interruptions of modishness into the poetic argument still get on one's nerves. When he remembers the changes time has made in the geography of the great world – red pieces gone for ever, and names of countries altered – if only, along with the Gold Coast becoming Ghana and Persia Iran, hell had *not* become Vietnam! In his portraits of himself as a middle-aged dog, there is more than a hint of Betjeman's sadness before the onsets of remembered flirtations:

> O my God,
> Morwenna, Julie, don't forget me, Kate.

('New diary')

He still identifies himself with mythical victims – in this case Orpheus torn to pieces by his fan-club. The end of this poem is pure cinema:

> Afterwards, the cyanosed figure
> on the ground, what was left of him,
> striped with blood, did not move,

and the women stood back silent,
most of them already smoking
and the others lighting up.

('The bereaved')

My impression is that some of his poems on patients are more decisive and cleaner, particularly 'my incurable cancer patient, the priest' who denounces miracles as OK for a doctor but quite impossible for him. In fact many of the poems on people, like 'The death of Aunt Alice', 'Peachstone', or 'Here', are satisfactory in a short-story sort of way. There is a new feeling for human courage in the face of death. But on the whole, with these shorter poems I feel that Abse's poetic vision is being tripped by the trap of the middlebrow, warped by what the blurb calls 'realistic and compassionate poems from his everyday experience' – what I would prefer to call the writing of 'representational poetry', which is as mistaken an aim as painting representational pictures.

Fortunately, 'Funland' itself, the title poem of the collection, is a real breakthrough into creative absurdity. In form, I suppose it is that very Anglo-Welsh thing, a radio ode, though it is not called one, having been broadcast on Radio 3 not Radio Wales. It is a long, surrealist-sounding poem using for its subject matter the inmates and weird happenings at a mental hospital. When I first read it I did not know it was about a mental hospital; I took it as a more or less abstract fantasy with characters like the 'masterful' superintendent who smiles in millimetres, draws the plans of the void and starts an arcane disquisition on bizarre secret weapons; or the tall handsome man they call Pythagoras who starts a society and is afraid it may turn into a religion unless they give it definition by having 'Thracians' to exclude. You can tell Thracians by their blue hair and red eyes; but there are also 'secret Thracians' in disguise. Then there is Fat Blondie, in her pink transparent night-dress, who spends most of the time in tears; and 'my atheist uncle' who wears black opaque glasses in order not to see the rubbish falling out of heaven; and a poet who chants 'Fu-er-uck Fu-er-uck' or 'Cu-er-unt Cu-er-unt' until he makes himself ill and has to be taken into the air. The happenings are wild and clearly the product of fierce schizophrenic fantasy, but they take place in a coherent, a created and fully realized world, where people accept that heaven's junk – like rusty angel's wings or Elijah's burnt-out chariot – various religious hardware – is perpetually crashing down outside the window.

The fantasy grows out of the special wish-fulfilments and reality substitutes of the patients, but is at the same time a reflection of the society in which we live. The characters all behave in zany ways with a solemn concentration that is both immensely serious, a matter of life and death, and really funny. One of the good things that the poem does is to suggest the levels of casualness at which bizarre behaviour can be taken for granted:

> And for some queer reason
> our American guest yells
> from time to time Mari-*an*
> if they give you chewing gum
> ............................... CHEW.

When the madness thins for a moment, we glimpse a return to sanity that is sad and frightening in a washed-out kind of way. The narrator from time to time remembers a love affair that he once suffered. Fragments of the true voice of feeling recur:

> We look left and right wondering
> who of us could be a secret Thracian
> wondering
> who of us would say
> with the voice of insurrection
> I love you
> not in a bullet proof room
> and not with his eyes closed.

Presumably, in the logic of the poem, to be a Thracian is to be sane; and to be sane is to be a victim.

For what is clear about Funland is that while people may behave as if they were acting from deep feeling, no one really feels anything but fear. The narrator writes a letter to someone nameless 'in white ink on white paper / to an address unknown':

> Oh love I write
> surely love was no less
> because less uttered or more accepted?

He then 'goosesteps' across the snow ('this junk of heaven') to post his blank envelope:

> Approaching the pillar box
> I hear its slit of darkness screaming.

Abse casually uses a word like 'goosesteps' – epitome of all that he hated as a Jew and a socialist – to describe the narrator's terrified progress to post a virtually non-existent love letter. The blank envelope, even, is feared for it is a proof of feeling and might give him away. The madness of Nazi Germany in all its unfeeling horror goosestepped with similar terror to that screaming slit of darkness.

That is typical of the way the words of 'Funland' gather more and more resonance as you read the poem:

> But Pythagoras is not happy.
> He wanted to found
> a Society not a Religion
> and a Society he says
> washing his hands with moonlight
> in a silver bowl
> has to be exclusive.
> Therefore someone must be banned.
> Who? Who? Tell us Pythagoras.
> The Thracians yes the Thracians.

Pythagoras is not only washing his hands like Pilate, he is paraphrasing Caiaphas the Chief Priest who gave counsel that one man should die for the people. The Thracians are excluded by a kind of lunatic racism – they have blue hair and red eyes – and feared for their atrocities and deadly cunning. Like the Jews under Nazism, all kinds of evil are attributed to them and particularly to the secret Thracians who go unnoticed:

> They are deadly cunning.
> Our water is polluted.
> Our air is polluted.
> Soon our orifices will bleed.

Of course 'Funland' is not about Nazism; it is about itself, a world behind locked gates, visited sometimes by 'strangers' who had once been lovers, sometimes by a scientific conference. It is a world where poetry –

> The last words Adam spoke to Eve
> as they slouched from Paradise –

has become a denatured, stammering chant 'Fu-er-uck Fu-er-uck' which Marian claims is an incitement not an expletive and which makes Fat

Blondie weep because it is so nostalgic. It is a hilarious parody of a poetry reading, but the background is bleak with desolation:

> After the interval
> the hall clatters raggedly into silence.
> Somewhere else distant
> a great black bell is beating
> the sound of despair
> and then is still.
> Cu-er-unt Cu-er-unt chants the poet.
> We applaud politely
> wonder whether he is telling or asking.
> The poet retires a trifle ill.
> We can all see that he requires air.

# 18

## An abdication from time:
## the Collected Poems of Raymond Garlick

~

Tony Bianchi has argued that the work of R. S. Thomas has called into
being for the first time a separate English-speaking readership in Wales;
but at the cost of making it permanently second best. R. S. Thomas was
perceived as cherishing all those positions that define the ethnic resurgence
of the Welsh-speaking middle class:

> a hostility to science and urban life as unWelsh; an elevation of rural
> values; an essentialist or ahistorical notion of nationalism, based on a
> selective view of the past and notions of an organic tradition; a belief in
> the importance of an elite in defending this ideal, of which the Welsh
> language is the embodiment; a view of the English-speaking Welsh as
> alienated and needing to align themselves with these values in order to
> overcome this alienation; and above all, the elevation of culture, literature
> and even 'taste' as the surrogate religion which informs these convictions.

The post-war Welsh-speaking intelligentsia, says Bianchi, adopted R. S.
Thomas as its 'honorary white' and used him as a point of reference by
which to distance or exclude other Anglo-Welsh writers of more dubious
allegiance.

> Institutionally and intellectually subordinate, an aspiring Anglo-Welsh
> intelligentsia acquiesced in this prescribed hierarchy in order to gain
> legitimacy. That collective acquiesence could not be realised, however,
> merely by the isolated reader's passive assent to a set of positions
> enunciated by the poet: rather, a whole readership had to be engaged as
> an active and conscious subject in the discourse. This, at bottom, was a
> formal problem. R. S. Thomas, in offering an answer to that problem,
> became the first Anglo-Welsh poet successfully to interpellate his

English-speaking readership within the discourse of cultural nationalism. ('R. S. Thomas and his Readers', in Tony Curtis (ed.), *Wales: The Imagined Nation* (Bridgend: Poetry Wales Press, 1986), 84–5)

Bianchi's structural analysis of how R. S. Thomas effected this interpellation in his most popular poems does not now concern us; but perhaps one can guess that R.S. did it almost in spite of himself. When R. S. Thomas seems to be addressing the reader ('Remember him, then, for he, too, is a winner of wars' etc.) I usually suspect he was really talking to himself; this is how the reader is drawn into the discourse, by becoming half of R. S. Thomas!

What has to be disputed is Bianchi's assertion that an intellectually subordinate Anglo-Welsh intelligentsia acquiesced in this prescribed hierarchy (and presumably in the ideology that went with it) in order to gain legitimacy. He notes poems by Bryn Griffiths, Harri Webb, John Tripp and Gillian Clarke that show Thomas's influence in their 'chronic long-sightedness'. It is certainly true that many of us were looking for a past we could identify with. My own 'Four Welsh personae' of 1954 – dramatic monologues where old Welsh poets like Gruffydd ab yr Ynad Coch, Dafydd ap Gwilym and Huw Morus talk about their art – ought to be mentioned at this point. Whether they were influenced by *Song at the Year's Turning* I don't know. It's more likely that I'd just been reading Gwyn Williams's *Introduction to Welsh Poetry*. Leslie Norris and John Ormond (a bit later) also tried to use the personages of early Welsh poetry to construct dramatic lyrics of their own. Neither they nor I have been drawn much into R. S. Thomas ideology.

There were (and are) other kinds of nationalisms around, besides those of us who weren't nationalist at all. Meic Stephens as a student told me he had no intention of learning Welsh, as he wanted to speak for English-speaking Wales. Raymond Garlick pinned his flag firmly to bilingualism. He wanted a European context for Wales. He actually supported television as a good thing because it made possible a pan-Welsh consciousness for the first time, and was thus a key to the creation of a Welsh state. All these nationalisms were overwhelmed not by R. S. Thomas (whom we disagreed with) but by the sudden people-power of the Welsh Language Society, demonstrating and going to prison for the language.

The initiative had passed out of our hands. We could only wish the boys and girls of Cymdeithas yr Iaith good or bad luck as the case may be, and get on with the job of creating an alternative culture, against the odds, for English-speaking Wales. The activists of the Cymdeithas made us temporarily irrelevant, but we did not give up the ideal of a bilingual nationalism – which actually remained Plaid Cymru policy. The trouble was, as nationalists we were outside the Welsh-language consensus – Garlick an Englishman, John Tripp a Cornish Welshman from the Valleys, myself an indeterminate English Welshman of Irish descent, and Jon Dressel (1934– ) a Welsh American. Garlick uses the term 'mestizo of cultures' to describe himself. A *mestizo* is a Spanish half-breed. We were half-castes, and we probably mistook the nature of the nationalism we were dealing with. To quote Bianchi again, the Welsh-speaking intelligentsia sought 'through a resurgent ethnicity to win a concessionary role on the fringes of the British state'. All the talk about a new and independent Welsh state proved in the event just my eye and Peggy Martin. It was not the Welsh-speakers – nor R. S. Thomas – but that part of the 'old' pre-Cymdeithas yr Iaith rump of largely English-speaking nationalists such as John Tripp and Raymond Garlick, who were totally discomfited by the Referendum vote in 1979.


Raymond Garlick would still be a significant figure in Anglo-Welsh poetry if he had never written a poem. He was born in London, but since his college days in Bangor (apart from a period in the sixties working in Holland) he has lived and taught in Wales all his life. He was the founding editor of *Dock Leaves*, later *The Anglo-Welsh Review*, which through the fifties and early sixties was practically the only outlet for Anglo-Welsh writing. He has argued consistently that English has been a literary language of Wales since the fifteenth century, and that its writers constitute no mere school but a literature, on a par with American or Australian, in English but not of England. This 'Anglo-Welsh' literature he has championed and chronicled as a contribution to European civilization and as a national heritage of the Welsh people.

Raymond Garlick's work as a poet shows a gradual loosening of his imagination from the ties of ideology. His early poetry, collected in *The Welsh-Speaking Sea* and *Blaenau Observed*, was that of a convert – to Wales, to Roman Catholicism, to what one can call 'educationalism'. Its characteristic *frisson* was that of a cultural fetishist – 'But O the joy of Welsh upon the street!' he exclaims about Tenby. His poem about going to Skomer ends: 'Then, praising God, I land.' 'And did you once see Shelley plain?' This element, celebrating (politely) the joys of his various faiths, has been tightened and tested over the years; but it still forms a very great part of his poetic purpose. The cover of his *Collected Poems*, an alphabet by Eric Gill once at Capel-y-ffin, looking like a sampler embroidered by the cherubim, gives you immediately the right sort of entry into his work. The alphabet is important to Garlick as a sacred object, not just as a medium of communication.

This early work tends to be in iambic pentameter. It seems to be innocent and Romantic, and to throw at you the big properties of our civilization. For example, John Cowper Powys in Blaenau Ffestiniog is told:

> You make us pause; survey ourselves again
> – catching a glimpse not merely of a town
> notorious as the native place of rain,
>
> but of a stage for human history
> superb as the theatre of Perikles.
> Poised amid peaks, we find our dignity.

Against this, there is set the picture of the poet himself. In this early work his physical deformity is seen as:

> a hustings for a heart wrapped in a wrack
> lusting for words to shape itself anew.

At this stage, the cultural *frisson* and romantic yearning of poetry is not yet there to be tied down, not to be schooled or splinted on to a new frame or surrogate skeleton for himself. Prosody is felt as a releasing process, in this early poetry, not as a reforming one. The crooked is not to be made straight by the poet's art, so much as released into freedom.

Garlick left Wales to teach in Holland in 1960, and his poetry changed with him. Short lines, often quatrains of iambic dimeters, now predominate. There is more conscious use of imagism:

> The secret adder
> flexed in the grass
> spits like a fuse
> as the noises pass.

But this is balanced by a much greater emphasis on moral and political point-making. His poetry begins to be conscious of opposition, to argue; to sound opinionated. It finds a mission in finding a European context for Wales. In political terms, of course, this was the correct strategy for the Anglo-Welsh intelligentsia. The European Community offers greater chance for local autonomy than the clattering nation-states of the past. It is noticeable that the United Kingdom and France, and even Spain, are much more tolerant of cultural nationalism in their minority peoples – the Welsh, the Bretons, the Catalans – now they are members of the EC. But the Welsh, as founder members of Great Britain, have been hard to convince of their European destiny. This has hit the Anglo-Welsh very badly. In any kind of political autonomy for Wales, their role would have been enormously enhanced. Instead of being poor whites, lowest of the low in the cultural priorities of the British state, without even the status of an ethnic minority, they would have been leaders and ideologues of a bilingual nation.

At this stage Garlick's attitude to himself and his work seems to change. Poetry and disability are still contrasted but now, he says, 'for me a poem is first a frame. / Form is the cane on which I lean.' He is much more conscious of the need to communicate. 'Art', he says, 'aspires to a telegram of images.' He does not only celebrate the values of civilization, he actively seeks to promote the kind of civilization he wants. His poetry – even in the sympathetic notation of the Dutch landscape – becomes inescapably political. The fact that his politics had not yet been tested in practice gives his work an air of armchair pontificating; but that is something all teachers are subject to, unless they're on their guard.

He returned to Wales, to a lecturing post in Carmarthen, in 1967. It was a very different Wales he came back to. A lot more was happening. The creation of the Welsh Arts Council had injected money into Welsh and Anglo-Welsh culture. *Poetry Wales* had spearheaded a nationalist revival of poetry. Above all, the young people of Cymdeithas yr Iaith Gymraeg, the Welsh Language Society, had responded to a lecture by Saunders Lewis on the fate of the language and were now taking direct action – acts of civil disobedience *à la* Gandhi.

Once again, Garlick's poetry changed. Up to then he seems not to have been very conscious of what a desperate little country Wales is. Like many Englishmen who come here, he looked for peace and quality of life – respectable, literary, moral values. He returned to Wales in a mael-strom. He was present at, and surprisingly well equipped to deal with, one of the contortions of the tragic peripeteia of Wales.

He had the vision, because he had so recently come back. Wales was vivid to him, both as memory and presence:

There's a spot in Bangor, between
the climb of the College park
and the old Bishop's palace –
I could lead you there in the dark.
On the map of my mind the place
is a paving-stone with the mark

of a cross. It's vivid today –
the scruffy hedge, the sudden stilled
ring of a passer-by's footsteps,
the sun going in, the air chilled,
and overhearing someone say
'Gandhi has been killed.'

Would the struggle keep to Gandhian principles and avoid violence and bloodshed? That was the main problem. And when the crunch came, it was not the protesters who were violent, but the police, the forces of law and order. The main tension in the new poetry that Garlick was writing back in Wales in the sixties was the one between his pacifism and the nationalist struggle. The resurrection of ancient Welsh heroic values from the *Gododdin* had its dangers. Poem on poem reflects on this revival, and on the need to save peace.

He had vision. He had an ideology of martyrdom. Christianity is such an ideology anyway, but for Catholics the period was dominated by the process at Rome leading to the consecration of the Elizabethan martyrs – English and Welsh – as saints of the Church. Garlick played a considerable part, in his radio-poem 'Acclamation' in celebrating this process. Martyrdom was a living force to him both for that public reason and for the personal anguish that his family was undergoing at that time, in the critical illness of his son.

He had a vision of Wales; he had a framework of ideas. He also had sufficient innocence to register the tawdry reaction of the state machinery to what was going on, as shock, amazement and horrified indignation. A more cynical person would have been disqualified. I expect nation-states to be oppressive, stupid, immoral and violent. Garlick did not, and therefore when they were his very English sense of fair play was outraged.

The poetry of outrage is still found in the *Collected Poems*. But what gave depth and reality to that poetry has been either excised altogether (as we shall see) or split among different topics. As these poems were originally collected in *A Sense of Time*, the outrage was only a part of an imaginative vision of what happened in the streets and lawcourts of Swansea; part of something much greater, part of God's dealing with the world, part of the order of love: martyrdom and finding, suffering and glory, pacifism and the Cross. It's that dimension (which I think is not only available to fellow believers) that makes the book a contribution to tragic vision. It is the book of Raymond Garlick's that I go back to, time after time. It transcends the play of his opinions, the expression of enthusiasms and distastes.

On the evidence of the new poems in the *Collected Poems*, subsequent to the trauma of *A Sense of Time*, Garlick's political direction was defeated in the Devolution Referendum; his religious faith did not survive the modernist reforms of Pope John XXIII, particularly the substitution of the vernacular for Latin in the liturgy; and his family in Llansteffan broke up, so that he lives now by himself in a flat in Carmarthen. This triple catastrophe has had very searching and profound effects on his poetry; both in the new poetry he has produced since it happened, and in the way he now looks at his poetic output as a whole, of which the *Collected Poems* is the definitive product.

On the positive side, his new poetry is marked by a strong desire to get things right. Autobiography has become his dominant mode. He acknowledges his Englishness – paradoxically sometimes using a rhythm reminiscent of R. S. Thomas who (John Barnie assures us) is the only *real* Anglo-Welsh poet. He writes of his childhood, being taken to the Mall to see the Trooping of the Colour and being gratifyingly irreverent; of his teachers; of himself as a teacher, 'Mr G of the Sixth . . . in full sail' – a real achievement this, mocking his own image:

> entering
> Rooms as though to unheard music,
> Wherever he goes order breaks
> Out, a clearway opens for him,
> Chattering stills. And should it not
> (Through inadvertence), he takes out
> His spectacles and slowly puts
> Them on, stares over them as if
> Transfixed by total disbelief . . .

Anglo-Welsh poetry is beridden by the teaching profession: it is not often we see through the earnest aspirations to the reality of the power struggle involved, or the actual feelings of being a good teacher. Garlick uses the old trick of third-person narrative here, and elsewhere, to distance himself from his life and to achieve equilibrium with his own past:

> His bitter hatred for his native
> Land, it said.
>
> He was appalled. How
> Hate the innocent earth, the hills'
> Elgar adagio . . .

Even more striking use of this device is found in the handful of lyrics right at the end of the collection, where he deals with the breakup of his marriage and his faith, and his resolution not to be 'born again'. These achieve a kind of benedictory effect, which is powerfully honest and has a kind of peace. In this new poetry his relationship to his own disablement also changes. Whereas in the past it had been contrasted with the poetry that would shape him into freedom, now the bitterness surfaces openly and becomes his subject matter:

> From boyhood into middle age
> Scarcely a single day had passed
> Without his flinching in distaste.

'If only', he cries, 'if only . . .' But at the end his surgeons set free in him 'strong, flawed life'. The poem is called 'The survivor': he no longer expects his poetry to do the surviving for him.

Indeed, the new poetry isolates survival and a sense of identity as its paramount values. Insofar as it still expresses Anglo-Welsh attitudes, it does so from a distance: the Welsh are (rather querulously, to my mind) censured for failing in both – as compared, for example, with the Dutch. The English-speaking Welsh are particularly disadvantaged. 'You're not really Welsh at all', the media-culture insists. In Wales Garlick finds himself finally unmasked –

> So
> Non-patrial, a mestizo
> Of cultures, see this worker-ant
> Unmasked now as an immigrant . . .

Identity and survival. This poetry, as Garlick's poetry has always done, reaches towards peace, towards equilibrium. If the cost is bitterness, old values jettisoned, old beliefs discredited, so be it. He will survive. He will retain his identity. As Voltaire remarked of God in another context, that is his *métier*.

These new poems should have been collected in a separate book, then we could have judged them for what they are, as fine poetry, as personal expression of an important human being in a particular time and place, and as a phenomenon of Anglo-Welsh culture *in extremis*. For it is apparent that the Anglo-Welsh movement is in crisis, and has been since 1979. The shock to our sense of purpose delivered by the Referendum is not within miles of being healed.

But in order to lay his poetry at the feet of his new gods, Identity and Survival, Garlick has not merely written new poems. That would be a positive thing, to be welcomed however much one may or may not agree with his viewpoint. For these poems are strong, valuable stuff. But there is a negative side. First, he has censored out nearly every reference to his Catholic beliefs; and second, he has arranged his poetry in what he calls a 'thematic' order. Together these decisions amount to a very strong and insistent filter on his literary career. It is all very well for a metaphysical poet like John Ormond to ignore chronology – though even with him it is a nuisance to people who want to come to terms with his development. With Garlick – as with Wordsworth – the strategy of 'thematic' arrangement is immediately felt as suspicious, simply because both of them have been involved in history, and both of them have changed their minds.

For there is no doubt that he has compromised with his 'sense of time' – ditched it, in fact, along with the Catholicism. Martyrdom was an important dimension of what he gave expression to in Wales. To leave it out denies history as much as he says those Welshmen were doing who voted against devolution. His faith in Christianity may only have been imagination, but imagination is what poetry is made of. To deny the proper sphere of poetry in the name of morality or politics or a change of religious belief is what we say dictators do, or intolerant churches. He has opted for an identity and a survival that is basically timeless. Clio, the muse of history, is not so easily set aside.

If one goes to Garlick's earlier books and looks at the role of Catholicism in them, one notices a fair amount that one is not all that sorry to lose. A good deal of it seems unreal: most of 'Acclamation' does not for more than a few lines at a time realize itself as felt experience. But even in 'Acclamation' the martyrdom provides a medium for what is going on now. It is (at the least) a repository of human worth that exists outside Raymond Garlick himself:

> These are the named ones, but I shall name
> as well those Protestant consciences
> of Wales who chose the scaffold and the flame:

Rawlins White, poor Cardiff fisherman;
William Nichol of Haverfordwest;
John Penry of Llangamarch, Puritan;

the Anglican Robert Ferrar, his last breath
drawn in Carmarthen. As I cross Nott Square
I make my act of sorrow for each death.

The names refuse to be just images in a book of poetry. Every one of them has a potential reality, ready to be opened to you in a relationship that is more than I-it – in Christian terms, the I-thou relationship of the Communion of Saints.

Catholicism in Garlick does at least have the function of opening up I-thou relationships. He is not a great religious poet, I think, but his religion makes him a better poet than he would otherwise have been. Does it matter to us, his readers, whether his experience was or was not of a genuine supernatural order? We have no means of telling that anyway. As poetry the experience he was in when he wrote *A Sense of Time* was so much greater than himself. To deal with it as he does in the *Collected Poems* amounts to a deliberate slighting of his vision, as castles were 'slighted' or destroyed by their defenders to prevent them being captured and used by the enemy. Why has he limited himself in this way? For survival's sake? Or for identity? Both of these deities seem to me to be another name for the ego – its opinions, its images, its fight to gain equilibrium and calm.

Raymond Garlick is not a timeless poet, any more than Wordsworth was. From the pieces expunged from the *Collected Poems* I remember him almost overwhelmed by the illness of his child ('A touch of white'); or his words to John Kemble, martyred in 1679:

What I remember, gentle
old man, is how you smoked
one final, wreathing pipe and
sipped a parting cup of sack,
savouring life and Hereford
until the hangman spoke the word.

It's that word, really, that I miss in the *Collected Poems*. No amount of propaganda for civilized life, or praise of the Netherlands countryside, makes up for its loss.

# 19

## The Referendum and the poetry
## of Jon Dressel

~

Anglo-Welsh is a very accurate term. It is a literary description, of course, not an ethnographical one. Anglo-Welsh literature is not books written by Anglo-Welshmen (though sometimes one wonders!) but books written within earshot of a frontier. It is the literature of a March. These days the March is not a geographical feature. It can be anywhere – through my backyard in Bangor where my children are Welsh-speaking but I am not – through a Cardiff shop or a Llangollen office. Most people in Wales live lives that at some point or other are different because of this insidious March, snaking along between them and the complacency of being completely Welsh or completely English. Nor is this Anglo-Welsh frontier limited to Wales: it can be felt in Birmingham or York, or for that matter in Illinois or New South Wales.

The literature of the Anglo-Welsh frontier already includes several American conscripts: Lynette Roberts, Joseph Clancy and now Jon Dressel. They should not be thought exceptional. Jon Dressel, born in Missouri, is no more exotic to us than David Jones, born in Kent. In fact, of the two, Jon Dressel is the more familiar. His first collection, *Hard Love and a Country* (Triskel Poets 20), showed him enthusiastically Anglo-Welsh in many of the accepted modes: poems about his Welsh relatives, ironic poems about English visitors, poems creating the archetypal 'Dai' – both the embodiment of everything wrong with Wales and at the same time a source of faith. Two poems commented wryly on the Dylan Thomas legend. In an American context these would no doubt be described as looking for roots; in an Anglo-Welsh magazine they were a very familiar presentation of the writer's credentials.

In 'Synopsis of the Great Yanklo-Welsh Novel' he tells how his grandfather 'given to choirs but hankering for cash / and air beyond Llanelli' settles in Illinois, and how

259

> one day Jon, short
> for Jones, comes to Llanelli, on whim,
> aged 27, at the sloshed-out end of a con-
> tinental tour; he has a religious ex-
> perience on Copperworks Road, chords sound,
> he knows who he is; he sells the family
> business, begins to write poetry ...

There you have much of the polarity of Dressel's poetry. On the one side, the hankering for cash and open spaces which lures Welsh people away – 'Why did you come to Pennsylvania to discover greed?' – but on the other, freedom, keeping the faith, knowing who you are, innocence:

> this is the dead end
> of Wales, unconfessed, alive, still saved.

As doctrine, it strikes me as over-simple. One is not quite sure whether Dressel isn't the Innocent Abroad rather than Wales the Land of Lost Content. But his enthusiasm is coupled with a sheer delight in language, a free-wheeling American fantasy; and it is this larger-than-lifeness, together with compassion for actual people in actual situations, which allows him to use the doctrine to produce poems which sometimes seem wiser than the doctrine itself.

One poem that does succeed like this is 'Children, night, Llansteffan'. The children in the village telephone booth – ironically with his own children among them – ringing up Carmarthen, Llanybri, anywhere but here, become embodiments of the hankering to get away, to leave 'the dead end of Wales'. He wants to go down to them and say, 'It's all right, Wales is a good place'; but it's no good, for he comes from the sound and glitter of places they have never known. He can't help them.

> The call ends; they move off, slowly,
> from the booth's cold light, one amorphous
> creature, murmuring, towards the dark
> of the bus shelter, till time to go home.

Light and dark, home and anywhere, childhood's restlessness and need for rest, are temporarily reconciled.

The contrast between ideology and the reality of Wales is most strident in poems which deal with individual neighbours Dressel knows in Llansteffan, like Jones the Stores, the Fishers and the shop girl. 'The shop girl' is a very self-conscious poem and really rather too prosaic, but it will do to pin-point my unease:

> There are worse places
> than Littlewoods. I have my paycheque
> and a boyfriend, a taste for Babycham
> and a vague vision of prams. Having
> no larger needs or illusions, I will
> be happy enough, and die, if I am lucky,
> at my ease with Sunday telly at the age
> of eighty-two. What is the dream
> of Wales to me? Even the poet who
> toys with me on this page understands
> that in my kept inertial dullness I am
> totally invincible, and make his hand go slack.

No, I want to say, life isn't like that. In Thatcher's Wales, does she still have her job at Littlewoods? Did her boyfriend marry her or is she a one-parent family on the dole? The poet is trying to bludgeon the poor girl with the past generations – but even a shop girl is not going to treat the past in this paper-tiger sort of way. She must have her own elderly, her own *mamgu*. I bet she doesn't think of her grandmother as 'lucky to die with Sunday telly at the age of eighty-two'. 'What is the dream of Wales to me?' the poet makes her ask. Nothing at all, I would have said, unless it relates to her life in Wales now. We are all of us missing out from the past. She is not exceptional in this. Wales is a past, yes, but it is also an infinitely complex present and future, a field full of folk, a field of exploitation and comfort, a rubbish heap and a forest just coming into leaf.

The lack of feeling for the girl as she is is perhaps exceptional, in that there is very little else in the poem to balance it. Other poems are certainly more compassionate and alive to the otherness of people. However, the feeling gap is present in many of these pieces, though usually not to such a marked degree. It is what makes me uneasy about 'A diary for St David's week, 1979', the centre-piece of Dressel's second collection, *Out of Wales*, from which 'The shop girl' comes. A Welsh translation or adaptation of this 'Diary' was unanimously awarded the Bardic Crown in the 1979 National Eisteddfod at Caernarfon, only to be disqualified as a collaboration. It is of course about the week of the Referendum in Wales as to whether there should be a Welsh Assembly in Cardiff with limited devolution of power. The subject set for the competition was 'Serch neu Siom' (Love or Disappointment).

The issue of devolution was clearly the main Anglo-Welsh question since the 1939–45 war. It is not surprising that many Anglo-Welsh writers felt bitterly disappointed at the result. The Nationalists fell hook, line and sinker into the trap: the Referendum stopped being a debate about how to control democratically the burgeoning and largely independent Welsh bureaucracy, and became a vote of no-confidence in Wales herself. Dressel's 'Diary' registers the grip of that no-confidence on the minds and hearts of those who suffered most from it. It is perhaps fitting that the only time when an Anglo-Welsh poet has come near to laying illicit hands on the holy of holies and winning a prize at the National Eisteddfod, should be in the wake of the Devolution fiasco. The issue was central to Anglo-Welsh perspectives as it never really was to Welsh-speaking Wales. This is not a matter of who supported what; simply that a Welsh Assembly automatically would have revolutionized the status of Anglo-Welsh writers while it would have left Welsh ones very much as it found them. It is also appropriate that an American Welshman should have done the deed, for only an American Welshman would have had the innocence or cheek to do it.

So far, so good. But at a time when the primary need was to seek clarity, to find comfort and not to give way to foolish despair, Dressel (at the time, I must admit, like me) was overwhelmed by it. The first poem, 'Sunday', sets the tone:

> in just four days there will be
> a stupendous aborting of the green force
> within us . . . and a season unimaginable
> and yet to be named, a season
> of the poisoned heart that hates itself
> will come to birth in the place of spring
> and lay us waste with ash for which we lust.

'Wednesday' invokes Llywelyn and Glyn Dŵr. 'Thursday' – Referendum Day – turns all the Welsh people in the town into sheep:

> Here the people
> smell of wet wool. I must not dwell on it.
> These are just my people.
> They are nothing more. These people
> smell like sheep. I cannot help it.
> They are sheep. They bleat.

The final apocalypse of disgust is reached in the 'Friday' poem. He explicitly compares the collapse of Devolution to the Conquest of Wales in 1282:

> Still, no day like this
> for seven hundred years.

> It is weather we the living
> have never felt before.
> The land is rotten.
> Rotten to its bowels.
> The trees ooze corruption . . .

Dressel finally invokes the memory of Gruffydd ab yr Ynad Coch (Gruffydd the son of the Red Judge) and his great elegy for the last Prince, a poem of cataclysmic grandeur mourning the collapse of independent Wales:

> Only the deep
> of the sea is clean,
> and it will not come,
> as it did not come for the Son
> of the Red Judge, to give relief, to end.

This is intemporate language. On 1 March 1979 the king of Gwynedd's head was not hoisted on a spear, exhibited on every town wall in Wales and finally left in the Tower of London. Neither did English soldiery pillage and burn their way through every *cantref* and township. Cradled babies did not scream any more loudly because of the Referendum. But that is the sort of thing that happens in Gruffydd the son of the Red Judge's poem. Not even metaphorically could the process of democratic choice, however warped by propaganda, be fairly referred to in those kinds of terms.

Ideology is in control and it is blinding the poet to what is really going on. It might be said that the Welsh people were not taking an opportunity that they should have taken; but there were (and I hate to admit this, myself) good and sufficient Welsh reasons for not taking it. One should ask oneself, does the model of colonial liberation really fit? Is Wales like Ireland? Is it even like Scotland, where union with England was agreed and can be revoked? Was Henry VIII the English monster that John Tripp pictures, swallowing Wales for a nightcap between wives? One ought to remember that the last time Welshmen (as Welshmen) fought against an English king, the Welsh won. They marched into London under the Red Dragon of Cadwaladr, the last ruler of independent Britain according to their legends. Britain, Great Britain, even the British Empire, are Welsh ideas, foisted on a rather bemused England by a dynasty very conscious of its British (i.e., Welsh) roots.

This is not to deny that many factors in Welsh life, and particularly in Welsh-speaking Welsh life, have affinities with colonial and post-colonial existence. These factors could eventually lead to separatism being adopted by the Welsh people and possibly even a war of liberation. It might be better for Wales (as I think) if she did cut herself free from her own ideological obsession with Britain; if she did, though, Arthur and Cadwaladr, Owain and Harri would be hated and prescribed names, almost like Quisling or Vortigern, as misleaders of the Cymry. But as of now, this has not yet happened. Wales still apparently regards herself as a founder member of Britain, and that means being an imperial nation in decline, tied to her destroyer in a symbiosis as old as Bosworth.

The Referendum was an intensely destructive thing, nevertheless. Wales has become much more boring since it happened, for it frosted so much that was just coming to fruition. Even the newspapers are conscious of this. Before the Referendum Wales had been news. There were reporters paid to take soundings, to send in reports of the struggle. That was a long time ago. The week of the 'no' vote changed all that. Dressel's poetry registers the awfulness of those days well enough; but it seems limited to the vision of shock, and the only comfort the poet can offer is that life goes on as usual and it will be all the same in a hundred years.

Jon Dressel has written social and political poetry about Wales which demands to be taken seriously. What vitiates his attempt is partly a political naïvety, partly a basic contradiction between form and content. The form is based on the personal-point-of-view, post-imagist and 'realist' Anglo-American lyrical tradition. The poem is a lens through which the reader can view a carefully framed and ordered fragment of experience, and so share with the poet the thrill of recognition and insight. On the other hand, the content of these poems is the social continuum, the interplay of people, and the desire to affect that interplay – to some extent – by what you are saying. The form demands I-it relationships to be dominant, the material demands I-thou. If you look at Gruffydd ab yr Ynad Coch's great elegy, what gives it point and control is the poet's former I-thou relationship to the dead prince. Similarly, in the greatest political poem of our century, Yeats's 'Easter 1916', it is the presence of Pierce and Connolly, MacDonagh and MacBride, as themselves and not just part of his experience, that makes it possible for the poet to write political poetry that lives in the real world, not in the private suburbs of intimate sensibility. The Welsh praise-tradition has many faults, and it would be naïve to suggest it holds the answer to all our problems, living as we do on this twentieth-century Anglo-Welsh March. But in this particular respect it has the edge on the Anglo-American tradition which all but drowns it out.

# 20

## Tony Curtis and the ways of death

~

Tony Curtis as a young, ambitious writer always seemed to be winning prizes, notable for his willingness to have a go. Sometimes this led to wonderfully embarrassing results. I treasure the poem welcoming Solzhenitsyn to Britain for its self-important and kindly bathos: 'Right now, you are tired – but in good shape.' More often one responded to an imagination ready to hijack a poem into virtue, rather than informing its creation as a whole. 'Killing whales' is a good example. A careful if rather pedestrian description seems to exist for the sake of its last few lines:

> In the ship's belly white flashes
> Pattern the darkness of a sonar screen.
>
> Circling the fleet, whales sing deeply
> Love to the hulls of factory ships.

The model of the snapshot *moralisé* (made explicit in the title of his first major collection, *Album*, and often in the poems themselves) is not one I find satisfactory. It represents an over-easy transformation of private experience into public art, all too often reminiscent of a lecture with slides.

Then one had registered a deepening imaginative power, chiefly associated with a remarkable sequence on the death of his father, a gradual focusing of vision on narrative, and, in the last few years, some really impressive poems usually about the rise of Hitler, the Holocaust and the Second World War.

The pattern seemed clear; but reading through Curtis's *Selected Poems* forced me to think again. In particular I realized that I had not given due weight to 'The deerslayers', a sequence of twenty-four four-line poems based on a folio of photographs by the American Leslie Krims, and originally published as a booklet by Cwm Nedd Press in 1977. To quote Curtis's dust-jacket on the booklet,

> I wrote these poems over a number of weeks, drawing each photograph at random out of the original folio box. Some photographs sparked off an immediate response and the poem was quickly formed; with others I had to work hard to see the depth of tension between Hunter, Dead Deer and Vehicle – the underlying structure of each composition.

Curtis in these poems has stopped using the photograph as a convenience, a sort of reach-me-down way of handling his material, and really taken seriously photography as an art. He has learnt the discipline of it. The 'depth of tension' between hunter, dead deer and car (present in the twenty-four photographs) has acted as a formal activator of a creative field. The poems arise out of this field as each photograph in turn is drawn out of the box. For the first time in Curtis, the whole is greater than the sum of its parts. Although the original or satiric aim of the photographer – he doesn't like the slaughter of wild animals for sport – is by no means lost, what emerges from the poetry is in fact more like a series of epitaphs on the slayers themselves. 'The buck's antlers close round you like claws', he says of one; or of another's trophy,

> its muzzle coming
> at your left side like a lover. Death's own kiss.

The ancient 'death and the maiden' theme where death is a lover coming for his bride is given added horror by the slang pun on 'coming'.

The 'empty-eyed' killings are done by people who are bored, obsessional, insincere, foolish. And yet there is a strange sort of compassion, a sense of *lacrimae rerum* which makes these poems not so much a diatribe against killing deer as a description of the human condition itself:

> Two loons: two loons with loon smiles.
> Two loons with loon smiles and check shirts perched on the hood.
> Two loons with loon smiles and check shirts perched on the hood
> with arms round 2 cold, dead doe. In the night.

The accumulative repetition like a party game (A, A+B, A+B+C . . .) has its own impact – the loons are made more foolish, the idiocy of their gestures more meaningless. But the way the pattern is released gives a force to the phrase 'In the night' that makes it so much greater than either the loons or their folly. Partly it is a matter of sound – the hollow d's, the long vowels, particularly the unexpected assonance on 'cold' and 'doe' with its hint of baby-like babble. Even the use of the numeral '2' after the fourfold 'two' written in full contributes a nuance to the typographical effect: it reduces what had been a pair into a statistic.

Again, in the last poem of all,

> Your grandson has the intense
> determined look of a future lawyer.
> Across the roof, that deer's white eye stretches to infinity.

The formal co-ordinates of hunter, dead deer and vehicle create a poetic field: the apparent monotony of design in fact makes possible a complex variety that opens out like the deer's white eye.

These quatrains must surely rank with the finest poems of their generation, and certainly so in Anglo-Wales. Why didn't one realize their quality before? Well, there are a few excuses. The pamphlet was badly produced, and made a half-hearted attempt to establish a random order on the poems by suggesting we should cut them up and juggle with them. That was a mistake on the poet's part: because the order in which he picked photographs out of the box was random, he assumed that the poems would work like that for the reader as well. But a poem has to introduce itself to us, a poetic field has to establish its own co-ordinates. To expect every quatrain to be able to do this, in a poetic sequence of such complexity, was to demand a *tour de force*. Sensibly, in *Selected Poems* Curtis has changed his mind. He has found a right order for the sequence, which is not the same as that tentatively put forward in the pamphlet.

I should judge that the experience of writing 'The deerslayers' was important to Curtis in three ways. First, it made him respect the photograph's integrity as an art-form. Second, it taught him to use tensions between centres of feeling – people, objects or ideas – as the co-ordinates of a poetic field. For example, in the very emotional circumstances of his father's last illness, he organizes his poetry in terms of the field of their relationship both with each other and with the circumstances they are in. Once again, the whole is greater than the parts. Indeed the parts only exist insofar as they are produced – almost randomly – by the poetic field of the whole; and insofar, therefore, as they reveal the whole.

Thirdly, 'The deerslayers' might well have uncovered for his imagination the main subject matter of his art – at any rate, up to now. This can roughly be described as 'ways of death' as one talks about 'ways of life'. In his sadly ironical 'Poem for John Tripp'[1] – ironical, that is, now John is dead – he quotes 'The Pardoner's Tale':

> John, we are under the weight of this thing
> And we wol slayn this false traytor Deeth
> clench the fist around the pen, we riotoures three:
> you and I and the third – our dead friends and fathers,
> on the road, at the desk, looking over our shoulders.

The idea of the dead subjects of their poetry as the third of the rioters who set out to kill death is a complex one: we recall that in Chaucer the two kill the one, who in turn posthumously poisons them. Curtis does not develop the idea, but perhaps something of it lies behind his poetry of death. The poet tries to kill death by fixing it in his art; but also, he has to extirpate the effect of the dead on himself, which otherwise would poison him. The poetry is a way of ridding himself (and us) of the accumulated grief, guilt, fear and longing that the dead can inspire. It is a way of 'letting go'.

That of course was the title of Curtis's last book of poems before the *Selected*. It was clearly a transitional volume. Alun Rees had already identified our source of unease in early Curtis in a very percipient review of *Album* in *Poetry Wales*: 'The pose he adopts is tough . . . a verbal cameraman dealing with reality in stark detail. Behind this persona, however, there is a nice man, a warm man, a neighbour to humanity . . .' And again:

> Curtis himself may be surprised at the number of Curtises revealed in this collection. There is Homo nostalgica of 'Davy' and 'The Circus Left'. There is Homo paternica ... decently worried about the children in his teacher's care . . . Homo peripatitica . . . Homo cabalistica . . . Homo lyrica, blest with the power to move himself and us . . .(vol. 10, no. 1)

The trouble with all these Homos – made feminine for the nonce by the reviewer – the trouble with all these Homines is not that they are various,

---

[1] The one in *Preparations* (Bridgend: Poetry Wales Press, 1980), not the long poem 'Thoughts from the Holiday Inn' composed after Tripp's death. It is perhaps surprising that he seems to include Tripp's father among the dead: John Tripp's father survived him by several months.

but that they are clichés, given to Curtis off the peg by the *Guardian*-cum-*Western Mail* culture he springs from. A lyric poet may indeed deal with subjective feelings; but the subject that feels them must be new-minted and thought through. It is Curtis's failure to create his own ego imaginatively that makes so much of his early poetry a collection of good bits rather than an *œuvre*. The creation of an imagined ego is analogous to, but not identical with, the ability to know oneself which the Greeks said was the beginning of wisdom.

He escaped from this problem in 'The deerslayers' by adopting the discipline of a camera rather than pretending to be a cameraman. In the poems about his father's death the reality of where he is, and where his father is, mostly crowds out the cliché selves. But in the first part of *Letting Go* it almost seemed as if he was not going to learn from these achievements. Certainly the title of the book gave one hope: for in these matters (as in greater) he that would find his life must lose it. But the old problem of the ego dogs him, like his grandmother's cactus:

> Time after time, when I'm sunk in work
> and stretch for a book, I'm spiked.
>
> The needles stab through shirts and
> wool and cloth. The jabs hook under the skin
> and days later inflame as spots that weep poison.
> I should move it. I should throw it out.
>
> But Gran, it's part of you in my life.
> One day I will, in turning to the shelf,
> thinking of quite different things,
> put my face right into it – that sure pain.

('My grandmother's cactus')

In the second and much better part of *Letting Go*, it is clear, he does take his own advice and throw it out. If he cannot create a satisfactory ego for himself, why not, like Browning, try other people's. The dramatic monologue – or the dramatic lyric, at any rate – was one way forward. He had made his poetry a medium for other voices as early as 'The spirit of the place' from *Preparations*, where the embodiment of the south Pembrokeshire coast sings of its mystery. The poem is in marked contrast to the rest of the book, and the absence of the cliché selves is refreshingly open to lyricism:

My weather eats the oiled guns of Castlemartin.

My surf rides in white, fucks fissures and caves.

I spread my legs in the cliff heather
move with waves.
My cries crack the headland's concrete bunkers,
spike the last war's ghost barrels.

Summer I twist lanes into blindnesses of faith.
I grit through carburettors till they phlegm to a stop;
my nails slough caravans into ditches.

I turn signs.

But the voice is too chant-like, too hostile to history and human process, to serve Curtis's permanent concerns.

The first poem in *Letting Go* that marks a decisive step forward is 'Trials'. It hits one like a whiplash. An American angrily asserts his German wife's innocence of the wartime atrocities with which she is charged. Here at last is a credible persona, whose imaginative reality shapes the utterance with stark inevitability:

I believe nothing of this.
Nothing.

Lies infest these proceedings like lice
– a court of blind revenge.
You talk to me of gas chambers
– show me them.
Photographs – faked.
A man in Dusseldorf wrote me –
Ah! You don't listen.

The man has been insulated from the horror of our history. He has lived with

a loving wife since the time she came
to the United States of America

(notice the plangency, the Pilgrim Fathers and all that) and now he is told she killed children, set a German shepherd to tear a pregnant woman apart. The plane of his and her normality will not accommodate it. Atrocity is something that happens in places like Phnom Penh, Uganda or Russia; not in real life, not done by all-American people like them. But the nightmare will not go away; the voice modulates from the passionate yet still prosaic, 'short-story' opening into something that only poetry can do – modulates seamlessly, without any of the feeling we often have in early Curtis that the imagination is 'hijacking' the prose:

> All I know is that for me
> it will be years more without her.
>
> Can you understand the horror of that?
>
> One night a blanket of snow
> thick over the State of New York; the lines
> down. I go with her in my dreams:
> she moves ahead of me, turning
> in the saddle, beckoning
> with her whip. She moves towards
> the smoke rising in the trees, past
> a straggling column of refugees.
>
> Hermine, my wife, my woman,
> my beautiful silver mare.

The snow, the lines down, the beckoning whip, the smoke rising and the straggling refugees create a strange confusion of wistfulness and guilty awareness, which she moves towards. Does he know, underneath, that she is a war criminal, for all his protestations; but that counts as nothing against the beauty of her animal being?

The man in his relation to his wife and she in her relation to the Holocaust inhabit a three-dimensional world; but it is dream-imagery that confirms and deepens this space into poetry. Curtis in his recent work is often very cunning in organizing space-time in this way. Sometimes he creates a 'field' by the overlapping of two occasions, two narrators. Sometimes, as in 'Two for luck' where he plots the behaviour of a man who is having a heart attack, he does it simply with the meticulousness of his narrative. Though the dramatic monologue is only one technique among many, it still seems a paradigm of what is happening: in very few poems of this group (mainly in *Selected Poems*, 11–38) does Curtis invoke the cliché selves that often seemed to squander his imagination before. Even when he uses 'I' as he does in 'Boxes', he does so for largely functional reasons, to throw the subject of the poem

– a reargunner nursing a mate with half his head blown off – into greater relief.

The convergence of two worlds, the normal one and an Otherworld usually of brutal death, is typical of Curtis. Sometimes the contrast is not with death but with love; and in one tender poem he reaches towards the mystery of his own conception through contemplating a photo of his mother as a land-army girl just before she met his father. But on the whole, 'ways of death' are where his imagination roosts. The blurb of *Selected Poems* rightly asserts that he is not an elegist: for elegy is a lament for a life or a way of life that has gone. Curtis aims at tragedy. He dares to attempt the vast tragic themes of our time. And, of course, this is not without risks. The material is so big and so emotional that it can dwarf the art that tries to deal with it. Or else, unless the poet comes clean, he may seem to be exploiting the misery of others: on a par, in fact, with a manufacturer of soap from human fat. And again, even if we do return to these places – Belsen, Auschwitz, Hiroshima – what we demand above all is the authentic record of a survivor. Anything else can seem at best irrelevant, at worst an impostor.

The tragic mode is rare in English lyric, though quite common in traditional ballad and folk-song. Folk-song generally ignores the general issues and dwells only on the personal. A song of the Napoleonic wars, for example, will pin-point a dying soldier on the battlefield sending a message to his girl that he loves her. Curtis usually chooses situations which have a more sophisticated relation to history than that; but essentially he too concentrates on the individual suffering and response. His subjects are specific and quite often named: 'The death of Richard Beatle-Seaman in the Belgian Grand Prix, 1939'. This specificity is one safeguard against the dangers we mentioned. Even dealing with an anonymous victim of the Holocaust, the whole effort is to create an individual situation, a gesture or predicament; and that was always the way of tragedy.

It is tempting to connect the problem of the cliché selves in Curtis with his confusion about Welshness:

> Growing up in Carmarthen through the 1950's I had always assumed that I was Welsh. This despite the fact that I was not sure what that entailed, apart from the fact that Carmarthen was undoubtedly *in* Wales; despite the fact, also, that no one in our house spoke Welsh. (*Wales the Imagined Nation*, 8)

But though this may have its place, it is certainly less than the disturbance caused by an ambitious provincial mind trying to catch up and overtop the fashions of the metropolis. That mind and its ambition, in turn, owed much to the extrovert south Walian communal norms in which it was nurtured and the models of poetic and professional achievement – particularly, perhaps, that of Dannie Abse from Cardiff – that were felt as available.

A more interesting question is the relation of the tragic vision of his more recent poetry to post-Referendum Wales. This is not the place to argue it, but twentieth-century Wales is no stranger to the tragic. Alone among the major dramatists of our time, Saunders Lewis has made tragedy his central concern; it is worth noting that he too has written about Nazi Germany as a tragic subject. I think perhaps we read *Siŵn y Gwynt sy'n Chwythu* as tragic monodrama, with Kitchener Davies's actual death as its catastrophe. Certainly the later narrative poems of T. Gwynn Jones and the stories of Kate Roberts (in their very different ways) are as close to the tragic vision as any non-dramatic work can be. In Welsh Wales, particularly, one has had both the sense of malign destiny and individual greatness pitted against it, that together form the recipe for tragic passion. The polarity of Welsh life is one of timid complacency on the one hand, and on the other heroic and tragic struggle against overwhelming odds. This is as true for Keir Hardie as for Saunders Lewis, for the miners' strike as for Cymdeithas yr Iaith. Though individual Englishmen may lead tragic lives, tragedy is not the dominant flavour of English (or American) culture. It is of Welsh. Welsh complacency is not apathy but a tragic backcloth to the heroic 'ways of death'.

Up to 1979, the dominant mode of Anglo-Welsh poetry was elegy, the chosen weapon of a new middle-class intent (as I have argued elsewhere) on taking over both from the chapel-dominated Welsh way of life and from English ruling-class hegemony. The elegy both laid claim to the inheritance of the Welsh Way of Life and asserted that it had died. The repercussions of the Devolution Referendum killed Anglo-Welsh elegy (and much else beside) stone dead. The elegists had always been a minority movement, and never in very close contact with contemporary Welsh feeling. To that extent the Second Flowering, as they called themselves, were less Welsh, not more, than the 'realist' movement – John Davies, Robert Minhinnick (1952– ) and others – that succeeded them. What seems to be happening is that an awareness of tragedy is finding expression, somewhat haltingly, in recent Anglo-Welsh verse. Glyn Jones – always a maverick voice – led the way with his devastating poetry of old age beginning with 'The common path' on 'private, middle-aged, rectal cancer' and 'what must not be comforted'. He takes his place, surely, in the line of great Welsh poets of old age and sickness, Llywarch and Guto'r Glyn the chief of them. John Davies turns to the tragedy of the American Indian on the Pacific Seaboard. Dannie Abse, who had for so long seemed an Anglo-Welsh poet only by courtesy, has moved into the focus, not only with his poems about patients and their 'ways of death' but also with the tragic extravaganza of 'Funland'. Nigel Jenkins (1949– ) can pick snowdrops and in the same breath remember the torture of children and their mothers in Bolivia. And for my part, the Falklands War realized in me an awareness that Wales has become, for our time, a place of tragedy, not to be elegized away.

Tony Curtis, therefore, in finding his imagination's roosting place in the tragedies of Nazi Germany and other avenues of death, may have been nearer to the quick of Welsh sensibility than we realize. Tragedy does not have to apologize for itself, or to come wrapped in the right political colours. Curtis's opportunist attitude to poetry – and even to the winning of competitions at which he is positively eisteddfodic – and his greater formal alacrity, have led him further towards the objectivity of tragic art than either Davies or Minhinnick. They remain poets of subjective lyric, more clotted into the subject matter of their own lives, nearer to the elegists they have displaced.

# List of authors
## and their major works

~

**Dannie Abse**, 1923– . Poet, dramatist and novelist.
Many volumes of poetry and prose including:
*Ash on a Young Man's Sleeve* (novel) (London: Hutchinson, 1954)
*Tenants of the House* (London: Hutchinson, 1957)
*Poems, Golders Green* (London: Hutchinson, 1962)
*A Small Desperation* (London: Hutchinson, 1968)
*Funland and Other Poems* (London: Hutchinson, 1973)
*Collected Poems 1948–76* (London: Hutchinson, 1977)
*Way out in the Centre* (London: Hutchinson, 1981)

**Euros Bowen**, 1904–88. Poet in Welsh.
*Poems*, selected and trans. by the poet (Llandysul: Gwasg Gomer, 1974)

**Ceiriog** (John Ceiriog Hughes), 1832–87. Poet in Welsh.

**Brenda Chamberlain**, 1912–71. Painter, prose-writer and poet.
*The Green Heart* (poems) (London: Oxford University Press, 1958)
*Tide Race* (prose) (London: Hodder, 1962)
*Poems with Drawings* (London: Enitharmon Press, 1969)

**Tony Curtis**, 1946– . Poet.
Several volumes of poetry including:
*Album* (Llandybïe: Christopher Davies, 1974)
*Letting Go* (Bridgend: Poetry Wales Press, 1983)
*Selected Poems 1970–1985* (Bridgend: Poetry Wales Press, 1986)
*Taken for Pearls* (Bridgend: Seren Books, 1993)

**Idris Davies, 1905–53. Poet.**
   *Gwalia Deserta* (London: Dent, 1938)
   *The Angry Summer* (London: Faber, 1943; 2nd edn. Cardiff: University of Wales Press, 1993)
   Islwyn Jenkins (ed.), *Collected Poems* (Llandysul: Gomerian Press, 1972)
   Dafydd Johnston (ed.), *The Complete Poems of Idris Davies* (Cardiff: University of Wales Press, 1994)

**John Davies, 1944– . Poet.**
   *At the Edge of Town* (Llandysul: Gomer Press, 1981)
   *The Visitor's Book* (Bridgend: Poetry Wales Press, 1985)
   *Flight Patterns* (Bridgend: Seren Books, 1991)

**W. H. Davies, 1871–1940. Poet.**
   *The Soul's Destroyer and Other Poems* (London: the author, 1905)
   *The Autobiography of a Super-Tramp* (prose) (London: Fifield, 1908)
   *Collected Poems*, various editions, the first as *The Poems of W. H. Davies* (London: Cape, 1940)

**Jon Dressel, 1934– . Poet.**
   *Hard Love and a Country* (Swansea: Christopher Davies, 1977)
   *Out of Wales* (Port Talbot: Alun Books, 1985)

**Caradoc Evans (David Evans), 1878–1945. Short-story writer.**
   *My People* (London: Melrose, [1915]).
   Other collections of stories, novels etc.

**J. O. Francis, 1882–1956. Dramatist.**
   *Change*, 1912 (first published London/Cardiff: Educational Publication Company, 1920)

**Raymond Garlick, 1926– . Poet, critic and editor.**
   *Dock Leaves*, later *The Anglo-Welsh Review* (ed.), 1949–61
   *A Sense of Europe* (Llandysul: Gomer Press, 1968)
   *An Introduction to Anglo-Welsh Literature* (prose) (Cardiff: University of Wales Press, 1970)
   *A Sense of Time* (Llandysul: Gomer Press, 1972)
   *Incense* (Llandysul: Gomer Press, 1976)
   *Anglo-Welsh Poetry 1480–1980* (ed. with Roland Mathias) (Bridgend: Poetry Wales Press, 1984)
   *Collected Poems 1946–86* (Llandysul: Gomer Press, 1987)
   *Travel Notes* (Llandysul: Gomer Press, 1992)

**Bryn Griffiths**, 1933– . Poet and anthologist.
Various books of poetry, including:
*The Mask of Pity* (Llandybïe: Christopher Davies, 1966)
*The Stones Remember*, (London: J. M. Dent, 1967)
*Welsh Voices* (ed.) (London: J. M. Dent, 1967)
*Scars* (London: J. M. Dent, 1969)
*Love Poems* (Western Australia: Artlook, 1980)
*Sea Poems* (Bullsbrook, W. Australia Veritas, 1988)

**Gwenallt** (David James Jones), 1899–1968. Poet in Welsh.
The poems about the Depression are from *Eples* (Llandysul: Gwasg Gomer, 1951). There are translations in Joseph Clancy, Gerallt Jones and Tony Conran.

**Gwili** (John Jenkins), 1872–1936. Poet in Welsh and English.
*Poems by Gwili* (English poems), (Cardiff: 1920)

**Gerard Manley Hopkins**, 1844–89. Poet.
R. Bridges (ed.), *The Poems of Gerard Manley Hopkins* (London: Oxford University Press, 1918. 3rd edn, ed. W. H. Gardner, 1948; 4th edn, ed. W. H. Gardner and N. H. MacKenzie, 1967)

**John Ceiriog Hughes.** See Ceiriog.

**Huw Menai** (Huw Owen Williams), 1888–1961. Poet.
*Through the Upcast Shaft* (London: Hodder & Stoughton, 1920)
*Back in the Return and Other Poems* (London: 1933)
*The Simple Vision* (London: Chapman & Hall, 1945)

**Islwyn** (William Thomas), 1832–78. Poet in Welsh.

**John Jenkins.** See Gwili.

**Nigel Jenkins**, 1949– . Poet.
*Acts of Union: Selected Poems, 1974–1989* (Llandysul: Gwasg Gomer, 1990)

**David Jones**, 1895–1974. Painter, poet and prose-writer.
*In Parenthesis* (London: Faber, 1937)
*The Anathemata* (London: Faber, 1952)

*Epoch and Artist* (prose) (London: Faber, 1959)
*The Sleeping Lord* (London: Faber, 1974)
*The Dying Gaul* (prose) (London: Faber, 1978)
Harman Grisewood and René Hague (eds.), *The Roman Quarry* (London: Agenda Editions, 1981)

**David James Jones. See Gwenallt.**

**Glyn Jones, 1905–95. Short-story writer, novelist and poet.**
*The Blue Bed* (stories) (London: Cape, 1937)
*Poems* (London: Fortune Press, 1939)
*The Dream of Jake Hopkins* (poems) (London: Fortune Press, 1954)
*The Dragon has Two Tongues* (prose) (London: Dent, 1968)
*Selected Poems* (Llandysul: Gomer Press, 1975; Bridgend: Poetry Wales Press, 1988)

**Sally Roberts Jones, 1935– . Poet and publisher.**
*Turning Away* (Llandysul: Gwsag Gomer, 1969)
*Strangers and Brothers* (Port Talbot: Alun Books, 1977)
*The Forgotten Country* (Llandysul: Gomer Press, 1977)
*Relative Values* (Bridgend: Poetry Wales Press, 1985)

**T. Harri Jones, 1921–65. Poet.**
The four separate volumes (1957–66) are included in Julian Croft and Don Dale Jones (eds.), *The Collected Poems of T. Harri Jones* (Llandysul: Gomer Press, 1977)

**Williams Ronald Rees Jones. See Keidrych Rhys.**

**Alun Lewis, 1915–44. Poet and short-story writer.**
*Raiders' Dawn* (London: Allen & Unwin, 1942)
*The Last Inspection* (stories) (London: Allen & Unwin, 1942)
*Ha! Ha! Among the Trumpets* (London: Allen & Unwin, 1945)
*Letters from India* (prose) (Cardiff: Penmark Press, 1946)
*In the Green Tree* (London: Allen & Unwin, 1948)
Ian Hamilton (ed.), *Alun Lewis: Selected Poetry and Prose* (London: Allen & Unwin, 1966)
Jeremy Hooker and Gweno Lewis (eds.), *Selected Poems of Alun Lewis* (London: Allen & Unwin, 1981)
Cary Archard (ed.), *Collected Poems* (Bridgend: Seren Books, 1994) (part of an ongoing uniform edition of his work).

**Saunders Lewis,** 1893–1985. Dramatist, poet and critic in Welsh.

Alun R. Jones and Gwyn Thomas (eds.), *Presenting Saunders Lewis* (Cardiff: University of Wales Press, 1973) (includes translations)

*The Plays of Saunders Lewis* (4 vols.), trans. Joseph P. Clancy (Llandybïe: Christopher Davies, 1985)

*Selected Poems*, trans. Joseph P. Clancy, (Cardiff: University of Wales Press, 1993)

**Roland Mathias,** 1915– . Poet, critic and editor.

*Break in Harvest* (London: Routledge, 1946)

*The Roses of Tretower* ([Pembroke Dock]: Dock Leaves Press, 1952)

*The Eleven Men of Eppynt* (short stories) ([Pembroke Dock]: Dock Leaves Press, 1956)

*The Flooded Valley* (London: Putnam, 1960)

*The Anglo-Welsh Review* (ed.), 1961–76

*Absalom in the Tree* (Llandysul: Gwasg Gomer, 1971)

*Vernon Watkins* (prose) (Cardiff: University of Wales Press, 1974)

*Snipe's Castle* (Llandysul: Gomer Press, 1979)

*Burning Brambles* (selected poems) (Llandysul: Gomer Press, 1983)

*Anglo-Welsh Poetry 1480–1980* (ed. with Raymond Garlick) (Bridgend: Poetry Wales Press, 1984)

*A Ride through the Wood* (criticism) (Bridgend: Poetry Wales Press, 1985)

**Menai.** See Huw Menai.

**Robert Minhinnick,** 1952– . Poet.

*Native Ground* (Swansea: Triskele, Christopher Davies, 1979)

*Life Sentences* (Bridgend: Poetry Wales Press, 1983)

*The Dinosaur Park* (Bridgend: Poetry Wales Press, 1985)

*The Looters* (Bridgend: Poetry Wales Press, 1989)

**Leslie Norris,** 1921– . Poet and short-story writer.

*Finding Gold* (London: Chatto & Windus, 1967)

*Ransoms* (London: Chatto & Windus; Hogarth Press, 1970)

*Mountains Polecats Pheasants* (London: Hogarth Press, 1974)

*Islands off Maine* (Cranberry Isles, Me.: Tidal Press, 1977)

*Sliding* (stories) (London: Chatto & Windus, 1978)

*Water Voices* (London: Chatto & Windus, 1980)

*Selected Poems* (Bridgend: Poetry Wales Press, 1986)

**John Ormond** (John Ormond Thomas), 1923–90. Poet and film-maker.
*Requiem and Celebration* (Swansea: Christopher Davies, 1969)
*Definition of a Waterfall* (London: Oxford University Press, 1973)
*Penguin Modern Poets 27* (with Emyr Humphreys and John Tripp) (Harmondsworth: Penguin, 1978)
*Selected Poems* (Bridgend: Poetry Wales Press, 1987)

**Pantycelyn.** See William Williams.

**R. Williams Parry**, 1884–1956. Poet in Welsh.
Translations of a number of poems in Joseph Clancy, *Twentieth Century Welsh Poems* (1982)

**A. G. Prys-Jones**, 1888–1987. Poet and anthologist.
*Welsh Poets* (ed.), (London: Erskine MacDonald, 1917)
*Poems of Wales* (Oxford: Basil Blackwell, 1923)
*Green Places* (Aberystwyth: Gwasg Aberystwyth, 1948)
*High Heritage* (Llandybïe: Christopher Davies, 1969)

**Ernest Rhys**, 1859–1946. Poet and editor.
*A London Rose* (London: Elkin Matthews & John Lane, 1894)
*Welsh Ballads* (1898)
*Wales England Wed* (prose) (1940)

**Keidrych Rhys** (William Ronald Rees Jones), 1915–87. Editor and poet.
*Wales* (magazine), 1937–40, 1943–49, 1958–60
*The Van Pool* (poems) (London: Routledge, 1942)
*Modern Welsh Poetry* (ed.) (London: Faber & Faber, 1944)

**Lynette Roberts**, 1909–95. Poet.
*Poems* (London: Faber & Faber, 1944)
*Gods with Stainless Ears* (London: Faber & Faber, 1951)

**Meic Stephens**, 1938– . Editor and poet.
*Poetry Wales* (ed.), 1965–73
*The Lilting House* (anthology of Anglo-Welsh Poetry, ed. with J. S. Williams) (London and Llandybïe: Dent and Christopher Davies, 1969)
*Exiles All* (poems) (Swansea: Christopher Davies, 1973)

*Green Horse* (anthology, ed. with Peter Finch) (Swansea: Christopher Davies, 1978)

*The Bright Field* (anthology, ed.) (Manchester: Carcanet, 1991)

**Dylan Thomas,** 1914–53. Poet, short-story writer and dramatist.

*18 Poems* (London: *Sunday Referee,* 1934)

*Twenty-five Poems* (London: Dent, 1936)

*The Map of Love* (London: Dent, 1939)

*Portrait of the Artist as a Young Dog* (stories) (London: Dent, 1940)

*Deaths and Entrances* (London: Dent, 1946)

*Collected Poems 1934–1952* (London: Dent, 1952)

*Under Milk Wood* (radio play) (London: Dent, 1954)

Ralph Maud (ed.), *Poet in the Making: The Notebooks of Dylan Thomas* (London: Dent, 1968)

Paul Ferris (ed.), *The Collected Letters of Dylan Thomas* (London: Dent, 1985)

**Edward Thomas,** 1878–1917. Poet and prose-writer.

*Poems* (London: Selwyn & Blount, 1917)

*Collected Poems* (London: Selwyn & Blount, 1920)

*Beautiful Wales* (prose) (London: A. & C. Black, 1905)

*The Happy-Go-Lucky Morgans* (prose), (London: Duckworth & Co, 1913)

R. George Thomas (ed.), *The Collected Poems of Edward Thomas* (Oxford: Clarendon Press, 1978)

**John Ormond Thomas.** See John Ormond.

**R. S. Thomas,** 1913– . Poet.

Many volumes of poetry, including:

*The Stones of the Field* (Carmarthen: Druid Press, 1946)

*An Acre of Land* (Newtown: Montgomeryshire Printing Co., 1952)

*The Minister* (Newtown: Montgomeryshire Printing Co., 1955)

*Song at the Year's Turning* (London: Hart-Davis, 1955)

*H'm* (London: Macmillan, 1972)

*Selected Poems, 1946–68* (London: Hart-Davis; MacGibbon, 1973)

*Laboratories of The Spirit* (London: Macmillan, 1975)

*Later Poems* (London: Macmillan, 1983)

*Collected Poems 1945–1990* (London: Dent, 1993)

**William Thomas.** See Islwyn.

**John Tripp,** 1927–86. Poet.
> Various collections including *The Loss of Ancestry* (Llandybïe: Christopher Davies, 1969) and the misleadingly titled *Collected Poems 1958–78* (Swansea: Christopher Davies, 1978)
> John Ormond (ed.), *Selected Poems* (Bridgend: Seren Books, 1989)

**Vernon Watkins,** 1906–67. Poet.
> *Ballad of the Mari Lwyd* (London: Faber, 1941)
> *The Lady with the Unicorn,* (London: Faber, 1948)
> *Selected Poems* (Norfolk, Conn.: New Directions, 1948; London: Faber, 1967); *I that was Born in Wales* (Cardiff: University of Wales Press, 1976); *Unity of the Stream* (Llandysul: Gomer Press, 1978)
> *The North Sea* (translations from Heine) (New York: New Directions, 1951)
> *The Death Bell* (London: Faber, 1954)
> *Cypress and Acacia* (London: Faber, 1959)
> *Affinities* (London: Faber, 1962)
> *Fidelities* (London: Faber, 1968)
> *Collected Poems* (Ipswich: Golgonooza Press, 1986)

**Huw Owen Williams.** See Huw Menai.

**Waldo Williams,** 1904–71. Poet in Welsh.
> Translations from his book of poems *Dail Pren* (Gwasg Aberystwyth) are in Gerallt Jones, Anthony Conran & Joseph Clancy. A bilingual selection of his poetry, *The Peacemakers*, selected, translated and introduced by Tony Conran, is to be published by Gwasg Gomer, Llandysul, in 1997.

**William Williams of Pantycelyn,** 1717–91. Hymn-writer, poet and prose-writer, mainly in Welsh but sometimes in English. Very little apart from some of the hymns has been translated.

# Bibliography

~

*Critical Books (A Brief Selection)*
Anthony Conran, *The Cost of Strangeness* (Llandysul: Gomer Press, 1982)
Glyn Jones, *The Dragon has Two Tongues* (London: Dent, 1968)
Jeremy Hooker, *The Presence of the Past: Essays on Modern British and American Poetry* (Bridgend: Poetry Wales Press, 1987)
Roland Mathias, *The Ride through the Wood: Essays on Anglo-Welsh Literature* (Bridgend: Poetry Wales Press, 1985)
M. Wynn Thomas, *Internal Difference: Twentieth-Century Writing in Wales* (Cardiff: University of Wales Press, 1992)

*Collections of essays*
Sam Adams and Gwilym Rees Hughes (eds.), *Triskel One: Essays on Welsh and Anglo-Welsh Literature* (Swansea: Christopher Davies, 1971)
Sam Adams and Gwilym Rees Hughes (eds.), *Triskel Two: Essays on Welsh and Anglo-Welsh Literature* (Llandybïe: Christopher Davies, 1973)
Tony Brown (ed.), *Welsh Writing in English: A Yearbook of Critical Essays*, 1 (Cardiff: New Welsh Reviews, 1995)
Belinda Humfrey (ed.), *Fire Green as Grass: Studies of the Creative Impulse in Anglo-Welsh Poetry and Short Stories of the Twentieth Century* (Llandysul: Gomer Press, 1995)

*Translations of Welsh poetry*
Joseph Clancy, *Twentieth Century Welsh Poems* (Llandysul: Gomer Press, 1982)
Anthony Conran, *The Penguin Book of Welsh Verse* (Harmondsworth: Penguin, 1967)
Tony Conran, *Welsh Verse* (2nd enlarged edn) (Bridgend: Poetry Wales Press, 1986)
Gerallt Jones, *Poetry of Wales, 1930–1970* (Llandysul: Gwasg Gomer, 1974)

# Index

~

Abraham, William, MP (Mabon), 3, 67
Abse, Dannie 184, 187, 203, 217,
    234–48, 273, 274
    'After the release of Ezra Pound' 239
    'bereaved, The' 236, 244–5
    'Black' 243–4
    'death of Aunt Alice, The' 245
    'Duality' 238
    'Elegy for Dylan Thomas' 179
    'frontier, The' 237
    'Funland' 245–8, 274
    *Funland and Other Poems* 243
    'Here' 245
    'In Llandough Hospital' 240–2
    'Letter to Alex Comfort' 236
    'Master' 238
    *Mavericks* 237
    'Miss Book World' 235
    'New Babylons' 236–7
    'New diary' 244
    'night out, A' 242
    'Not Adlestrop' 242
    'old commitment, An' 243
    'Peachstone' 245
    *Poems, Golders Green* 239
    'second coming, The' 236
    *Small Desperation, A* 240, 242
    'smile was, A' 235
    'Surprise! Surprise!' 242–3
    *Tenants of the House* 238, 239
    'trial, The' 236, 238–9
    'victim of Aulis, The' 236
    'water diviner, The' 239
Archard, Cary 164
Arány, János 67
Arnold, Matthew 68

Auden, W. H. 137, 139, 180, 218, 235,
    237

Baillie 75, 85
Barnes, William 66, 67, 83
Barnie, John 255
Barrett, Elizabeth 166
Barrie, J. M. 36
*Battle of Maldon, The* 173
Bell, Idris 25
Bender, Todd K. 88
Betjeman, John 188, 244
Bevan, Aneurin 60, 217
Bianchi, Tony 148, 190, 249, 250, 251
Blake, William 133, 154, 181
    *Songs of Innocence* 21
Bottomley, Gordon 39
Bowen, Euros 111
    *Cerddi*, 129, 181
Bradshaw, Alice Ann 71
Brook, Rupert 93
Browning, Robert 123, 205, 269
Brownjohn, Alan 236
Büchner, Georg: *Woyzeck* 131
Buckley, Wilma: 'Song of Pwyll' 25
Buckmaster, Celia 170
Butler, Susan: *Common Ground* 205

Cameron, Norman 118
Ceiriog 10, 11
Chamberlain, Brenda 165, 166–7, 177
    *Alun Lewis and the Making of the*
        *Caseg Broadsheets* 165
    *Tide Race* 165
Chartism 8
Chatterton, Thomas 130

Chaucer, Geoffrey 89, 153
  'Pardoner's Tale, The' 268
Clancy, Joseph 150, 259
Clare, John 165, 166
Clarke, Gillian 166, 217, 250
Cleverdon, Douglas 106
Coleridge, Samuel Taylor 67, 194
  'ancient Mariner, The' 21, 116, 132
Cook, A. J. 67
Cooke, W.: *Edward Thomas: A
    Critical Biography* 39
Corcoran, Neil: *Song of Deeds, The*
    107
Cox, Brian 199
Crane, Hart 114
Curtis, Tony 234, 235, 265–74
  *Album* 265, 268
  'Boxes' 271
  'death of Richard Beatle-Seaman in
    the Belgian Grand Prix, 1939,
    The' 272
  'deerslayers, The' 265–8, 269
  'Killing whales' 265
  *Letting Go* 269, 270
  'My grandmother's cactus' 269
  'Poem for John Tripp' 268
  *Preparations* 268, 269
  *Selected Poems* 265, 267, 268, 271,
    272
  'spirit of the place, The' 269–70
  'Thoughts from the Holiday Inn'
    268
  'Trials' 270–1
  'Two for luck' 271
  'welcome, A' 265
Cymru Fydd 3, 8
Cynddelw 81, 84, 91

Dafydd ap Gwilym 81, 149, 150–1,
    153, 185, 186, 229, 250
Davies, Aberpennar *see* Davies, Pennar
Davies, Aneirin Talfan 153, 181
Davies, Idris 2, 3, 8, 9–11, 12, 27, 29,
    42–55, 58, 60–4, 65, 142, 163,
    177, 203, 206, 218
  *Angry Summer, The* 9, 11, 43, 45–6,
    60–3
  *Gwalia Deserta* 6, 9, 43–51
  *Selected Poems* 43

'Tonypandy' 46
*Tonypandy and Other Poems* 43,
    177
Davies, John 29, 235, 273, 274
Davies, Kitchener 180, 273
*Sŵn y Gwynt sy'n Chwythu* 273
Davies, Pennar 110, 177, 181
  *Dock Leaves* 180
Davies, Rhys 149, 157, 200
Davies, W. H. 12–21, 26, 32, 65, 112,
    146
  *Autobiography of a Super-Tramp*
    12, 18
  'blind child, A' 17
  'child's pet, A' 20
  *Complete Poems* 17
  'Dying' 17
  'Facts' 19–20
  'homeless man, The' 17
  'Hope abandoned' 16
  *Nature Poems* 17
  *New Poems* 16, 17, 18
  Poem 583 13
  'soul's destroyer, The' 13–15, 16
  *Soul's Destroyer, The* 15, 17
  'ways of time, The' 17
Davies, Walford 129, 131, 138, 139, 182
de la Mare, Walter 37
Debussy, Claude 117
di Pietro, Fr 79
Dickinson, Emily 165, 166
Dixon, Richard Watson 75, 78, 89
Donne, John 29, 91
Dressel, Jon 251, 259–64
  'Children, night, Llansteffan' 260–1
  'diary for St David's week, 1979, A'
    261–3
  *Hard Love and a Country* 259
  *Out of Wales* 261
  'shop girl, The' 261
  'Synopsis of the Great Yanklo-
    Welsh novel' 259–60
Dunbar, William: 'Done is a battell on
    the dragon blak' 90
Dyer, John 31

Earle, Jean 29
Eastaway, Edward *see* Thomas,
    Edward
Edwards, O. M. 32

Eliot, T. S. 92, 109, 113, 120, 124, 141, 163, 164, 177, 183, 189
  'Ash Wednesday' 130, 136
  'Burnt Norton' 140, 183
  'East Coker' 183
  *Four Quartets* 136, 140, 154, 183, 228
  'Gerontion' 123, 137
  'hollow men, The' 130
  'Little Gidding' 46, 62, 140
  'waste land, The' 109, 123, 136, 137, 154, 182
Evans, Caradoc 3, 32, 149, 157, 200
  *My People* 25, 111, 112–13
Evans, Evan 67
Evans, George Ewart 157
Evans, Margiad (Peggy Whistler) 157, 165, 166–7

FitzGibbon, Constantine 119
Francis, J. O.: *Change* 112
Frost, Robert 32, 39
Frye, Northop 92, 93, 94, 109
Fussell, Paul 98

Gardner 80
Garfitt, Roger 186
Garlick, Raymond 12, 205, 249–58
  'Acclamation' 254, 257
  *Blaenau Observed* 251
  *Collected Poems* 251, 254, 255, 258
  *Dock Leaves* 200
  *Sense of Time, A* 254, 255, 258
  'survivor, The' 256
  *Welsh-Speaking Sea, The* 251
Geoffrey of Monmouth: *History of the Kings of Britain* 72
George, Daniel 17
Gerontion 124
Gill, Eric 252
Ginsberg, Allen: 'Howl' 152
Glewlwyd 98
*Gododdin* 254
Goodwin, Geraint 157
Grahame, Kenneth 36
Graves, Robert 163, 164, 165, 189, 218
  *White Goddess, The* 163
Gray, Thomas 24, 86
  'bard, The' 67
  'Elegy' 136

Griffith, Llywelyn Wyn 157
Griffiths, Ann 6
Griffiths, Bryn 218, 222, 250
Grisewood, Harman 105
Gruffydd ab yr Ynad Coch 250, 263, 264
Gruffydd, Dr Geraint 85
Gruffydd, W. J. 25
Guest, Lady Charlotte 67, 71
Guto'r Glyn 162, 274
Gwalchmai 85, 86, 87, 88, 89, 90–1
  'Gorhoffedd' ('Exultation') 69–70
Gwenallt (D. Gwenallt Jones) 54, 55, 61, 64, 233
  *Eples* 55
  'meirwon, Y' ('The dead') 55–60, 63, 230–2
Gwili (John Jenkins) 29, 30, 32
  *Poems* 31

Hague, René 95, 105
Hardie, Keir 3, 273
Hardy, Thomas: *Jude the Obscure* 48–9
Hart-Davis, Rupert 188
Hedd Wyn 10
Herbert, George 29, 90
Heseltine, Nigel 157
Hogler, Raymond L. 203, 204
Holbrook, David 131, 137, 203
Homer 63
Hooker, Jeremy 148
Hopkins, Gerard Manley 12, 66, 68, 71, 72, 74–91, 109, 113, 130, 160, 173, 190, 205
  *Poems*, no. 28 79
  *Poems*, no. 135 88
  'wreck of the *Deutschland*, The' 79, 86, 87, 88–90
Horace 170
Housman, A. E. 49, 205
  'Bredon Hill' 28
  *Shropshire Lad, A* 48
  'To an athlete dying young' 48
Humphreys, Emyr 177, 200, 206
  'Roman dream, A' 214
Huw Menai 21–4, 65, 146
  'When Time the sculptor . . .' 22–4

Ieuan Glyn Geirionydd 24
Iolo Morganwg 67, 73
Islwyn 8, 16, 21
   *Storm, Y* 8

James, Henry 93
Jenkins, Iswyn 60
Jenkins, Nigel 274
Jenkins, Randall 184, 185
Jiménez, Juan Ramón 111
Johnson, Dr Samuel: 'On the death of
   Mr Robert Levet' 241
Jones, Bobi 148
Jones, Daniel 129, 130, 132
Jones, David 71–3, 92–108, 109, 110,
   113, 163, 164, 190, 200, 201–3,
   206, 207, 259
   *Anathemata, The* 92, 97, 105–8,
     109
   'Book of Balaam's Ass' 101
   'fatigue, The' 101–3
   'hunt, The' 154
   *In Parenthesis* 69, 71, 92–100, 105,
     106–7, 114
   *Roman Quarry and Other
     Sequences, The* 105
   *Sleeping Lord, The* 105
   'tutelar of the place, The' 103–4
Joyce, James 10, 92, 93, 94, 106, 109
   *Finnegans Wake* 106, 154
   *Ulysses* 109
Jones, Fr John Hugh 78
Jones, Glyn 10, 12, 51, 54, 114, 138,
   142–62, 163, 177, 179–80, 188,
   200, 273
   'Bethania' 161
   'Biography' 152–3
   'common path, The' 162
   'Cwmcelyn' 158
   *Dragon has Two Tongues, The* 21,
     143, 148, 149, 156, 157, 180
   'dream of Jake Hopkins, The' 158
   *Dream of Jake Hopkins, The* 149,
     153, 155–6, 177
   'Easter' 158–9
   'Esyllt' 143–5
   *Learning Lark, The* 155
   'Maelog the Eremite' 146
   'Merthyr' 156–8
   'Morning' 142–3

'Nant Ceri' 159
*Poems* 145, 147, 152, 153
'Rain' 147–8
'seagull, The' 150, 151
*Selected Poems* 150
'Sketch of the author' 145, 147, 152
'Spring bush' 159
'Superior' 160
'thrush, The' 151
'Wounds' 152
Jones, Gwyn 22, 54, 157, 177, 181, 200
Jones, Jack 54, 206
Jones, James 71
Jones, Lewis 11, 54, 206
Jones, Sally Roberts 217, 218
Jones, T. Gwynn 25, 67, 109, 190, 273
Jones, T. Harri 178, 179, 181, 217,
   218–25, 226
   'Back' 225
   *Beast at the Door, The* 218
   *Colour of Cockcrowing, The* 221
   'Cotton Mathers remembers the
     trial of Elizabeth How: Salem,
     Massachusetts' 223
   'Girl reading John Donne' 223
   'Lucky Jonah' 222, 223
   'My grandfather going blind' 219
   'My grandmother died in the early
     hours of the morning' 220–1
   'One memory' 221, 223–4
   'Rhiannon' 219
   'Sawmill incident' 224
   'Spoiled preacher' 224–5
   'storm in childhood, A' 221–2

Kafka, Franz 93
   *Trial* 92
Kavanagh, Patrick: 'Epic' 229
Keats, John 35, 89, 130, 139, 181, 203
   'Hyperion' 116
   'Ode to a nightingale' 116, 182
Kemble, John 258
Kitchen, Paddy 80
Krims, Leslie 266

Larkin, Philip: *Less Deceived, The* 136
Lawrence, D. H. 13, 33, 52, 114, 143,
   145, 159, 203

Lewis, Alun 3, 27, 40, *52*, 54, 114, 137,
    163, 164, *165*, 175, 177, 188,
    193, 200, 206, 218
Lewis, C. Day 180
Lewis, C. S. 95
Lewis, Richard 16
Lewis, Saunders 29, 100, 110, 113, 190,
    191, 207, 253, 273
    'Golygfa mewn caffe' 110–11
Lilly, Miss Gweneth 84
Lloyd George, David 3, 67
Lloyd, Howel 74
Llywarch Hen 153, 162, 229, 274
Lowell 232

*Mabinogion* 71, 72
Mabon 3, 67
Madog 67
Mallarmé, Stéphane 111, 124
    'Après-midi d'un faune, L'' 123
Marlowe, Christopher 120, 130, 183
    *Faustus* 123
    *Tamburlaine* 123
Marvell, Andrew 170
    'To his coy mistress' 126
Mathias, Roland 131, 148, 188, 200–15
    *Anglo-Welsh Literature: An
        Illustrated History*, 201
    'Brechfa Chapel' 212
    'Burning brambles' 212
    *Common Ground* 207, 214
    'flooded valley, The' 213–14
    'For Jenkin Jones, prisoner at
        Carmarthen, these' 207
    'Grief and the circus horse' 205
    'letter, A' 207
    'Memling' 207
    'remonstrance of John Poyer, The'
        214
    *Ride through the Wood, A* 181,
        201, 205, 206
    'Snipe's castle' 212
    'Testament' 215
    'They have not survived' 215
    'Tide-reach: A sequence of
        Pembrokeshire poems written
        for music' 214
Maud, Ralph 131
McKenna, Siobhan: 'Anna Livia
        Plurabelle' 154

Minhinnick, Robert 273, 274
Morgan, Derec Llwyd 6, 44
Morris brothers 67
Morris-Jones, Sir John 9, 67, 109, 190
Morus, Huw 250
Muir, Edwin 237
*Myvyrian Archaiology* 85, 88, 90

Nennius 92
Nicholson, Norman 137
Noble, Helen 30, 32
Norris, Leslie 30, 40, 177, 218, 226–33,
        234, 235, 250
    'ballad of Billy Rose, The' 226, 229
    'Early frost' 226
    'evening by the lake, An' 229
    *Finding Gold* 226
    *Loud Winter, The* 226
    'old house, An' 226, 227, 229, 230
    'Ransoms' 230
    *Selected Poems* 229, 230
    'small war, A' 213, 229

Ormond, John (Ormond Thomas)
        177, 181, 184, 217, 218, 234, 250
    'Cathedral builders' 185, 187
    'City in fire and snow' 184–5
    'Elsewhere' 186
    'section of an elegy, A' 186–7
Ovid 123
Owen, Daniel 6
Owen, Goronwy 67
Owen, Wilfred 40, 86, 93, 96, 136, 137

Pantycelyn 2, 4, 8, 9, 10, 11, 24, 58
Parry, R. Williams 25, 27, 29, 67, 243
    *Haf a Cherddi Eraill, Yr* 27
    'llwynog, Y' 27–8
Parry, Thomas 67
Patmore, Coventry 75, 83
Pikoulis, John 38, 163, 164, 165, 167
Plato 110
Pope, Alexander: 'Eloisa to Abelard'
        123
Pound, Ezra 32, 92, 109, 110, 137, 190
    *Cantos, The* 109
Powys, John Cowper 201, 252
Prys-Jones, A.G. 25–6, 69, 146
    'ballad of Glyndwr's rising, A' 26

Pugh, Shenagh 166
Raine, Allen (Anna Puddicombe) 111
Rattigan, Terence 154
Rees, Alun 268
Rent, Arthur 79
Rhymers' Club 68
Rhys, Ernest 26, 68–71, 72, 112, 190
    *London Rose and Other Rhymes,*
      *A* 69
    *Song of the Sun* 69
    *Welsh Ballads* 69–70
Rhys, Keidrych 42, 163, 164, 167, 175,
    176, 177, 178, 188, 189, 205
Rhys, Sir John 74, 83
Rilke, R. M. 242
Rimbaud, Arthur 131, 182
    *Illuminations, Les* 117–18
Roberts, Kate 273
Roberts, Lynette 114, 163–76, 177,
    189, 259
    'Argentine railways' 171
    'Crossed and uncrossed' 167,
      168–70, 171–2
    'Cwmcelyn' 158
    'Earthbound' 175–6
    'Gods with stainless ears' 158
    *Gods with Stainless Ears* 164, 165
    'Low tide' 171, 174–5
    'new perception of colour, The' 167
    'Poem from Llanybri' 164, 171, 175
    *Poems* 164, 167, 177
    'Raw salt on eye' 171
    'Rhode Island Red' 172–3
    *Village Dialect* 163
Rossetti, Christina 166
Rousseau, Henri 166

Sassoon, Siegfried 40, 96, 136
Seeger, Pete 47
Shakespeare 30, 120, 151
    *King Lear* 154
    *Hamlet* 123, 127, 183, 199
    *Macbeth* 123
Sharp, Cecil 36
Sharp, William 68
Shaw, George Bernard 12
Shelley, Percy Bysshe 10, 42, 46, 181
Sitwell, Edith 163, 168, 180
Smart, Christopher: 'For I will
    consider my cat Jeoffrey' 155

Southey, Robert 67
Spender, Stephen 180
Stephens, Meic 218, 250
Stevens, Wallace 189
Stravinsky, Igor 205
Swinburne, Algernon 113, 130

Talfan, Aneirin *see* Davies, Aneirin
    Talfan
Taliesin 66, 91, 98, 130
Taylor, Jeremy 31
Tennyson, Alfred, Lord 13, 18, 205
Thomas, Fr A. 75, 78, 83, 84
Thomas, Caitlin 119, 134–5, 139, 141,
    183
Thomas, Dylan 2, 9, 10, 25, 27, 29, 51,
    52, 54, 58, 92, 113, 114, 117,
    118–20, 121–41, 142, 152–3,
    157, 163, 164, 168, 178–87, 188,
    200, 203, 206, 209, 218, 219,
    226, 227–8, 234, 242, 259
    *18 Poems* 55, 119, 121, 122, 124–30,
      135–9, 180, 182, 183, 204, 205
    'After the funeral' 122
    'Altarwise by owl-light' 120, 121,
      122, 125
    'And death shall have no dominion'
      122
    'As yet ungotten I did suffer' 182
    'Ballad of the long-legged bait'
      132, 204
    *Collected Poems* 178, 179, 180
    *Deaths and Entrances* 122, 140,
      177, 180
    'Do not go gentle' 122
    'Especially when the October wind'
      122, 204
    'Fern Hill' 122, 141, 158, 180, 184,
      204
    'force that through the green fuse,
      The' 135
    'hand that signed the paper, The'
      122, 131
    'Holy Spring' 204
    'hunchback in the park, The' 122,
      133, 139, 204
    'I, in my intricate image' 136
    'I make this in a warring absence' 13
    'I see the boys of summer' 53, 135
    'I sent my creature scouting on the
      globe' 182

'If I were tickled by the rub of love'
124–6, 127–8, 135, 154, 182
'In country sleep' 204, 205
'In my craft or sullen art' 122
'Into her lying down head' 139
'Lament' 122
'Lie still, sleep becalmed' 133–4
'Lie still, you must sleep' 131–2,
135
'Light breaks where no sun shines'
125, 180, 204
*Map of Love, The* 121, 122, 139
'My world is pyramid' 135–6,
137–8
'Not from this anger' 139
'Out of the sighs' 123–4
'Over Sir John's Hill' 122, 204
'Poem in October' 122, 133,
139–40, 141, 178, 184, 188, 204,
227
'Poem on his birthday' 204
'refusal to mourn, A' 122
'This side of the truth' 122
*Twenty-five Poems* 69, 121, 122,
138
*Under Milk Wood* 153
'When, like a running grave' 135
'winter's tale, A' 122, 133, 140, 184,
204
Thomas, Edward 12, 17, 27–41, 53,
114, 228, 229
'As the team's head-brass' 35, 39
'ash grove, The' 30
'Beauty' 33
'child on the cliffs, The' 30
*Collected Poems* 36
'coombe, The' 30
'Gone, gone again' 34, 37
'Home' 38
'Liberty' 35
'Lob' 35, 36, 37
'Out in the dark' 40
'Old man' 46
'owl, The' 33
'Roads' 33–4
'Shieling, The' 39
'sun used to shine, The' 39
'Two houses' 36–7
Thomas, Gwyn 54, 206
Thomas, Helen 17

Thomas, M. Wynn 41, 112, 148, 197
Thomas, R. George 36, 39
Thomas, R. S. 12, 177, 187, 188–99,
200, 205, 206, 207, 209, 213,
219, 220, 225, 234, 249, 250, 255
'Chapel deacon' 198
'country clergy, The' 195, 196
*H'm* 197
*Laboratories of the Spirit* 197–8
*Llwybrau Gynt, Y* 197
'Man and tree' 191
'minister, The' 153
'moon in Lleyn, The' 197
*Neb* 198
'old Cumberland beggar, The' 194
'old language, The' 191
'peasant, A' 194
*Poetry for Supper* 195
*Song at the Year's Turning* 178,
188, 196–7, 250
*Stones of the Field* 177, 188
'To a young poet' 130
'Welsh landscape' 190
'Reservoirs' 213
Thomas, Revd William *see* Islwyn
Thompson, Francis 113–14, 130
'hound of heaven, The' 130
Thomson, Professor George 169
Treece, Henry 130
Tripp, John 217, 218, 234, 250, 251,
263
Tudur Aled 80, 81–2, 84, 91

Vaughan, Henry 65
Verlaine, Paul 143, 182
Villon 153
Virgil: *Aeneid* 107
Voltaire 256
Watkins, Vernon 51, 54, 55, 114, 119,
134, 135, 142, 163, 177, 181,
185, 187, 188, 205, 206, 200–2
'collier, The' 205–6
*Lamp and the Veil, The* 177
Webb, Harri 181, 234, 250
Welsh Folksong Society 6
Welsh Home Rule Movement 3
*Welsh Poets* 25
Wheale, Nigel 165
Whitman, Walt: 'Out of the cradle
endlessly rocking' 155

Widsith 98, 158
Williams, Gwyn 150, 190
   *Introduction to Welsh Poetry* 250
Williams, Ifor 67, 109, 190
Williams, Raymond 37
   *Country and the City, The* 35–6
Williams, Waldo 191
   'heniaith, Yr' ('The old language')
     191–2
   'Preseli' 193
Williams, William, of Pantycelyn *see*
   Pantycelyn
Williams, William Carlos 189, 199

Wordsworth, William 13, 18, 27, 96,
   154, 181, 194, 196, 257
   'Highland reaper, The' 182
   *Lyrical Ballads* 123
   'Michael' 193
   'Old man travelling' 194
   *Prelude, The* 116, 182, 193
   'Resolution and independence' 116

Yaughan, Fr Renelm 78
Yeats, W. B. 10, 68, 71, 189
   'Easter, 1916' 264
   'Rose of the world' 71
   *Wanderings of Oisin, The* 68